DATE DUE

The Autonomy Myth

The Autonomy Myth

A Theory of Dependency

Martha Albertson Fineman

THE NEW PRESS

NEW YORK
LONDON

© 2004 by Martha Albertson Fineman

Published in the United States by The New Press, New York, 2004
Distributed by W. W. Norton & Company, Inc., New York

LIBRARY OF CONGRESS CATALOGING-IN-PUBLICATION DATA

Fineman, Martha.
   The autonomy myth : a theory of dependency /
Martha Albertson Fineman.
       p. cm.
   Includes bibliographical references and index.
   ISBN 1-56584-760-1 (hc)
     1. United States—Social policy—1993–   2. Family policy—
United States.   3. Autonomy (Philosophy)—United States.
4. Social justice—United States.   5. Equality—United States.
I. Title.

HN59.2.F56 2004
361.6'1'0973—dc21   2003051302

The New Press was established in 1990 as a not-for-profit alternative to the
large, commercial publishing houses currently dominating the book
publishing industry. The New Press operates in the public interest rather than
for private gain, and is committed to publishing, in innovative ways, works of
educational, cultural, and community value that are often deemed
insufficiently profitable.

The New Press, 38 Greene Street, 4th floor, New York, NY 10013
www.thenewpress.com

In the United Kingdom: 6 Salem Road, London W2 4BU

Composition by dix!

Printed in the United States of America

10   9   8   7   6   5   4   3   2   1

Contents

Acknowledgments

As a preliminary matter, I want to thank all the people (too numerous to mention) who questioned my ideas about dependency and encouraged me to expand them after the publication of *The Neutered Mother, the Sexual Family, and Other Twentieth Century Tragedies* (Routledge, 1995). Their interest and probing provided the initial incentive to develop a theory of dependency and collective responsibility.

The wonderful students who worked on this project as it was transformed from miscellaneous articles and drafts into a "proper book" deserve special thanks: Sarah Brady, Homa Dashtaki, Victoria Hadfield, Joanne Roman, and, in its very final (and very hectic) stage, Luke Zachary Fenchel. Many people commented on early drafts of this book. In this regard I am particularly indebted to: Terence Dougherty, Jack Jackson, Douglas A. Kysar, Risa Lieberwitz, Benjamin Meier, Adam Romero, and Teemu Ruskola.

Preface

This book was begun before, but completed after, September 11, 2001. The tragic events of that day have changed much in the United States of America. Particularly disheartening has been the deviation in the direction of political rhetoric and attention to domestic concerns. Prior to September 11, massive tax cuts that benefit the wealthiest among us ate into the budget surpluses of the 1990s. Criticism about such measures and the administration that pushed them forward was mounting in the summer of 2001. In particular, there was growing concern about looming and ballooning deficit projections. Democrats were beginning to argue that the wealth the surpluses represented could have and should have been directed toward addressing some of the increasing inequality in opportunity in the United States.

Post–September 11, the political environment is consumed with the need for "homeland security" and overtaken by allocations for military spending that supported a "preemptive" war

with which many in the United States and most of the world dis-
agreed. The debates about the topics of concern in this book—
need and dependency, families and state, welfare and the
dimensions of the social contract—have been largely muted,
victims of a war mentality that defines the threats to the United
States as external, terroristic, and violent. But these problems
remain. Unaddressed, they will continue to undermine the
health and general well-being of the United States, even as they
are displaced in our national consciousness by more dramatic
concerns.

The issues surrounding dependency remain constant, a part
of everyday reality for many who struggle to survive in America
and in the world. Dependency has not disappeared; it may even
have been exacerbated by the "war" against terrorism that we
now wage. Publication of this book at this time is undertaken
with that realization in mind.

M.L.A.F.
Ithaca, New York

Introduction

This book examines some of the core myths of American society as they are interwoven through political rhetoric and popular ideology at the beginning of the twenty-first century. One of its major premises is that our particular way of thinking about the desirability and attainability of autonomy for individuals and families has seriously limited the ways in which we think about equality. Ideas about individual autonomy and self-sufficiency create this limitation, as do corresponding institutional arrangements that support privatization and the market as an absolute good and governmental action and regulation as presumptively bad. One consequence of this has been the conceptual separation of the family from other societal institutions and the assignment to it of primary responsibility for the dependency of those deemed not autonomous and independent.

Contrary to this trend, I argue for the adoption of an intergenerational and cross-institutional notion of collective responsibility for dependency. In doing so, I examine the rhetorical and

ideological underpinnings of dominant American societal constructs, including the ways in which these concepts are played
out in existing institutional relationships. My focus is primarily,
though not exclusively, on the law and on legal constructions of
society and its institutions.

Law is one important manifestation of the state. In this book
I conceive of the state as a complex of coercive legal and institutional relationships that situate individuals, as well as complex
societal organizations such as the family, in relation to one another. In this regard, I look at theories that delineate the relationship between state and individual, as well as those that posit
(or assume) an appropriate role for the state in regard to the regulation of concurrent societal institutions and arrangements,
such as the market and the family.

Rejection of the idea that there is some collective responsibility for dependency is not surprising in a society such as ours.
American political ideology offers an iconic construct of the autonomous individual and trusts the abstraction of an efficiency-
seeking market as an ordering mechanism.[1] We have an historic
and highly romanticized affair with the ideals of the private and
the individual, as contrasted with the public and the collective,
as the appropriate units of focus in determining social good.

After all, the very concept of the private defines the domain
of the individual—an unregulated space where individual freedom reigns and in which each would-be king can construct *his*
castle. If a child is part of that landscape, it is deemed a private
matter, not the occasion for public subsidy or support.[2] Children
are considered to be like any other item of consumption, a matter of individual preference and individual responsibility.

The idea that the private is generally preferable as a means of
responding to need and dependency has become more and
more firmly enmeshed with our sense of social justice during the
past few decades—informing the unwritten "social contract"
that guides and gauges the relationship among individuals, soci-

etal institutions, and the state. As it evolves, what may be referred to as a distinctively American version of the social contract seems to be expanding along the private axis.

Privatization is increasingly seen as the solution to complicated social problems reflecting persistent inequality and poverty.[3] The rhetoric surrounding many current policy debates urges previously public concerns to be transferred to the magic realm of the private solution. From welfare reform to the construction of ideal educational or prison systems, the assertion is that the private market can better address historic public issues than can the public government.

My argument in this book is a mirror image of such arguments about the perceived advantages of the private sector's taking over tasks historically located within the public sphere. I am arguing for the assertion of collective or public responsibility for dependency—a status or condition that historically has been deemed appropriately assigned to the private sphere.

The theory of dependency I set forth develops a claim of "right" or entitlement to support and accommodation from the state and its institutions on the part of caretakers—those who care for dependents. Their labor should be treated as equally productive even if unwaged, and should be measured by its societal value, not by economic or market indicators. The fact that dependency work has been un- or undervalued in the market is an argument *for* governmental intervention and restructuring to mandate adjustment and market accommodation, as well as more direct reparations.

PART ONE: FOUNDATIONAL MYTHS: AUTONOMY, DEPENDENCY, AND SOCIAL DEBT

Chapter one develops the idea of foundational American myths, particularly political myths. It looks at the myth of autonomy in the United States, with its attendant ideals of independence and self-sufficiency. I am particularly interested in the role the autonomy myth plays in political and popular rhetoric, as well as in national ideology. In these discourses, autonomy is understood in very narrow terms, linked to economic self-sufficiency and a sense of separation from others in society. I discuss how this conception of autonomy places it in conflict with a full, substantive sense of equality—equality that would guarantee more than mere sameness of treatment or opportunity and access.

A discussion of autonomy as being in opposition to a fuller sense of equality is important. The rhetorical and ideological rigidity with which contemporary policy debates have been conducted makes it particularly difficult to assert the claim of any collective responsibility to assure at least a minimal standard of economic and material equality for all citizens. This difficulty is illustrated most clearly (though not exclusively or even primarily) in the struggle over welfare payments to poor mothers and children. In those debates, the core components of America's founding myths, such as the sacredness of autonomy and individual responsibility, have been reflected in simplistic notions of individual independence and self-sufficiency. These notions have become mantras for many, ossified and used as substitutes for analysis, eclipsing rather than illuminating debate.

Chapter two proceeds from the assumption that we must complicate the way we think about some of the basic concepts that have been effectively employed in recent political maneuvers to undermine the comparatively minimal guarantee of a social safety net for the poor and dependent in the United States. In this regard, I challenge the rhetoric that creates dichotomous pairs of desirable versus stigmatized positions, such as independence/dependence and self-sufficiency/subsidy.

In place of such simplistic and inaccurate characterizations,

Chapter two presents a theory that understands dependency as both universal and inevitable—all of us were dependent as children, and many of us will become dependent as we age. These characteristics of universality and inevitability support an argument for the reallocation of responsibility for dependency across societal institutions, away from primary reliance on the family. Such a reallocation is essential if equality is to be realized because caretaking carries with it a derivative form of dependency—the need for resources on the part of the caretaker in order to perform her care work. As developed in chapter two, if those resources must primarily come from the family, gender inequality will be hard to undo. Dependency must not be structured as in competition and incompatible with the ideal of equality—it is merely one of the human and societal circumstances that must be addressed as part of achieving equality.

This theory of universal dependence encapsulates the notion that subsidy is also universal—we all live subsidized lives—as well as the idea that subsidies come in many different forms. Yet, not all subsidies are labeled as such. Specifically, I argue that while the state provides what we think of as subsidies, such as those supplied by the tax code, caretakers provide a subsidy to the larger society and its institutions. Far from being independent, the state and the market institutions that it protects and fosters are dependent on the caretaking labor that reproduces society and populates its institutions.

Caretaking thus creates a "social debt," a debt that must be paid according to principles of equality that demand that those receiving social benefits also share the costs when they are able. Far from exemplifying equal responsibility for dependency, however, our market institutions are "free-riders," appropriating the labor of the caretaker for their own purposes.

PART TWO: INSTITUTIONALIZING AUTONOMY—THE MARITAL
FAMILY AS SOCIAL POLICY AND POLITICAL IDEOLOGY

The introduction to part two sets out the traditional "separate
spheres" understanding of society within legal discourse in
which the family is positioned as a unique and private arena. I
argue that this is an incorrect and unsustainable conception.
The family is contained within the larger society, and its contours are defined as an institution by law. Far from being separate and private, the family interacts with and is acted upon by
other societal institutions. I suggest the relationship is not one of
separation, but of symbiosis. It is very important to understand
the roles assigned to the family in society—roles that otherwise
might have to be played by other institutions, such as the market
or the state.

Chapter three examines the family in the rhetoric of those
policy proponents who are concerned with the future of civil society in the United States. This chapter presents a case study in
the treatment of family matters. Marriage is considered central
to the concept of family, and family is perceived of as the foundation of society. Civil societarians argue for policies that promote marriage, a position that is increasingly popular among
diverse sets of groups. I examine these arguments and their
bases, concluding that the most telling aspect of these theories is
what is left out—the growing inequality in access to resources
that has characterized American society over the past several
decades. Blaming the plight of children on their parents' marital
status without seriously considering how governmental and employer actions (or lack thereof) contribute to and compound that
plight is just bad policy analysis.

Chapters four and five look at marriage as a societal institution, first in chapter four by looking at the history of marriage
and then in chapter five by asking what marriage actually means

as an institution, both to individuals and to society. There are many reasons that individuals may marry, and historically the state has also had a catalogue of justifications for its regulation and for the privileging of the institution. I argue that in a diverse and secular society, it is impermissible for the state to privilege one form of sexual affiliation over others, and thus to make marriage the core connection in the institution of the family.

These chapters continue to explore the significance of the state's imposition of responsibility onto the family, as initially developed in chapter two. If we want our families to shoulder responsibility for dependency then we must look directly at that task and build policy to foster and facilitate caretaking. Certainly, we should not be creating policy directed to and organized around marriage. Census figures and other statistics clearly indicate that both sex and reproduction are no longer confined to marriage. People are forming all sorts of different types of intimate entities. Why create policies based on a seriously weakened family affiliation—the marital couple—when it is really caretaking that we as a society should want to ensure? Society has a responsibility to adjust to these changing patterns of behavior by guaranteeing that the emerging family forms are supported in performing the tasks we would have them assume.

PART THREE: EQUALITY AND FAMILY—AUTONOMY WITHIN
THE FAMILY AND THE ASPIRATION TOWARD EQUALITY

Chapters six and seven consider existing institutional arrangements, presenting feminist critiques of the family, as well as a critique of feminists who either ignore or minimize the role of the family in their theorizing. Feminists have paid particular attention to the institution of marriage and the roles of husband and wife, but they typically assume that the family can easily be transformed so as to achieve equality within it. Family issues tend to be analyzed as oppressive and in need of reform, so that women are able to act as equals in the workplace and other public aspects of life. The family reforms have been successful, at least on a rhetorical level, with the law now gender-neutral, and old assumptions, such as a maternal preference for custody of small children at divorce, impermissible.

The problem with many feminist analyses is that they have failed to realize the degree to which the possibility for the transformation of the family is dependent on corresponding radical and massive transformations of the workplace and accompanying ideological shifts that validate assumption of responsibility by the state in an unstigmatized manner. Women's aspirations for themselves have indeed been transformed, but these aspirations cannot be realized in the context of institutions that continue to assume that all workers are unencumbered individuals with no caretaking responsibilities and that the state is not responsible for regulation and amelioration of the excesses of the market and its institutions.

These chapters argue that one problem with the privatization of dependency is the continuing unequal and gendered division of family labor, which burdens women more than men. Within the family there is a delegation of responsibility for dependency; caretaking has traditionally been and largely remains gendered work, assigned to those in the family roles of wife, mother, grandmother, sister, daughter, and daughter-in-law.

Of particular relevance to the debates about dependency are feminist attempts to show how the dichotomous concepts of public and private, which are reflected in the division of society into separate spheres, have significant political implications. These concepts represent more than mere labels; they have tremendous political and practical implications. They interact as ideological channels for the allocation of societal resources, including the resources of power and authority.

PART FOUR: THE AUTONOMOUS INDIVIDUAL AND
THE AUTONOMOUS FAMILY WITHIN THE SOCIAL CONTRACT

Designation of some institutions in legal discourse as "public," while others are considered "private," has implications for the manner and method of state regulation and the perceived legitimacy of collective subsidy. These classifications also shape the contrasting norms of interaction and expectation within and between societal institutions that we designate as being part of either sphere. I discuss this interaction in chapter eight through the lens of social contract theory.

The social "contract" is a metaphor for consent of the governed—the idea that people have consented to the current arrangement of the government and its regulation of and relationship to other societal institutions. This fiction of a social contract implies that the current situation is fair, because autonomous individual members of society implicitly agree to it through their participation in that society.

Using the concept of social contract allows me to introduce the idea of social change and the importance of background conditions to our assumptions about the status quo. I argue that the basic institutions of society—family, market, and state—have changed to such a degree that we can no longer believe in either the fairness or the successfulness of existing arrangements in which the family is designated as the primary repository for dependency.

Chapter nine links the changes already discussed in regard to the family to the transformations in the workplace that have taken place over the past several decades. This chapter describes the much more tenuous employment relationship that now exists in the United States. The degree of change in family and work calls into question the historic terms of the social contract and mandates that it be revised, with the state and the market assigned some share of responsibility for dependency and caretaking.

CONCLUSION AND POSTSCRIPT: REVITALIZING THE STATE:
AGAINST PRIVATIZATION; FOR PRIVACY

Chapter ten serves as the conclusion for the book, making the argument that there is a need for a responsive state, a state with which to address the dilemmas presented by the changes in other institutions in regard to dependency. In this chapter, I address the state in its relation to societal institutions as well as its relation to the individual.

Defining the appropriate relationship among the state, societal institutions, and individual citizens is important for several reasons. In the first instance, American foundational documents such as the Constitution are understood as conferring limits on state authority, serving to establish a space for citizen freedom and autonomy. This dimension of the relationship of the state to the individual is of particular relevance in today's political climate, in which many are suspicious of governmental intervention into private matters.

The rhetoric of economics, which is increasingly the language of government and policy-making, warns us that society and its market institutions operate efficiently only when unregulated individuals are free to act to maximize their interests. Competition produces the best results for all, as the inefficient, and therefore "inferior," are swept away in a free market free-for-all.

But there are also affirmative aspects to the historic relationship between state and individual—protections offered by the state against arbitrary actions on the part of governments and fellow citizens in some contexts. Theories about law and justice compete with "scientific" economic concepts in an effort to establish guidelines for assessing which formal governmental actions affecting individual behavior may be condemned as inappropriate intervention, as contrasted with necessary regulation, and which may be tolerated as providing a necessary corrective to a sometimes harsh, unfettered free market.

Unfortunately, the political and governmental institutions that should be facilitating and encouraging debate and reconsideration have been stalled in partisan and polarizing rhetoric. The methods and tactics they employ are actually impeding understanding and exploration. A new understanding of autonomy would enable us to appropriately and fairly assign responsibility for dependency in a way that promotes substantive equality.

However, it is not enough for the responsiveness of the state to come only in the form of policy directives and regulatory measures. The state must also assume responsibility for the creation of structures where truly democratic debate and deliberation can occur. An important concern when articulating the idea of a collective responsibility for dependency is the fear that the government may become too far-reaching in its ability to impose the collective will over the rights of individuals—the prospect of collective control. Collective responsibility for dependency should not concede the individual's right to control intimate decisions, such as whether and when to reproduce, or how to form one's family. The postscript of this book develops the idea of entity or family privacy. Family privacy currently works to shield individuals within the marital family from governmental supervision and regulation absent abusive or neglectful conduct. I argue for a new version of family privacy that would attach to the caretaker/dependent unit, free from any dictates as to family form, and based instead on the caretaking function.

Pursuant to the goal of more equitably distributing the responsibility for dependency across societal institutions, this postscript supports the revisioning of the family undertaken in this book—a revisioning in which the individual family would no longer be viewed as the primary repository for dependency. The effort and resources of the family would be supplemented by those of other societal institutions, which would also assume some of the responsibility for shouldering the burdens dependency entails. The critical question for policymakers and politicians would then center not on how to eliminate dependency (a futile objective), but on how to order society so that dependency needs are met and satisfied in a manner that is both "efficient," offering, in the economist's sense of that term, the greatest benefit and the least detriment to the largest group of persons, and "just," meaning that social costs and benefits are distributed with reference to individual and institutional actions and capabilities.

The Autonomy Myth

PART ONE

Foundational Myths: Autonomy, Dependency, and Social Debt

A Dystopian Fantasy

Imagine for a moment what changes would have to be made to our society in the United States in order to really foster our self-proclaimed national ideals of autonomy, independence, and self-sufficiency. This exercise is intended to focus attention not on those subsidies received by "the other"—the welfare mother or the homeless addict—but on those, perhaps more subtle, advantages conferred on the rest of us. I contend that if we seriously want a world in which each individual is assumed to stand alone, to rise or fall on her or his individual merit, and to be beholden to no one for her or his success, we must shape our policies so as to facilitate that model of society. As it stands now, we give lip service to these ideals in a society in which policy and law protect and perpetuate existing and historic inequality, a nation where some individuals are subsidized and supported in their "independence," while others are left mired in poverty or burdened by responsibilities not equitably shared.

For example, a society that imposed the ideals of self-sufficiency and independence on all its citizens would certainly institute close to a 100 percent inheritance tax on all large estates. Otherwise, the beneficiaries would be tempted to forgo work and live off their unearned windfalls, exhibiting neither independence nor self-sufficiency.[1] It seems obvious that inherited wealth carries with it the potential to corrupt individual initiative. Not only do we risk putting into place a system of disincentive, by allowing inheritance of large estates we also distort the very meaning of meritocracy, making success a transferable commodity rather than the result of individual accomplishment. People should not be deprived of the opportunity to rise above the mediocre masses, demonstrating their own inherent merit and worth, simply because they are burdened by the wealth of their fathers. We should provide an equal opportunity for everybody to live the American Dream, pulling themselves up by their own bootstraps. To do this, we must ensure that the laces are relatively equal in length and strength.

Of course, inherited wealth is not the only distorting factor that interferes with individual independence and the realization of a true meritocracy. There are also existing unequal economic and social advantages, and it is unlikely that they will ever be totally eradicated within our capitalist system. I struggled with how to address this fact and concluded that a lottery system would be the most appropriate and just way to distribute social goods. This is not the same thing as imagining a society from behind a "veil of ignorance," as does philosopher John Rawls, whose work is discussed in the introduction to part four. Rawls's veil is supposed to prevent the searcher for justice from knowing what characteristics she or he as a single rights-claiming individual would possess, thus facilitating the creation and acceptance of a system in which justice is done abstractly for all individuals without regard to background and status. I think it is important, however, for a social theorist to directly confront the reality of privilege, which is conferred by social contexts. The reality of inequality mandates the rotation of individuals into existing, known, and accepted structural disadvantages in order to more equitably distribute them.

A lottery would not eliminate differences in social conditions, but certain advantages and disadvantages would be allocated by chance, rather than by accident of birth. Although this might eventually ensure a much more level playing field, I am willing, for purposes of this exercise, to concede that true or pure social equality is not attainable. If that is so, and if we believe that each individual can demonstrate merit and ability independent of the burdens presented by social and economic contexts, we can at least democratize or randomize the process whereby benefits and burdens are distributed. Therefore, if we wanted to put each individual to the test, we might at birth assign each child a Social Security number, along with a list of professions they might legitimately pursue, appropriately grouped into categories such as "service worker" or "professional." We could also assign the schools the child would be permitted to attend—if there were too many assigned to an institution, admission would also be by lottery. If an individual were not inclined to be satisfied with her or his educational or job allotment later in life, she or he would have to find a willing person with whom to bargain or trade in order to alter the luck of the draw, perhaps leading to a "free market" for careers and educational advantages. To further equalize contexts, perhaps each child (and her or his parents, should they want to stay with the child) should be compelled to spend some significant amount of time in a number of different neighborhoods while growing up; two or three years in wealthy Marin County, California, would be balanced by equivalent time in a poverty-stricken neighborhood in New York City or rural Alabama.

The point of this exercise is not to suggest seriously that this is what we should do, but to have us think about how much context does matter for *all* of us. We do not begin our lives in equal circumstances. We begin in unequal ones. Society's winners and losers become so in some large part because of benefits and privileges or disadvantages and burdens conferred by family position in a society with extreme and unequal distribution of social and economic goods. In such a society, the approach to a resolution to this type of inequality is not found in simplistic and hypothetical prescriptions or ideological placebos of independence, autonomy, and self-sufficiency.

Chapter One

Exploring Foundational Myths

A litany of terms accompanies our approach in the United States to policy-making regarding family and poverty. These terms have mythic dimensions. As defined in *The New Webster's Encyclopedic Dictionary of the English Language,* three concepts are particularly relevant to this book:

Autonomy: 1) independence or freedom, as of the will or one's actions. 2) the condition of being autonomous; self-government or the right of self-government: independence.

Independence: 1) not influenced or controlled by other; thinking or acting for oneself. 2) not depending or contingent upon something else. 3) not relying on another for aid or support. 4) refusing to be under obligation to others. 5) possessing a competence: financially independent . . .

Self-sufficiency: 1) able to supply one's . . . own needs without external assistance. 2) having extreme confidence in one's own resources or powers.

These concepts are strung together, representing complementary ways to think about the position or power of individuals and institutions. They are often grouped together in an attempt to present a picture of someone or something that has autonomy (freedom), which is demonstrated by independence (self-determination or reliance) and results in self-sufficiency (financial or material sufficiency). Their antonyms, particularly dependence and subsidy, are highly stigmatized terms as applied to individuals and institutions in American society.

I. INTRODUCTION

At the beginning of the twenty-first century we find an American society that, at least in its political rhetoric and imagination, is seriously incapacitated in dealing with some of the most important social welfare problems facing its citizens today. We live in the richest country in the history of the world, yet at least one out of every five children lives in poverty.[2] The elderly and disabled fare little better. Over 10 percent of Americans aged sixty-five and older are classified as poor, as are one-third of adults with disabilities.[3] Most working-age adults with serious disabilities face a dilemma, in that if they find an employer who will provide accommodation for their disability they will lose the necessary health benefits they receive under Social Security. Over thirty million Americans lack health insurance.[4]

The list of relative and absolute deprivation could go on and on, but rather than setting out a catalogue of existing inequities, I want to explore the ways in which we have become incapacitated conceptually and politically by looking at the rhetoric and ideology of contemporary American politics. An understanding of equality as a substantive promise to our least advantaged citizens has been sacrificed to a shallow sense of autonomy. Our incapacity to fashion solutions leading to a more just and equal society is reflected in our political discourse. The very language of our politics and politicians is mired in a simplistic rhetoric of individual responsibility and an ideology of individual autonomy.

Taking responsibility is understood narrowly, as being accountable for oneself and one's dependents only. This sense of responsibility is also primarily economic in nature. The autonomous individual is anchored in a world of paid labor either directly, as a worker, or indirectly, through marriage to a wage earner. Autonomy is the absence of economic dependence on outsiders, particularly on the government. At the same time, autonomy is seen as the reward conferred by the government for economic self-sufficiency.

Autonomy thus connotes on an ideological level that an individual who conforms to the dominant notions of independence and self-sufficiency is both freed *from* the prospect of regulatory governmental action and freed *through* governmental structures from interference by other private actors. The freedom through the government is the nonintervention point stated in positive terms—the right to be let alone is also the guarantee of privacy. In establishing and adhering to a norm of nonintervention and regulation for those individuals deemed self-sufficient, the state grants them autonomy.

I argue that this sense of autonomy is on a collision course with another important aspiration in the American constellation of political ideals—the promise of equality of opportunity and access to societal goods and services. It is so because it posits that state delivery of subsidy creates dependency and evidences a loss of autonomy in the recipient, notwithstanding that for the poor and many of the struggling middle class, some infusion of economic and other resources is essential if they are to be able to take advantage of the access and opportunity that society provides formally.

In America, equality is not understood as it is in some other societies, as a state or quality of being—participation in the "good life" of the community and sharing in society's benefits, at least in terms of entitlement to basic social goods. Equality in this substantive sense means that there is some floor beneath which individual citizens may not sink, a floor constructed by the state because the status of being human demands a degree of resources and dignity. This type of equality is viewed in other societies as a necessary precondition for the exercise of self-governance or autonomy, which the government is at least partly responsible to secure.

Instead, in America, while there is a great deal of rhetoric about equality, in policy-making it seems a second-level concern. In our political process equality is cast as though it is a subset or outgrowth of autonomy. Equality is manifested in mere formal or legal guarantees of sameness of treatment for individuals. Inherent in sameness of treatment is the absence of affirmative governmental measures designed to raise the unequal to a more equal position. Thus, equality is not an aspiration about achieving a state of being for all citizens, but the obligation to neutrally provide opportunity or access. In a society such as ours where there is existing inequality, the guarantee of access and opportunity means little for many. In this way, our ideas about autonomy interfere with the development of a concept of equality as a substantive goal or objective with positive material and social implications.

In the pages that follow, I look at some of the core concepts of American mythology, focusing on autonomy with its attendant notions of independence and self-sufficiency. I insist that we have an obligation to reexamine these concepts in the contexts presented by our contemporary society and the needs and aspirations of people today. We must view these historic ideals with the complexity that passage of time and resulting changes in societal structures and aspirations have added, perhaps redefining them in the process. A commitment to a process of ongoing reexamination of core concepts would be a recognition that even if we were absolutely confident (which we are not) that we know the *historic* meanings of those concepts, the demands of justice, as well as concerns about the legitimacy of government, require that our implementation of foundational principles resonate in the *current* realities of our lives.

Every society has well-developed foundational myths associated with its origin and the nature of its national character.[5] By "myth," I mean "a legendary story that invokes gods and heroes and explains a cultural practice or phenomenon."[6] The mythical stories of a nation—its dreams and the heroes who populate them—both reflect and incorporate the historic values and visions a society hopes to embody at home.[7] They also represent an assertion of the place of the nation within the larger context of the world of nations by articulating what are self-reflectively viewed as its asserted distinct, important, or powerful contributions.[8]

One such construct, which will be discussed in more detail in chapter eight, is the idea of the "social contract"—the theory that modern states exist because individuals, who are free by nature, joined together and decided to create an agency—the state—to act on their mutual behalf.[9] The idea of the social contract is particularly relevant to the constellation of American foundational myths, because the stories of the American Revolution, the Declaration of Independence, and the establishment of the Constitution emphasize the very same concepts. The language of the Preamble of the Constitution is a classic expression of a social contract:

> We the People of the United States, in Order to form a more perfect Union, establish Justice, insure domestic Tranquility, provide for the common defense, promote the general Welfare, and secure the Blessings of Liberty to ourselves and our Posterity, do ordain and establish this Constitution for the United States of America.

These famous words of the Preamble are a classic example of a foundational myth: they embody the principle that American society is based on a democratic political system, which was voluntarily created by "We the People" through the Founding Fathers.[10]

A. Myth and Purpose

In his classic book *Myth and Reality,* Mircea Eliade argued that there are many varieties of myth. Religious myths, for example, deal with gods and worship, and natural myths deal with the stories of natural phenomena. Eliade's research focused on primitive and archaic societies, but the principles also apply to modern myths. However, unlike the primitive societies, advanced societies also develop political myths, which are based on the same principles and differ from other types of myth only in subject matter.[11] Like the myths described by Eliade, political myths do not merely entertain; they promote practical purposes.[12] They are based on the story of a society's beginnings, but they also explain the present and provide a vision of the future.[13] Political myths "[tell] the story of how a political society was founded, and [express] the values and aspirations of those who benefit . . . from the continued existence of that society."[14]

In addition to their historic aspect, foundational stories are also epic in nature, relating in poetic terms a series of majestic achievements over time. This epic characteristic enhances the stories' mythic quality, as well as the perception that the values and personal attributes represented are stable and legitimate aspirations irrespective of the passage of time or changing societal circumstances.[15]

Foundational stories are about people. Eliade said that myths tell the story of "the fabled time of the 'beginnings' . . . [and] the actors in it are Supernatural Beings and mythical Ancestors." A myth is more than just a story about our origins; it also "supplies models for human behavior ... it expresses, enhances, and codifies belief; it safeguards and enforces morality ... and contains practical rules for the guidance of man."[16] The Preamble of the Constitution reminds us of the "time of beginnings" of the United States. The Founding Fathers are the mythical ancestors who provide an exemplary model for independent and democratic behavior, and classic "American values"—justice and liberty—are given as reasons for establishing the new state.

As a myth, the story may not present a strictly accurate historical account of the past, but it preserves the significance of the event.[17] There is no historical evidence that George Washington ever cut down a cherry tree or uttered the words "I cannot tell a lie," but the story is a mythical expression of the value of honesty, modeled by a mythical ancestor. Other societies also have their own foundational stories: the Norman invasion of England, the Great Trek of the Afrikaners, and the Russian myth of the October Revolution are all examples of political foundational myths.[18]

The traits of the Founding Fathers and ancestors are often presented in mythic terms, as though they were unwavering and unchanging over time.[19] These characteristics become cultural and ideological absolutes, cast as not only desirable but also essential to instill in the current generation within individual citizens in order to preserve the very identity of the nation.[20] One aspect of the classic Roman foundation myth was that as descendents of the Trojans, the Romans inherited the valuable qualities of the Trojans.

In his study of political myths, Henry Tudor explains a process applicable in analyzing the role of myth in American constitutional discourse: "the foundation[al myth] ... established the character of the Romans as a people, and it was in terms of their character that they explained their rise to greatness."[21] Romans looked to their own mythical ancestors as examples to follow, just as Americans uphold the model of the Founding Fathers. The Roman author Ennius wrote: "On men and on manners of olden times stands firm the Roman state."[22] These characteristics provide the imagery of the language of politics and exemplify the aspirations of the nation for its citizens.[23] In this way, purported historical attributes and characteristics become mythical and manifest their status as foundational.

Because foundational political myths are typically complex and multidimensional, they can be made relevant to shifting patterns, incorporating or accommodating changes within societies. A foundational myth evokes a particular theme over time—that the current greatness is the result of specific deeds by the mythical ancestors—but the historically particularized versions of each story may be used for different, even contradictory political purposes as time passes and the political needs of the state evolve. On the Roman foundation myth, Tudor has observed: "as the myth was transmitted from one generation to the next, its meaning and content changed giving us a series of individually distinct versions. A political myth is not a world-view which somehow persists unchanged through all its particular manifestations."[24]

In fact, the circumstances of a nation and its people are always evolving and fluid. Nevertheless, politicians using political foundational myths ignore this or see it as undermining adherence to the core values the stories reflect.[25] It seems that the nature and form in which the values are manifested is deemed to be independent of any societal context.

In fact, politicians often present these stories as if they persist unchanged. The myths' status as foundational means that certain values escape an explicit and self-conscious examination by the society that holds them out as the conceptual structures defining their national "character."[26] Tudor has commented that "[b]ecause a myth has nothing specific to propose and gives no reasons for what it asserts, it eludes the critical efforts of 'intellectualist philosophy.' Unlike a program or a prediction, a myth cannot be refuted." [27] Thus, there is little impetus to consider the appropriateness of the values for our contemporary citizen and society. [28]

Ironically, at the time of the Declaration of Independence, the term "independence" meant freedom from the need to work for wages paid by another. Not relying on a wage constituted independence, and those members of society who had to work for their living were considered "wage slaves." [29] Wage earners were actually considered to have forfeited their economic independence: "however voluntary the transaction, to work for wages was to be dependent, to lose the autonomy requisite to citizenship—the autonomy associated with title to property." [30] The abolitionist movement, the Civil War, the Industrial Revolution, and the rise of charity reform all converged to change the prevailing understanding of dependency. Eventually wage work was considered a manifestation of independence along with property ownership enjoyed by the "independently wealthy." [31]

B. Mythical Politics

The tendency of political myths to evade self-conscious reconsideration by each new generation is unfortunate. Times and circumstances change and evolve, sometimes dramatically. When societal change is sweeping and profound, it affects aspirations and expectations as well as behavior. In the wake of change it may be that certain foundational myths need adjustment in order to be made compatible with contemporary circumstances and situations. Altered social realities may require the explication of a more nuanced understanding of a cherished national characteristic or value. It is also sometimes the case that changing contexts and circumstances will cast historically compatible foundational aspirations in tension with one another.[32] In such a case, there is also a need for realignment in order to regain a sense of consistency among cherished objectives, a reconsideration of the very nature of our goals and values and the weights historically conferred upon each in relation to others.

Such a project would require express consideration of the nature and function of the current versions of our foundational myths because they do not stand alone and are not easily identifiable. Political myths operate in extremely complex cultural contexts and are usually embedded and interwoven into "the framework of a general ideology," combined with philosophy, history, and science.[33] As a result, they are difficult to examine critically, as they are only one element of a series of mutually supporting points of view.[34] Change in understanding is slow. However, the excavation and reevaluation of the current versions of our political myths is a crucial project because such myths may be used rhetorically to bolster positions that are fundamentally incompatible with healthy social programs. Reconsideration is important because, while myths can be used for many, even contradictory purposes, they tend to operate in a conservative manner. They are more often used to preserve the status quo than to inspire change.[35]

While myths tend to support conservative policies, they can be used progressively and actively. Political myths can be powerful tools in forging many types of social policy. In our current ideological climate, however, they are most often wielded by those in power, who argue for curtailment of emerging family forms, as well as of progressive welfare policies perceived to be undesirable because they support those forms. By evoking the language of foundational myths—words such as "autonomy," "independence," "justice," and "liberty"—political players may shield a very radical agenda from societal scrutiny. When discussing the application of political myths, Tudor observes that "emotive words such as 'equality,' 'dictatorship,' 'elite' or even 'power' can often, by the very passions which they raise, obscure a proper understanding of the sense in which they are, or should be, or should not be, or have been used."[36]

Of course, foundational myths are conveyed not only in political contexts. In fact, they must be part of the day-to-day ideological context of life in order to become truly fundamental—embedded in the sense of national character. Our values are thought to be transmitted within our society's basic institutions, such as the family, and handed down from generation to generation. The values are typically assumed to be coherent in nature, as well as both perfectly clear to and perfectly attainable by the successful citizen growing up within the appropriately functioning family. Correctly transmitted, values become intuitive or second nature.[37] This explains why there is such concern when institutions such as the family begin to change their historic (or mythical) nature and form—we fear that the values will not be properly instilled or will be distorted or destroyed within deviant family configurations.[38]

II. THE RELATIONSHIP BETWEEN THE "RULE OF LAW" AND FOUNDATIONAL MYTHS

In the United States, our foundational beliefs and aspirations historically were and continue to be profoundly shaped by the fact that the nation was created through a process of democratic liberation from an oppressive monarchy. The heroes of our story of national origin were the Founding Fathers, who set up a system of government based on the consent of the governed—a democracy. The foundational principles in this story were not only the ideal of democracy, but also concepts such as equality, liberty, and due process of law. Law in this context is essential to democracy, equality, and liberty—it provides the assurance that a free people will be treated equally, not arbitrarily, and that their liberty and freedom will be guaranteed against governmental encroachment and violation by others. We are proud to proclaim that we have a system based on "the rule of law, not on the rule of men."

This idea—that the law is objective and universally applied—means that the law can be offered as a "neutral" mediator in controversies, whether they occur between state and citizen or among citizens. This perception that the law is the framework for the expression and protection of our individual rights complements the belief that other core values are timeless and unchanging and therefore appropriately monitored and protected from and through governmental action and attention. The notion that law protects us is an important part of the story that ours is a legitimate and just system of government, to which it would be only natural to consent.

A. Autonomy, Independence, and the Individual

The centrality of independence to the construction of individual American identity is reflected in the mythic and foundational document the Declaration of Independence. While it declares freedom for a fledgling nation, it nonetheless sets forth as a "natural" principle that every *individual* is endowed with *inalienable rights,* such as the right to life, liberty, and the pursuit of happiness. The Constitution of the United States and the Bill of Rights more fully develop the concept that individual rights define the relationship between government and citizen. Self-government (autonomy) is the ideal and defines the individual subject of liberal political discourse.

The specific provisions of the Bill of Rights restrain the government in regard to the individual, whose liberty and equality are thereby guaranteed. Government may not implement its will or even the will of the majority so as to interfere with protected spheres of action, such as individual speech or individual right of assembly. When the government does act, it must do so with restraint and according to principles of due process. Individual liberty interests are what are protected—autonomy entails being left alone to satisfy our own needs and provide for our own families without undue restraint.

Through the concept of states' rights, our Constitution also incorporates the idea of a limited sphere for the national, as contrasted with the local or state, government. This concept is embodied in the idea of federalism. Our foundational documents set up a federation of individual states that have joined together and ceded power to the national government. But the national is a limited sovereign.

States' rights are in part a continuation of individual rights against governmental intrusion. The least offensive government is assumed to be the one closest to home. The states are closest to the citizen and thus presumptively more within the democratic individualistic ideal. The Constitution, therefore, structures the relationship between these individual states and the national government. The Bill of Rights restrains the government in regard to the individual.

Consistent with eighteenth-century liberal political theory, the foundational concepts of our society, as well as the documents enshrining them, conceptualize the individual as a rights holder—separate from, but potentially in competition with, other rights holders. Rights holders are autonomous human beings, protected in their individuality from encroachment by other individuals on their rights. But our particular constitutional ordering also implies that freedom from external rules and regulations generated by government is inherent in individual autonomy. Autonomy is synonymous with a concept of self-

governance, and is characterized by self-sufficiency and independence, individual qualities that are seen as prerequisites for
individual freedom of will and action.

Our all-American hero is therefore the autonomous individual, protected by law from unwarranted interference with his
rights by other individuals and by government on any level, and
free to conquer the frontier, be it westward or upward into space.
The rhetoric of individual freedom and rights incorporating an
ideally restrained and limited government permeates our society. We believe that this is the natural order of things, guaranteed to us as citizens of the United States.

As part of this rubric of individual rights, our entrepreneurial
spirit cannot and should not be contained and restrained—freedom for the individual requires freedom from governmental
regulation and control. This belief creates a complicated set of
hurdles for reformers to overcome when they seek to argue that
there is a need for governmental action in order to remedy inequity and equalize existing unequal conditions.

B. Autonomy

Autonomy is indisputably important in our constellation of
foundational myths, perhaps more centrally so today than ever.
However, in recent years the myth of autonomy has become
opaque and illusive. This is partly because this myth does not
encompass only one situation or circumstance where we set up
autonomy as a paramount objective, but confuses and speaks in-
terchangeably about several different aspects of the concept.
Autonomy is the term we use when describing the relationship
between the individual and the state. Autonomy in this regard is
individual freedom from state intervention and regulation, the
ability to order one's activities independent of state dictates. In
particular, we think of an economically self-sufficient individual
as autonomous in relation to society and its institutions.

But families also have the expectation of autonomy placed on them in today's political culture. An autonomous family is a family perceived to be self-sufficient, providing for the needs of its members. The autonomy of the family in relation to society is expressed in the idea that it occupies a "separate sphere," and is a "private" institution governed by distinct rules. This type of autonomy, along with the individual variety, underlies our current political culture.

There is a third type of autonomy that is also relevant. This is the autonomy of individuals *within* the family, for which feminists have fought by exposing domestic violence and child abuse. This way of thinking about autonomy separates out individuals from the family unit and asks that their interests be considered separately and protected even against other members of that family unit. This version of autonomy undermines the other two, in that the individual who is encroaching on the welfare or safety of another family member can find his autonomy compromised by the state's intervention on behalf of the person in danger (on the side of her autonomy as an individual independent from her place within the patriarchal family). In such contexts, the family is treated not as an autonomous and separate entity, but merely as another societal institution subject to regulation and the imposition of norms generated from the outside.

It is important for us to examine foundational concepts such as autonomy in all their manifestations and permutations and to see how they are being used rhetorically and ideologically in society. What does a resort to the rhetoric of autonomy mask? Whose interests are served when it is invoked? Indeed, what does it mean to those who invoke it, as well as to those against whom it is invoked? In considering these questions, it is important to note that not all three versions of autonomy are considered equally desirable in our current political climate. Individual autonomy is the type most brandished about by politicians. Family autonomy is still assumed to be the natural order of things, and the idea of the state's intervening to protect the autonomous interests of a member of the family against another member is deeply contested by certain groups in society seeking to preserve the traditional, "autonomous" family.

Notions of individual autonomy have been powerfully employed in shaping policy. In recent years, the myth of individual autonomy has been spun out in very individualistic terms by those invoking such phrases as "independence" and "self-sufficiency" to describe the ideal citizen. Independence and self-sufficiency are terms that refer to characteristics that are perceived as attainable and as complementary in our political and civic discourses. Even the targets of the imposition of independence are convinced of its appropriateness, as evidenced by the "testimony" of mothers on welfare who mimic the rhetoric that condemns them as pathologically dependent. They accept the assertion that independence and self-sufficiency are inexorably tied to paid work.

In a very simplistic sense in contemporary America, individual autonomy is linked with economic notions. Independence and self-sufficiency are characteristics of an idealized economic status. Attainment of that economic status, in turn, is a necessary precondition for the conferral or recognition of any other type of independence or autonomy by the system. Only if we are economically self-reliant can we be considered independent. Because we are able to supply the economic resources necessary to meet our needs, we are self-sufficient. In this way, independence and self-sufficiency "buy" for us the right to self-governance and "control" over will and actions. They earn for us our autonomy.

C. Manifesting Equality
Equality guarantees that the same rules will apply to us all, uninfluenced by our station or status in life. Of course, the original American notion of equality applied only to white, male, and

propertied citizens, belying the universality of equality in regard to the exercise of political and civil rights. However, equality progressed in the epic of American law as more and more people were eventually assimilated to the original ideal. The Civil War addendum to our story added the Thirteenth, Fourteenth, and Fifteenth Amendments, abolishing slavery and adding black males to those entitled to political equality. The suffragette struggles led to the Nineteenth Amendment, adding women to the ranks of voters. Political equality was manifested in a very direct manner—equivalent treatment. The idea was "one person, one vote"—people were to be treated the same.

Even beyond the political situation, our conceptualization of the ideal of equality has been based on an antidiscrimination or sameness-of-treatment principle. This is certainly apparent in the juridical or civil sense of equality (equality before the law). Different treatment is suspect, unless there is some legitimate basis for distinguishing among individuals or groups. The history of law in the twentieth century involved the expansion of legal rules to extend equal treatment, access, and opportunity to more and more individuals. Currently, gay men and lesbians seek protection within this antidiscrimination paradigm, arguing for access to institutions such as marriage and for protection in employment and public accommodations.

The American march toward greater and greater equality has resulted primarily in an increase in the numbers of persons considered to be entitled to equality in treatment or access to existing categories of social goods, not in an expansion of our understanding of the substantive nature of equality. We gain the right to be treated the same as the historic figure of our foundational myths—the white, free, propertied, educated, heterosexual (at least married), and autonomous male. We do not gain, however, the right to have some of his property and privilege redistributed so as to achieve more material and economic parity. We have not altered our understanding of the concept of equality beyond mandating sameness of treatment, equality in access, and opportunity with the mythic male. We have merely expanded the group to whom this version of equality is to be applied.

Of course, political equality and the idea of equality under law are significant aspects of the protection and guarantees owed to the citizen by the state. But it is important for us to ask whether these forms of equality (freedom from discrimination and a guarantee of sameness of treatment by the government) are sufficient to actually ensure an appropriate level of substantive equality in today's world. Retelling our foundational story for an audience confronting the problems and contexts of the twenty-first century might posit a world in which we were promised more in terms of securing equality than just sameness of treatment in the political and juridical relationship between the government and the governed.

One could argue that concepts such as equality require constant mediation between articulated values and current realities. In trying to understand the current contexts that shape our expectations for equality, we might also want to consider changes wrought by advances in technology and knowledge that have influenced the structures of society. So, too, we may want to take into account pressures and opportunities, reflecting on challenges to our concept of equality generated externally through our interactions with other nations. We must be attentive to evolutions in our concepts and understandings of what we consider "just" and "fair." Our views on justice should be evolving as societal knowledge, realizations, aspirations, and circumstances change.

A second line of inquiry would place equality in the context of other societal aspirations and ideals. How do our contemporary aspirations for equality relate to our pursuit of other values, such as autonomy? How does our definition of terms such as dependency and self-sufficiency shape our sense of what constitutes equality? Equality rests side by side with other foundational concepts that set out further expectations for the citizen in regard to the state, as well as ordering the relationships among diverse societal institutions, such as the family and the market. In fact, these other foundational concepts have had a profound effect on the way in which equality has been understood historically, actually shaping the course and direction of its legal history and limiting the potential scope of the concept. Paramount among the limiting values in this regard are contemporary ideas about individual freedom, which is reduced to the idea of autonomy with its complementary components of individual independence and self-sufficiency.

III. EQUALITY OR AUTONOMY—SHIFTING FOUNDATIONS

Foundational myths, while rhetorically constant over time, may actually convey very different aspirations, values, and concepts from one generation to the next or across different groups within society at any one time. This presents a dilemma to the idea of equality, which is typically stated in abstract, timeless phrases and encapsulated in ringing terms, such as "justice for all" or "equality under the law." There is yet another equality dilemma lurking—when foundational concepts are in fact little more than unrealizable myths, they can have real and negative societal consequences. The idea of individual autonomy is used as a measure against which to judge the appropriateness of both individual and governmental actions. It also sets standards for the functioning of societal institutions, such as the family, the market, and the state.[39]

A. Meaning and Myth

Foundational myths and the concepts they promote are in fact abstractions. Terms such as autonomy and equality have no independent meaning or definition and can be understood in conflicting and incompatible ways. These concepts often become battle cries for diverse political movements.[40] Their amorphous, overarching, and imprecise nature means that they can be used simultaneously by those holding disparate positions in regard to any proposal.[41]

The foundational myth of individual autonomy can be understood to mandate that there be "equality of opportunity" so that each individual can succeed or fail according to her or his own merits and initiative. But it is not clear exactly what equality of opportunity might entail in the way of either individual or regulatory effort and action. For example, equal opportunity can be used to justify the institutional creation of an affirmative action program to "equalize" the possibilities for people who are members of historically excluded groups, while simultaneously serving as a rallying cry for those resisting such schemes because they give members of certain groups an "unequal advantage."

The first group would be arguing that their individual aspiration for autonomy is frustrated and the whole ideal twisted if existing systems of privilege and power prevent them from competing on equal footing with those who have not been historically excluded. Those resisting affirmative action would argue, in contrast, that "special" treatment for some in society compromises the autonomy of others and is a "perversion" of the principles of independence and self-sufficiency, signaling the very end of meritocracy.

Likewise, one may assume that a modern marriage is a "partnership" and that both parties should be treated equally should the marriage end in divorce. However, there are many different interpretations of "equal" treatment in such contexts. One could argue that equal treatment means the family assets should be divided in half, which would constitute a version of equal treatment at the moment of divorce, and that there should be no ongoing entitlement to the future wages of the primary wage earner.

On the other hand, particularly if there are children, one could argue that the assets should be divided so that the party who is assuming caretaking responsibilities—usually the mother—is able to maintain a living standard similar to that of the other spouse. In addition, one could argue that periodic payments should continue for a substantial period of time to supplement the reduced amount the caretaker will be able to earn working for pay due to the demands at home. It could be said that this would be the only way to treat the caretaker-child unit equally and ensure their future autonomy.

Both approaches to this problem would be based on the principle of equality and a desire for autonomy. However, the focuses of the approaches are different. Husband and wife in this situation have conflicting and incompatible equality and autonomy interests. Equality for caretaker and child, allowing them to achieve autonomy, comes at the expense of equal treatment of the noncaretaker and some compromise of his (or her) autonomous ability to decide the nature and extent of his obligations. Depending on which perspective we take, we would get very different divisions of marital assets and imposition of ongoing financial responsibility after divorce.

Opponents of the equality-of-result approach resist the idea that equalizing results may require unequal treatment in some circumstances. Paradoxically, they may also resist the imposition of sameness of treatment in other circumstances. Considering equality across families, the point should be made that at a minimum there is no equality possible so long as only some individuals bear the burdens of family and reproduction in society. Nor can there be equality for families so long as the foundational relationship continues to be marriage, which is limited to heterosexuals and excludes other intimate relationships that are not based on sexual affiliation.

This latter point is important. The status of marriage and the institution of the marital family is the way that many social goods are delivered to individuals in American political culture. The state subsidizes this form of family. Social goods, such as insurance and old-age pensions, are structured through the workplace and the family, rather than directly from the state, as is typical in social welfare democracies, such as those of Western Europe. The family is a mediating institution, and access to it is critical for claiming social benefits.

This doesn't mean that we recognize the marital family as a subsidized institution that is dependent on state largesse. In fact, our very particularized and superficial type of autonomy has become the standard applied in judging societal institutions, such as families, as well as individuals. Economic independence and self-sufficiency are set up as transcendent values, attainable for all social units and for all members of society. Offered in negative comparison to independence and self-sufficiency are the ideas of dependence and subsidy. As discussed more fully in chapter two, dependence is negatively compared with the desirable status of independence, and subsidy is vilified as a failure to meet the meritorious goal of self-sufficiency.

B. Rethinking Autonomy

The very terms of autonomy—as exemplified by economic independence and a detached notion of self-sufficiency—might well be redefined or reimagined in the public mind. Independence is not the same as being unattached. Independence from subsidy and support is not attainable, nor is it desirable; we want and need the webs of economic and social relationships that sustain us.[42] A different understanding of autonomy and what it entails is needed. It is not beyond our current ability to imagine a new concept of autonomy, one that recognizes that the individual lives within a variety of contexts and is dependent upon them.

Certainly popular culture seems open to the idea. This can be seen in the popularity of books and educational programs by Stephen Covey, author of *The Seven Habits of Highly Effective People*.[43] Covey's work is based on the theory that all of nature, human life, and society are *inter*dependent. He suggests that there is a continuum of maturity, from dependence, to independence, to the eventual realization that we are all interdependent.[44] He observes: "the current social paradigm enthrones independence. It is the avowed goal of many individuals and social movements. Most of the self-improvement material puts independence on a pedestal, as though communication, teamwork, and cooperation were lesser values. . . . But much of our current emphasis on independence is a reaction to dependence—to having others control us, define us, use us, and manipulate us."[45] Covey thus implies that there is a connection between the emphasis on independence and the stereotypes and social stigma attached to dependence.

Aside from the inroads into the national psyche that might be provided by pop psychology, there are important arguments and debates that must occur in political and policy circles about the interrelationship between autonomy and equality. Specifically, we should not define our aspiration for equality in the shadow of autonomy. Rather, we must begin to think of autonomy as possible only in conjunction with the meaningful and widespread attainment of equality. For example, some degree of equality (equalization) of resources so that there is a floor below which no citizen shall fall would seem to be a prerequisite for the achievement of autonomy. Autonomy is only possible when one is in a position to be able to share in society's benefits and burdens. And sharing in benefits and burdens can only occur when individuals have the basic resources that enable them to act in ways that are consistent with the tasks and expectations imposed upon them by the society in which they live.

The expectation that one should achieve this form of autonomy—autonomy supported by a societal commitment for the provision of basic social needs—should be every person's birthright. Autonomy in this sense concedes that there is an inherent dependence on society on the part of all individuals. While some, having benefited by history and circumstances, may have the current means and methods that make it fair to expect them to achieve autonomy, others have been disadvantaged and are deserving of some societal support.

In addition, this form of autonomy concedes that the concept only has meaning in situations in which individual choices are not made impossible, constrained by inequalities, particularly those inequalities that arise from poverty. The goal of autonomy must be supported through an understanding of collective responsibility for basic needs.

Chapter Two

Dependency and Social Debt:
Cracking the Foundational Myths

I. INTRODUCTION

Ideals of independence and self-sufficiency historically have been complementary themes in our political discourse. Both of these core concepts seem subsumed within the contemporary manifestation of the ideal of autonomy, giving it content. Invoking autonomy, we create and perpetuate cultural and political practices that stigmatize and punish those among us labeled dependent. Dependency is thus cast as a societal problem in need of drastic measures to remedy. However, only some interrelationships among individuals and institutions are seen as constituting dependency. In recent years, much of the content of dependency has been provided by debates in the welfare context.

Specifically, in our political rhetoric and policy we stigmatize with the label "dependent" the welfare mother who is unemployed and trapped within poverty. Her need for resources in order to undertake her caretaking responsibilities mandate she resort to public support in the form of government subsidy. Her circumstances are deemed to be her fault and the solutions within her control—she is told that she can marry or she can work, perhaps do both to relieve her situation. Her dependency, as conceptualized of her own making, means she is undeserving of a "handout." Disciplined into self-sufficiency, she is abandoned to assume responsibility for herself and her children.[1]

The rhetoric surrounding the welfare mother evidences a narrow conception of self-interest in which each person is permitted only to care about his or her own circumstances and those of his or her family. This has led to a rending of the social safety net in the United States. The illusion that independence is attainable for all leads to increased resistance to responding to the obvious dependency of others, as the better-off taxpayer detaches himself from the poor and struggling in society. Economist Frank Levy of the Massachusetts Institute of Technology sums up the consequences of such a narrowed perspective when he notes that prosperous Americans "have caught on to the fact that they can do better if there is no redistribution of income, and since power correlates with income, they are in a position to push the argument."[2]

This self-interest may not be considered selfish or greedy if those same Americans can convince themselves that we are all capable of becoming economically "self-sufficient" and "independent," regardless of the socioeconomic circumstances of our lives. Those who need the government subsidy of welfare payments or other programs simply are not "taking responsibility" for themselves, a premise exemplified by the current political rhetoric about the poor.

Ironically, at the same time that we stigmatize mothers on welfare, we commiserate with industries that experience other forms of "disaster" that we define as outside of individual control. American politicians apply differing standards of self-sufficiency to different situations. Hence we "bail out" some who run amok economically, such as farmers, airlines, savings and loan associations, and highway construction firms. Sometimes the cash transfers such entities receive are justified as being in the national interest—an investment to secure jobs, ensure national defense, or otherwise promote the "American way." At other times, the government is seen as playing the role of an insurer, such as when it responds to disasters that occur when houses built on floodplains or over fault lines are destroyed through predictable natural occurrences.

We rationalize assistance for ill-conceived or no-longer-sound business reasons and view as necessary and appropriate disaster assistance for "acts of nature," but bristle at providing relief for the disasters that have resulted from decades of neglect and discrimination—disasters manifest in inner cities and rural poverty pockets. Governmental response in the former cases is seen as a matter of investment or preservation, an entitlement, not a grudging response to dependency, as it would be if the subsidy were going to impoverished mothers and their children.

In an ultimately disastrous manner for our families, we valorize activities associated with work for wages and the accumulation of wealth, while we take for granted dependency work and the production of human beings. Yet raising the future generation is certainly of at least equal value and significance to society as that of the economic activities we subsidize and facilitate. As the argument in this chapter indicates, not only is dependency inevitable, reliance on governmental largesse and subsidy is universal. We delude ourselves when we think that many (perhaps any) endeavors in our complex modern society can be undertaken in an autonomous and independent manner.

II. THE RHETORIC OF DEPENDENCE AND INDEPENDENCE

Given where we as a nation stand on theoretical and moral grounds, one of the most important tasks for those concerned with the welfare of vulnerable members of society, particularly poor mothers and their children, is the articulation of a compelling and complex theory of dependency. I do not underestimate the difficulty of this task. Dependency is a particularly unappealing and stigmatized term in American political and popular consciousness. The specter of dependency is incompatible with our beliefs and myths. We venerate the autonomous, independent, and self-sufficient individual as our ideal. We assume that anyone can cultivate these characteristics, consistent with our belief in the inherent equality of all members of our society, and we stigmatize those who do not.

Politicians, social conservatives, and advocates of small government use the labels of "dependency," which signifies the condition of being dependent, and "subsidy," which denotes a governmental handout, in an accusatory, simplistic, and divisive manner.[3] The mere invocation of the term "dependency" prompts and justifies mean-spirited and ill-conceived political responses, such as the 1996 welfare "reform" designed to "wean" women and their children from the "cycle of dependency" and "free" them for the world of work. These "reforms" were compounded in the reauthorization process begun in 2002.

The force of the rhetorical assault has served to derail or limit contemporary policy discussions about important issues of public welfare. Condemnation or pity are considered the appropriate responses for those unable to live up to ideals of autonomy by acting in an independent and self-sufficient manner. However, the very idea of an independent individual is fashioned upon unrealistic and unattainable (dare I even say, "undesirable") premises.

A. "Inevitable" and "Derivative" Dependency

It is puzzling, as well as paradoxical, that the term dependency should have such negative connotations. Far from being pathological, avoidable, and the result of individual failings, a state of dependency is a natural part of the human condition and is developmental in nature. Understood from this perspective, developmental dependency should at least be regarded as both universal and "inevitable," and for these reasons, certainly not deserving of generalized stigma.[4] All of us were dependent as children, and many of us will be dependent as we age, become ill, or suffer disabilities. Surely this form of unavoidable and inescapable dependency cannot be condemned. Historically, such dependents were called the "deserving poor," and thus deemed worthy of society's largesse.

Dependency is not only of the biological or physical sort discussed so far, and this type of dependency does not exhaust the potential range of situations in which we depend upon others. There are additional forms of reliance that might be characterized as "dependency," such as economic, psychological, or emotional dependency. In fact, these other categories may accompany the physical or biological form that I am labeling "inevitable." One lesson, therefore, is that the term dependency encompasses more than one set of relationships or circumstances. It is far from a simplistic, one-dimensional idea—it must be understood to be a complex and multifaceted concept, potentially taking many different forms. My concern in this book is in the first instance with the form of dependency that I label inevitable. Its universality and inevitability position this form of dependency at the center of the arguments made in this chapter about the obligation of society and its institutions.

Paradoxically, undertaking dependency—caring for an inevitable dependent—generates a different form of dependency in the caretaker. I label this form of dependency, often overlooked in policy discussions or collapsed into stigma, "derivative dependency." Derivative dependency arises when a person assumes (or is assigned) responsibility for the care of an inevitably dependent person. I refer to this form of dependency as "derivative" to capture the very simple point that those who care for others are themselves dependent on resources in order to undertake that care.

Derivative dependency has both economic and structural dimensions. The economic issues are related to the fact that within families, caretaking work is unpaid.[5] The structural dimension is due to the fact that caretakers do their caretaking within societal contexts and rely on some institutional accommodation or noneconomic resources to assist in their labor. Far from structurally accommodating or facilitating caretaking, workplaces operate according to premises that mean that domestic dependency labor is incompatible with the norms and practices of paid labor. For those who have assumed the responsibilities of caretaking, current workplace expectations compete with the demands of dependency and, in this regard, caretaking interferes with or even precludes participation in the paid labor force.

Derivative dependents, as a result of the dependency work they are doing, have a need for monetary or material resources. They also need recourse to institutional support and accommodation, and have a need for structural arrangements that facilitate their caretaking. Dependency work is demanding. The norms of sacrifice and selflessness are clear—and costly. It is important to emphasize that, unlike inevitable dependency, derivative dependency is *not* a universal experience. Derivative dependency is inherent in the status of caretaker, but not all of us perform that role. In fact, many people in our society totally escape the burdens and costs that arise from assuming the role of a caretaker, and perhaps are even freed for other pursuits by the caretaking labor of others.

In our current understanding, inevitable dependency, as well as the derivative dependency it generates, is considered to be a private matter. It is the family, not the state or the market, that assumes responsibility for inevitable dependency. In this regard, the institution of the family frees the market to act without consideration or accommodation for dependency. The state is cast as a default institution providing minimal, grudging assistance should families fail. Each individual family is ideally responsible for its own members' dependency, and resort to collective resources is considered a failure, deserving of condemnation and stigma. In fact, the failure to adequately provide for its members can move a family from the private to the public sphere, where it may be regulated and disciplined.[6]

The assignment of responsibility for dependency to the family in the first instance, and within the family (mainly to women) in the second, operates in an unjust manner. Meeting the needs of dependents has significant material implications for the caretaker. One result of this privatization of inevitable dependency is the frustration of our aspirations toward gender equality. It has proven difficult, if not impossible, to break unequal historic patterns of gendered division of labor within the family when the family is also saddled with almost exclusive responsibility for dependency. Within the family, dependency work typically continues to burden women more than men. In the pattern of long-standing tradition, caretaking continues to be delegated to women—assigned as the responsibility of the person occupying the gendered role of wife, or mother, or grandmother, or daughter, or daughter-in-law, or sister.[7]

B. Dependency and Responsibility

In considering how to shape our social policy in a more focused and sophisticated manner, we must begin to distinguish among various forms of dependency. As noted earlier, unlike biological dependency, economic, psychological, and emotional dependencies are not generally understood to be universally experienced. This distinction suggests that these forms of dependency may appropriately be treated differently than forms that are considered inevitable or developmental. The characteristic of universality, which indisputably accompanies inevitable dependency, forms a theoretical basis upon which to construct a claim that society as a whole must respond to the situation of the inevitable dependent.

The universal nature of inevitable dependency is central to the argument for the imposition of societal or collective responsibility.[8] The realization that this form of dependency is inherent in the human condition is the conceptual foundation upon which can be built a claim to societal resources on the part of the caretakers of inevitable dependents, in order to facilitate their care. Justice demands that society recognize that caretaking labor produces a good for the larger society. Equality demands that this labor must not only be counted, but also be valued, compensated, and accommodated by society and its institutions.

Society has not, however, responded to the caretaker by counting, valuing, compensating, or accommodating her caretaking. Instead of a societal response, inevitable dependency has been assigned to the quintessentially private institution—the traditional, marital family. As discussed more fully in part two, the marital family is an institution that has been considered to occupy a "separate sphere." It is conceptualized as placed beyond and protected from intervention by the state. Dependency, through its assignment to the private, marital family, is hidden—privatized within that family, its public and inevitable nature concealed.

Our attitude toward family follows scripts rooted in historic and, therefore, contingent ideologies, particularly those of patriarchy and capitalism. It is naturally assumed that the family is the repository for dependency and that collective societal responsibility is therefore unwarranted and inappropriate. The family assigned this essential societal task is also believed to have a "natural" form. It is organized legally as though reproductive biology necessarily determined the social organization of the family unit. The core of the family in policy is the heterosexual couple, formally united in marriage.

In addition, and consistent with the policy of privatizing dependency, the economic resources necessary for undertaking caretaking tasks are to come from the family. Historically the breadwinner (the spousal complement to the caretaker) provided these resources. Through such complementary gendered arrangements, each individual private family was ideally and ideologically perceived as able to assume responsibility for its own members and their dependency. A need to call on collective resources, such as welfare assistance, has therefore been considered a family as well as an individual failure.

Consider how this plays out in the debates about child care for working parents. The current child-care system is not designed to provide affordable child care for all working families, but simply to promote the self-sufficiency of poor families.[9] The language of the recent reforms is consistent with maintaining the myths of self-sufficiency and autonomy by requiring that families, in order to continue receiving aid, be engaged in activities that will lead to their self-sufficiency.[10] Even President Bush's support for maintaining the funding for Temporary Aid to Needy Families (TANF) is driven by the ideal of "the great soul of America."[11] He feels that TANF will be the tool that will help needy families get into, and stay in, the workforce. He consequently aims to have over 70 percent of welfare recipients be self-sufficient within five years.[12]

Even those who agree that the societal role of families is evolving with the current capitalistic market insist that there is no child-care crisis and that government intervention will only lead to an institutionalized form of child care.[13] Their solution is to let the market evolve to suit the needs of society.[14] These commentators are very instrumental in their approach and hold on to myths of independence and self-sufficiency, which create a stigma regarding welfare and welfare recipients. Essentially, the libertarian argument against child-care subsidies is that the current situation is what the market is willing to bear, and that people are willing to accept these conditions. Even commentators who feel that there should be no stigma surrounding dependency feel that the goal of programs such as TANF should be to help recipients achieve self-sufficiency.[15]

What is seldom mentioned in media and public discussions are the racial and class implications of this system. In thinking about the privatization of dependency and the role of the family, our history of racism should also be a relevant and expressed context for debates. Women who work outside the home need to make child-care arrangements—arrangements that typically entail the employment of other women to do that care. But consider the nature of this work, which while it occurs in the paid labor force also too often merely substitutes for unpaid family labor at the exploitation of a woman of a different race and class, who is paid low wages and given few, if any, benefits.[16] Since the resources for child care come from the family, wages are depressed, as family resources are needed for provision of other basic goods and services. Ironically, a good deal of the training for work that is occurring in the wake of welfare reform is for positions in child care.

III. DEPENDENCY AND CHOICE

People operate in society, expressing preferences as structured by and through existing societal institutions. Choices are made in social relations that reflect long-standing cultural and social arrangements and dominant ideologies about gender and gender roles. The beliefs about the appropriateness of arrangements function at an unconscious (and therefore unexamined) level. Our notions of what are "natural" behaviors channel our beliefs and feelings about what are considered appropriate institutional arrangements. We know what constitutes the good mother, the ideal husband, and the perfect marriage. When individuals act according to the scripts culturally crafted for these roles, consistent with prevailing ideology and institutional arrangements, we may say that they have chosen their own path. Choice is problematic in this regard. Ideology and beliefs limit and shape what are perceived as available and viable options for all individuals in a society.

The notion that it is an individual choice to assume responsibility for dependency work and the burdens it entails allows us to ignore arguments about our general responsibilities. Choice trumps any perceived inequity and justifies maintenance of the status quo. We ignore the fact that choice occurs within the constraints of social conditions, including history and tradition. Such conditions funnel individual decision making into prescribed channels, often operating along practical and symbolic lines to limit and close down options.

Women historically have been identified with the role of mothering, and presumed to have the responsibility for children.[17] Women who choose not to have children are seen as having made a nontraditional, even unnatural choice.[18] Even when women choose to have children they are expected to care for their children at home.[19] Negative media attention to alternative modes of child care, such as placement with nannies or day-care facilities, has instilled a fear in many people that only parents can properly, safely, and conscientiously raise a child. In the cultural context that places caretaking primarily on mothers, this creates further pressure for women to stay at home and raise their children.[20] Even the public school system is structured in a way that is not consistent with families in which women work. The structures remain even though the historic assumption that most mothers remain at home to take care of their children after school and during holidays is no longer valid.[21]

Whenever we use individual choice as a justification for ignoring the inequities in existing social conditions concerning dependency, we also fail to recognize that, quite often, choice of one status or position carries with it consequences not anticipated or imagined at the time of the initial decision. We assume that people who are derivative dependents (caretakers or mothers) voluntarily assume that status—they "consent"—but we fail to ask why and how is it that only some in our society are asked to undertake the sacrifices that caretaking entails. Further, even if we may say that a woman "chose" to become a mother (societal and family pressures aside), does this choice mean she also has consented to the societal conditions accompanying that role and the many ways in which that status will negatively affect her and her children's economic prospects?

A resort to individual choice should not be the end of the matter if what we are seeking is social justice or fairness. Even if someone does "consent" in the sense of taking risks or forgoing opportunities to undertake dependency work, should that let society off the hook? Should society tolerate the situation of dependency within the family and the mandated personal sacrifices a caretaker typically encounters under current societal arrangements? In other words, are some conditions just too oppressive or unfair to be imposed by society even if and when an individual openly agrees to or chooses them?

In response to the argument that caretakers should be compensated for their labor, I have been struck by two contemporary and quasi-economic retorts based on the idea of choice. I refer to one as the "Porsche preference." This argument states that if someone prefers to have a child, this preference should not be treated differently than any other choice (like the choice to own a Porsche). Society should not be responsible for subsidizing either preference—if you can afford to own a Porsche or have a child, fine, but you can't expect the rest of us to chip in.

I do not accept the basic premise that children are merely another commodity. The nature of children hopefully distinguishes the choice to reproduce from the whims of the auto fan. Further, it seems to me that a decision to have a child sets up a qualitatively different relationship between the decision maker and the collective or state. As I argue in the next section of this chapter, caring for dependents is a society-preserving task—care of children in particular is essential to the future of the society and all of its institutions. It is a different sort of "preference," providing a social good as well as individual satisfaction.

Responding to this type of reasoning, some have argued that the consumption of Porsches is also essential to society. Consumption leads to jobs and the creation of stockholder wealth, just like a preference for children.[22] Accepting only for argument's sake the troublesome premises of this kind of argument through analogy, it seems clear that the appropriate comparison is not between the *consumers* of children and of Porsches, but the *producers* of children and of Porsches. If we make that kind of comparison, my arguments for subsidy for caretakers are supported by the analogy. The producers of Porsches are subsidized (heavily) through regulatory measures, such as tariff and tax policy and labor regulations, as well as directly, such as when communities bid for location of plants or lawmakers slash taxes and make investments in services to entice businesses with roaming eyes.

Further, when we think of just who are the consumers and who are the producers for purposes of comparison, it is important to remember that the government and the market are the consumers for the products of caretaking labor. And they are not paying a fair price; in fact, they are paying very little.[23] Not subsidizing the caretaker in this kind of comparison is the equivalent of the consumer's stealing the Porsche that its manufacturer so lovingly created and skillfully constructed.

The second argument about choice is also framed in economic terms. I label this the "efficiency as exploitation" excuse for not requiring society to pay a fair share of the necessary care work. This argument is really nothing more than the assertion that if caretakers allow themselves to be exploited—unpaid or underpaid—then this must be the most "efficient" solution. Voluntary assumption of the costs of caretaking and dependency should not be disturbed.

Sometimes this is expressed as simply the result of women's having a greater "preference" for children; as such, they are willing to make other sacrifices—that is simply what the market will bear. Aside from creating situations that negatively affect society overall, a free market in care work is not working. It has resulted in poverty, which generates other social ills. I think the implications of this laissez-faire approach to important issues of social policy also demonstrates how little economics has to offer to considerations of justice.

IV. THE DEPENDENCY DEFICIT—A SOCIETY IN DEFAULT

As it now stands in this society, derivative dependents are expected to get both economic and structural resources within the family. The market is unresponsive and uninvolved, and the state is perceived as a last resort for financial resources, the refuge of the failed family. A caretaker who must resort to governmental assistance may do so only if she can demonstrate, through a highly stigmatized process, that she is needy.

A. Deficit
Unfortunately, in many situations, neither the economic nor the structural supports for caretaking are adequate. Within families,

caretaking work is unpaid, expected to be gratuitously and un-complainingly supplied. Even when non–family members, such as nannies or nurses, supply caretaking labor, the family remains primarily responsible for the care. Furthering the assumption that this type of work is not valuable, the wages are supplied from family funds, not through social subsidies, ensuring that the pay remains low.[24]

In some atypical instances, employers offer a more communal approach to caretaking or the state assumes some responsibility, such as with company-sponsored child care or home health aids provided by public funds. However, such nonfamily assistance is not compelled (and in fact is contradicted) by our understanding of who is responsible for dependency. This sort of assistance is viewed as "generous," an unexpected benefit supplementing the primary responsibility of the family.

If we measure success by poverty statistics, it seems clear that many families are failing in their socially assigned task as the repository for dependency. Many caretakers and their depend-ents find themselves impoverished or severely economically compromised even if they are operating within the context of a marital family. Suzanne W. Helburn and Barbara R. Bergmann illustrate that even with both parents working full-time at mini-mum wage, taking into consideration the required poverty-line expenditures, they are unable to pay the cost of licensed child care.[25] As can be expected, single working mothers have an even more difficult time making ends meet and providing for child care than families with two adults present.[26]

For others, divorce or the death of a primary wage earner can prompt an economic freefall into poverty. Some women in these situations are in worse positions than women who remain single, since they have cut back on their career commitments as a result of the partnership, to raise children or to allow the partner to advance his career.[27]

Even families that "conform," in that they are both intact and economically self-sufficient, are often suffering a crisis either in caretaking or from work demands, or both. Most two-parent households must send both parents into the workforce in order to make ends meet, all at the cost of quality time spent with their children.[28] In some two-parent households the child care or after-school care is designated to one parent, and the other parent spends less time with the child or children.[29]

B. Assessing the Costs of Care

Direct costs associated with caretaking burden the person doing the dependency work. Caretaking labor interferes with the pursuit and development of wage labor options. Caretaking labor saps energy and efforts from investment in career or market activities, those things that produce economic rewards. There are foregone opportunities and costs associated with caretaking. Even caretakers who work in the paid labor force typically have more tenuous ties to the public sphere because they must also accommodate caretaking demands in the private.[30]

In addition, there are psychological or spiritual costs resulting from the attenuated and compromised relationships a caretaker is forced to have with both the market and family (if she works in both), or from the need to choose, thus sacrificing one to gain the other.[31] The caretaker is caught within social configurations and institutional arrangements that are unjust.

Further, most institutions in society remain relatively unresponsive to innovations that would lessen the costs of caretaking. Caretaking occurs in a larger context, and caretakers often need accommodation in order to fulfill multiple responsibilities. For example, many caretakers also engage in market work.[32] Far from structurally accommodating or facilitating caretaking, however, workplaces operate in modes incompatible with the idea that workers also have obligations for dependency. Workplace expectations displace the demands of caretaking—we assume that workers are those who are free to work long and regimented hours. These costs are not distributed among all beneficiaries of caretaking (be they institutional or individual). Unjustly, the major economic and career costs associated with caretaking are typically borne by the caretaker alone.[33] If she is lucky, the caretaker is able to persuade her partner in the private family to share the costs with her, spreading them out a bit. But the costs remain confined to the family in a world where market institutions assume workers are unencumbered by family and dependency, and the government assumes that (functioning) families provide for basic needs.

There are penalties that dually responsible workers currently suffer, while market institutions are relieved of responsibility for dependency. It is important to note here that while caretaking remains gendered in practice, it is the caretaking itself, not the gender of the caretaker, that is inherently disadvantageous in our system. When men do care work, they also suffer costs. It is the caretaking itself that institutions are free to punish. These penalties must be removed, and there must be a more equitable distribution of responsibility for dependency among the primary societal institutions of family, market, and state.

C. Default—Accruing a Social Debt for Social Goods

I argue that caretaking work creates a collective or social debt and that each and every member of society is obligated by this debt. Furthermore, this debt transcends individual circumstances. In other words, we need not be elderly, ill, or children to be held individually responsible. Nor can we satisfy or discharge our collective responsibility within our individual, private families. Merely being financially generous with our own mothers or duly supporting our own wives will not suffice to satisfy the share of the societal debt we generally owe to all caretakers.[34]

My argument that the caretaking debt is necessarily a collective one is based on the fact that biological dependency is a universal and inevitable phase in the human condition and, therefore, is of necessity a collective or societal concern. Individual dependency needs must be met if we, as individuals, are to survive, and our aggregate or collective dependency needs must be met if our society is to survive and perpetuate itself. The mandate that the state (collective society) respond to depen-dency, therefore, is not a matter of altruism or empathy (which are individual responses often resulting in charity), but is a matter that is primary and essential because such a response is fundamentally society preserving.

If infants or ill persons are not cared for, nurtured, nourished, and perhaps loved, they will perish. We can say, therefore, that they owe an individual debt to their individual caretakers. But the obligation is not theirs alone—nor is their obligation confined only to their own caretakers. Social justice demands a broader sense of obligation. Without aggregate caretaking there could be no society, so we might say that it is caretaking labor that produces and reproduces society. Caretaking labor provides the citizens, the workers, the voters, the consumers, the students, and others who populate society and its institutions. There are essential tasks to be performed in every society that are legitimate state concerns. One of these is the response to dependency.[35] The fact that biological dependency is inherent in the human condition means that it is of collective or societal concern.

Society-preserving tasks, such as dependency work, are commonly delegated. The delegation is accomplished through the establishment and maintenance of social institutions. For example, the armed services are established to attend to the collective need for national defense. But delegation is not the same thing as abandonment. The armed services are structured to be the responsibility of both some designated members (volunteers or draftees) and all members of society (taxpayers and voters).[36]

This dual and complementary responsibility is consistent with our deeply held beliefs about how rights and obligations are accrued and imposed in a just society: societal obligations have both an individual and a collective dimension. Certain members of society may volunteer, be recruited, or even be drafted for service, but they have a right to be compensated for their services from collective resources. They also have a right to the necessary tools to perform their assigned tasks and to guarantees that they will be protected by rules and policies that facilitate their performance. Caretakers should have the same right to have their society-preserving labor supported and facilitated. Provision of the means for their task should be considered the responsibility of the collective society.

V. THE RHETORIC OF SUBSIDY AND SELF-SUFFICIENCY

In popular and political discourse, the idea of "subsidy" is the equally stigmatized companion to dependence, the opposite of the ideal of self-sufficiency. In fact, dependency is assumed if an individual is the recipient of certain governmental subsidies, such as welfare. The specter of dependency serves as an argument against subsidies in the form of governmental social welfare transfers. Policymakers, who argue for the goal of independence, favor the termination of subsidy so the individual can learn to be self-sufficient.

But a subsidy is nothing more than a process of allocating collective resources to some persons or endeavors rather than other persons or endeavors, because a social judgment is made that they are in some way "entitled" or that the subsidy is justified.[37] Entitlement to subsidy is asserted through a variety of considerations, such as the status of the person receiving the subsidy, their past contribution to the social good, or their need. Often, a subsidy is justified because of the position the subsidized group holds or the potential value their endeavors have for the larger society. Sometimes the benefits we receive are public and financial, such as direct governmental transfer programs to certain individuals or business entities, such as farmers or sugar growers.[38] Public subsidies can also be indirect, such as the benefits given in tax policy.[39] Private economic subsidy systems work in the forms of foundations, religions, and charities.

A. Types of Subsidy

Typically, a subsidy is thought of as the provision of monetary or economic assistance. However, a subsidy can also be delivered through the organization of social structures and norms that create and enforce expectations. A subsidy can also be nonmonetary, such as the subsidy provided by the uncompensated labor of others in caring for us and our dependency needs as individuals, as well as members of a larger dependent society. Taking this observation into account, along with the ideas of inevitable and derivative dependency, it seems obvious that we must conclude that subsidy is also universal. We all exist in contexts and relationships, in social and cultural institutions, such as families, which facilitate, support, and subsidize us and our endeavors.

In complex modern societies no one is self-sufficient, either economically or socially. Whether the subsidies we receive are financial (such as governmental transfer programs or favorable tax policy) or nonmonetary (such as the uncompensated labor of others in caring for us and our needs), we all live subsidized lives.

In fact, all of us receive both forms of subsidy during our lives. Those who adhere to the myths of autonomy and independence must recognize that the uncompensated labor of caretakers is an unrecognized subsidy, not only to the individuals who directly receive it but, more significantly, to the entire society.

The interesting question is why some subsidies are differentiated and stigmatized while others are hidden. Subsidies to market institutions and middle-class families are called "investments," "incentives," or "earned rewards" when government supplies them, but deemed "gifts," "charity," or the product of "familial love" when they are contributions of caretaking labor. The actions of our government thus far reflect the inconsistent and hypocritical stance taken with regard to subsidy. The family is to be self-sufficient, but the situation of others is viewed sympathetically.

B. Subsidy and Politics—Contemporary Comparisons

Curiously, the negative stigma of subsidy reflected in its companionship with dependency does not carry over to the rhetoric surrounding corporate welfare, or subsidies to businesses or industries. Corporate welfare, or state action that benefits a specific firm or sector, may take the form of grants, tax breaks, real estate, loans, or government service. Robert B. Reich, President Clinton's labor secretary, documents the emergence of business subsidies and bailouts in *New Deals: The Chrysler Revival and the American System*. The congressional bailout of Chrysler Corporation in 1980 marked the beginning of a series of outright rescues of American mega-firms that included Lockheed, railroad companies, and, at the end of the 1980s, the savings and loan industry.

Policy leaders have come to take for granted the necessity of assistance to large corporations. By the 1990s, this amalgam of cash payments, special rules, and tax subsidies totaled somewhere between $30 and $100 billion a year.

These subsidies exist in various forms, but exemplify a political and rhetorical acceptance for government intervention on behalf of American firms. This goes beyond the motto "what is good for General Motors is good for the country." In fact, Reich traces this conception of assistance to a nineteenth-century law-yer, Jay L. Torrey. Torrey urged Congress to accept an analogy: "When a vessel is labouring at sea, nothing will more surely sink her than to leave untouched the broken masts and loose spars which every wave is using as a battering ram to pound her to pieces and carry her to the bottom."[40] This influential compari-son resulted in reforms in bankruptcy law, and ultimately an ac-ceptance of state assistance for firms deemed to be too valuable to be let go under. Ironically, this sympathy for the firm arose dur-ing a time of "tough love" (or worse) for the American family.

The same politicians who seem to be out of touch with the ac-tual situation of welfare recipients by insisting on their self-sufficiency[41] choose to disregard these myths when it comes to matters such as the farm subsidy.[42] These conflicting concepts of autonomy and subsidy were highlighted recently when, on the very same day that certain Democratic senators joined with Re-publicans in proposing stricter requirements for welfare recipi-ents, the House of Representatives passed a bill that would provide large subsidies to America's farms.[43] The language used in each case is revealing: the agricultural bill is named the Farm Security and Rural Investment Act, and ironically was described by President Bush as establishing a "reliable *safety net* for our Nation's farmers and ranchers."[44] The president emphasized that the act would provide the "support" that "[h]ardworking . . . farm and ranch families" deserve. Obscenely, because the House voted down a motion that would cap payments at $275,000 a year per farmer, the result is that three-quarters of the subsidy payments will go to the largest and richest 10 percent of farmers—in other words, to agribusinesses, not to the "hard-working farm and ranch families" who deserve support.[45]

On the same day, a dozen Democratic senators "declared that Congress must adopt 'tougher work requirements' " so that by 2007, 70 percent of welfare recipients must be engaged in work and other supervised activities, an increase from the current requirement of 50 percent.[46] Unlike the Farm Bill undertaken earlier, welfare reform *does* allow states to cap their payments, so that if a child is born to a mother already receiving welfare payments, she will not receive any additional funds to support and feed that child.[47] For example, New Jersey has implemented a system whereby a woman on welfare receives a basic $488 per month with an additional $64 for each child. But if a woman on welfare gets pregnant and has a child while receiving assistance, she receives no additional cash allotment for the new baby.[48] It was argued that to provide the funds would create an incentive for reproduction.

VI. CONCLUSION

The societal arrangement whereby dependency was the responsibility of the private family may have made some sense when marriage provided (and assumed) a certain population for the family. If we have both a caretaker and a wage earner who make differentiated but complementary contributions—one providing the caretaking and emotional resources, the other the material necessities—then perhaps dependency can be handled within this family. But what about the situation of millions of families that do not conform to that (some would say antiquated) ideal? And what about the costs to individuals within families that do conform—the losses of opportunity and access because of the burdens of caretaking? Further, what about the responsibility of the rest of us—society and its institutions? How is it just that we appropriate the labor of caretakers and refuse to contribute a fair share of the burdens associated with that care?

The myths about autonomy, independence, and self-sufficiency both for individuals and for families have only been able to flourish and perpetuate themselves because dependency has been hidden within the family. When certain families reveal the fallacy of the assumption that they can adequately manage their members' needs, we do not reexamine the premises, but demonize those families as failures. Therefore, those in need of economic assistance are viewed as deviating from the stated norm of independence and self-sufficiency. It is time to rethink "subsidy," as well as "autonomy" and "dependency."

If caretaking is society preserving, and therefore productive, work, the political and policy questions should focus on an optimal reallocation of responsibility for dependency across societal institutions. Reallocation in this scheme may be provided through economic transfers to caretaking units, as well as by the provision of structural supports that accommodate caretaking responsibilities within workplaces so that those who both work for wages and work for love or duty do not have to compromise one to do the other.

In chapter ten I build upon these suggestions. In the section that follows I explore the rhetoric of marriage in policy discourse by focusing on adherents to the civil society movement, often called "communitarians." I also look at the roles assigned to marriage and the marital family and ask what functions marriage, *per se,* actually performs and which of those functions should be considered essential and appropriate for our diverse and secular state.

PART TWO

Institutionalizing Autonomy

Existing Societal Arrangements

The significance of the family as a societal construct is revealed by its position as a primary terrain for the cultural wars in which our society is increasingly mired. The chapters in this section look at the relationship between our legal and policy understandings of the family and our concepts of autonomy and independence. An essentialized, traditional notion of the family supports a static set of cultural, social, and economic relationships, most significantly confining responsibility for dependency to the local and intimate levels of society. The stakes are very high for those who want to maintain the status quo and not disturb the role of the family as the primary repository for dependency—a role that alleviates other societal institutions from assuming any responsibility in that regard.

This section develops the argument that it is not only the individual but also the family that is cast as ideally independent in our scheme of things. The autonomy of the family is assumed in discussions placing it on a different plane than other societal institutions. In this regard, society is often presented as though it were constituted by "separate spheres." The "public" and the "private" spheres are cast as complementary social spaces, each connoting a distinct area of human interest and activity. Within this scheme of division, the family represents the quintessentially private institution, separated from the market and its functions, on one hand, and the quintessentially public state, on the other. In this sense, the family is perceived as autonomous, with some of its members having overlapping interaction with the public sphere. This family/state model can be diagrammed thus:

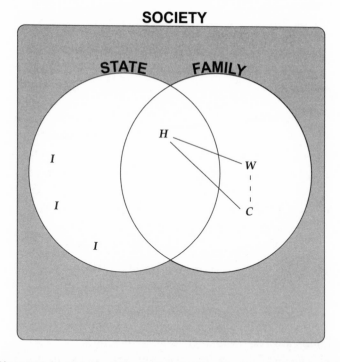

Diagram I. I = individual; H = husband; W = wife; C = child. The configuration of the Family drawn here is that of the common law, in which the Husband was the head of the Family and owed obedience and services by Wife and Child. The common-law Family was hierarchical and patriarchal.

Not only is the family perceived as occupying the private sphere, it is also conceptualized as embodying values and norms that are very different from those of the institutions occupying the public sphere, particularly those of the market. Family relationships are cast as different in function and form than relationships existing in the public world. According to this conceptualization, families are altruistic institutions held together by bonds of affection. A division of the world into "public" and "private" realms also indicates that the family is defined as both separate and necessary for achieving a balance or wholeness.

The notion that the family is private and separate has had a tremendous impact on the way the law has developed. Ongoing family functioning has been shielded from outside scrutiny through the legal doctrine of family or entity privacy. However, it would be a mistake to think that the conceptual organization of "separate spheres" means that the marital family exists outside of the regulatory reach of the government and its laws, cocooned within the protection of the family privacy doctrine.

If we look at the family from the perspectives of its formation as a legal entity through marriage, and its dissolution as a legal entity through divorce, it is clear that the family has always been heavily regulated by the state. What have historically been deemed private were the day-to-day interactions of an existing, legally defined, and recognized family. But it is the state through its regulation and recognition of the status of marriage that brings the family into legal existence.

The three chapters in this section address the institution of marriage from different perspectives. The "traditional" family is built around this institution. The law tells us who may marry and, in so doing, defines the circumstances under which a sexual union and its offspring will be considered legitimate and entitled to the special treatment afforded the marital family in our society. Once the marriage is established, the state must be a party to its dissolution; it dictates the terms under which divorce may occur and under which property and ongoing economic responsibility for the ex-spouse or children may be allocated.

We may speak of a marriage "contract," but it is a contract in which the state is an active party, defining the terms and consequences for the other parties—husband and wife. Until the institution of the prenuptial agreement, which occurred only recently, men and women entering the institution of marriage were not free to make individualized agreements about the terms and consequences of their relationship. Marriage rules concerning the character of property and support obligations applied to *all* couples at divorce. These rules were more than mere default. State-imposed rules defined the responsibilities and consequences attached to marriage and structured the relationship between husband and wife. Individuals were unable to make a legally enforceable alternative to the state rules.

Further, as the discussion in chapter two indicates, any serious consideration of the marital or traditional family in America must also consider its public and essential function with respect to dependency.[1] Expectations for family responsibility for dependency relieve the state of some obligations it might otherwise have to assume. This section demonstrates that thinking of the family as manifesting a separate sphere facilitates this arrangement.

While it is true that law initially defines the family, controlling entry into the privileged status, once it is formed and given content, the family is a powerful construct. Family has symbolic significance to many groups within society and can be manipulated by politicians and others with ideological objectives to mobilize a variety of constituencies. In addition, perceived family strengths (or weaknesses) can be utilized to place pressure on political institutions. The adjustments and accommodations that may result can alter the very nature of the state's relationship to the family and the individual.

The family is currently subsidized on both a material and a cultural level in its traditional, preferred (marital) form. Supporters argue the legitimacy of allocating public resources to the marital family. Such subsidy is facilitated and enhanced by the symbolic position the preferred family has in political rhetoric and American ideology. One implication of this preference for the marital family form is the demand for access to marital status by those who are in unions that do not conform to the ideal form. The more favored the preferred family is, the more pressure is generated from outsiders to the institution demanding entry into or expansion of the subsidized family category.

Because of the interactive relationship between the family and other institutions within society, it is much more accurate to view the family not as existing in or constituting a separate sphere, but rather, as being a constructed institution contained within the larger society. As such, the extent and functioning of other societal institutions profoundly affects the nature and shape of the family. By the same token, the nature and functioning of the family profoundly affects other societal institutions, particularly the state. This interrelationship is more fully explored in chapter eight on the social contract. It is diagrammed on the next page.

The metaphor of "symbiosis"[2] seems more appropriate to describe this model of the family in relationship to the state than does the separate spheres imagery. The family is located within the state—family and state are interactive and define one another. Alterations in the scope or nature of one institution will correspondingly alter the scope or nature of the other.

Note also in this diagram that there is an outermost ring labeled "society." This reflects a recognition that the state as I perceive it does not occupy the entire social space. Of course, the state may contract or expand, and this process will inevitably have an impact on those "voluntary" arrangements or structures that coexist in this relatively unregulated space. It is this

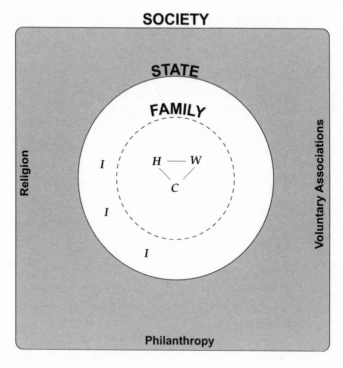

Diagram II. The Family depicted in this diagram is the egalitarian family the modern version of the marital arrangement in which Husband and Wife are viewed as equals and the Child has an elevated, if somewhat subservient, position. Within the larger society, the Family coexists with market and nonmarket institutions, some having greater impact on the family than others. Voluntary and private institutions, such as religion, can and do have effects on specific, individual Family units, but it is the more structured and dominant institutions the ones we cannot avoid or opt out of that must be part of a comprehensive consideration of the Family and its place in society. Here I am referring to the relationship between Family and State, but later chapters address the market, which is most certainly a dominant societal institution with which the Family must deal. The line drawn around the Family is the demarcation of family privacy, which sets the entity apart from other societal institutions. It is porous since, in the egalitarian family, the state will intervene to prevent abuse or neglect. In the common-law version of the Family, the privacy line would be more intact.

space that is occupied by organizations such as religious or philanthropic entities. However, in this book I am concerned with those institutions that are clearly contained within and defined by the state. It is those institutions that are correctly understood as "coercively constituted," in that they are creatures of the state. While law may affect voluntary entities, it is those institutions, such as the family and the market, that are actually created and constituted as coherent institutions through law. Their very existence as objects of state regulatory concern comes into being through law: it is law that gives them consequence and meaning even outside of the wishes or demands of their members.

Of course, these various state-constructed entities may spill over into the voluntary field. There is a well-developed sense of family in religion, for example. So, too, individuals and groups outside of the regulated space may clamor for entry into it, willing to trade the freedom of nonlegal status for the benefits of the legal and privileged institutional form. Such overlapping interest on the part of the coercive and voluntary realms in regard to an entity such as the family might provide an occasion for tension, even for transformation or adjustment in state rules. In this way these coercive institutions are potentially dynamic in nature. The state has the authority and power to monitor (or impede) their transformations.

If this model of the family/state relationship is accurate, it has important implications for public policy. In the first instance, it indicates that the family's relationship to the state is not fixed or static. State policies can profoundly affect the form and functioning of the family. Correspondingly, if the family is constructed through interaction with the state and society, the family cannot be posited as a "natural" entity with a form that is constant over time and culture. Nor can a preferred family form be assumed essential to family functioning, such as caring for children or providing emotional and psychological support for members. Instead, the state defines the nature of the preferred family as a *political* matter. Definitions of what constitutes a family can change, and perhaps will inevitably change, in response to political and social pressures.

Altered state regulation, support, and subsidy for the preferred family may affect that family; it may empower it or create tensions and pressures that lead to demands for accommodation or regulation of other institutions with which the family interacts. Changes in the family can spur changes in other societal institutions, such as the workplace. As a societal institution within the state, the family competes with other institutions for allocation of state resources, including political and ideological capital. Since other societal institutions are also inherently state constructs, existing in law and grounded in state regulatory authority, the state, acting through law, can mandate accommodation and change in those institutions.

In the chapters in this section, I first look at the treatment of the marital family undertaken by those adhering to a "traditional" perspective. The marital family is used in an ideological manner, exemplified here by communitarians seeking to strengthen the institution.

In discussing the communitarian position, as contrasted with the libertarian position, Amitai Etzioni expresses the movement's commitment to values that would be considered "progressive" in most circles:

> [C]ommunitarians (at least the more enlightened among them) favor new communities, in which all members have the same basic moral, social, and political standing. In these communities, values are reformulated and policies evolve in a free dialogue and exchange in which ideally all participate, and particular groups do not impose their values. Whereas traditional communities were often homogeneous, new communities seek a balance between di-

versity and unity. As Gardner notes: "To prevent the wholeness from smothering diversity, there must be a philosophy of pluralism, an open climate for dissent, and an opportunity for subcommunities to retain their identity and share in the setting of larger group goals."[3]

I choose this group rather than the "easier" targets of the Southern Baptists or the Promise Keepers (which are discussed in chapter four) because it is important to realize how deep the ideological commitment to the institution of marriage runs. Its mere existence as an option for the organization of one's intimate life impedes the imagination of theorists, limiting and directing approaches to social problems even for those truly concerned with children and poverty. Even "progressive" reformers and politicians stress the centrality of the heterosexual marital relationship in their visions for a just society. Marriage is positioned as the primary affiliating circumstance, the core family relationship in these discourses.

Those who cling to the norm of the traditional, heterosexual marital unit often conclude that the nuclear family is in "crisis" because of the tendency of many marriages to disassemble and dissolve. Some in the "crisis camp" further claim that society is also in a state of crisis as a result of the instability in the institution of marriage.[4] Others are concerned by the crisis they perceive in increasing visibility of "deviant" relationships, such as nonmarital heterosexual cohabitation and same-sex relationships. These are entities that "compete" with marriage, and many in such relationships are claiming that their sexual affiliations are entitled to the benefits and privileges previously extended only to marriage.

I think the sense of crisis resulting from increasing diversity in family formation is unwarranted. Not only can the form of the preferred family constructed within our (or any) society be reconfigured, it has been reconfigured in the past to reflect evolving and different sets of expectations and aspirations. We see this clearly in the transformation of the marital family from a hierarchical unit with well-defined gendered roles to the "partnership" between equals expected to share responsibilities and rights in all areas of life that is described in chapter four. This transformation indicates just how sweeping the changes in our beliefs about the institution of marriage can be and have been.

Chapter five looks at the marital family from a functional perspective, raising the question of how the changing nature of family roles and relationships between husbands and wives should affect the way we think about the institution of marriage. A sense of past transformation is the appropriate context for the current struggle over what will be the form of tomorrow's preferred family. The arguments that family should not be coterminous with marriage are not a threat to the family, but rather a recognition that an intimate entity can function and flourish even without the marital connection as its core intimate tie.

What I do think constitutes a crisis is the lack of coherent or serious policy discussion about the process of change in family form that we are undergoing. We need ways of reflecting upon and absorbing the changes that are occurring in the wake of altered patterns of intimate behavior and family formation. Change has introduced some instability in regard to the institution of the traditional marital family, but instability alone does not constitute a crisis.

We must approach this time of change in a thoughtful and considered manner, asking what functions we want our families to perform and how the society and its institutions can assist in carrying out those responsibilities. Even without the occasion of far-reaching change that we now encounter, it seems that families and society would benefit from periodic self-conscious reflection. We should consider the continued viability and desirability of historic assumptions about the family as an institution, as well as debate about directions for the future.

We are at a point where we must accept that the relationship between marriage and popular conceptions about the family has changed substantially over the past four or five decades. This change is reflected in the disengagement of marriage from the concept of family in many people's minds. Sexuality is no longer thought only appropriate when confined to marriage. Couples live together without marriage, but in marriage-like domesticity. Reproduction and child rearing have also escaped from the marriage box, with rising divorce rates and instances of unwed motherhood, combined with a rise in gay and lesbian lone parenting, increasing the number of children raised in single-parent households.

It is time to build our family policy around these emerging norms, to focus not on form but on the function we want families to perform. Certainly one of the most important functions assigned to the family is that of caretaking. If we were to conceive of family as organized around this relationship, we would model it as seen on the next page.

I also argue that the transformations in our expectations and aspirations for our families cannot be undone. Families as practicing units (as contrasted with legally defined entities) in all likelihood will only continue to change, deviating further from the traditional form. Those who try to use law to push new and emerging forms of family into old molds seem doomed to frustration and failure. Our energy should be turned from obsessing over the changing nature of marriage to rethinking the expectations and assumptions we have for the family of the future.

The new and emerging family may not function in all regards in the same way as did the traditional marital ideal. However, we must ensure that family policy addresses the needs of the new

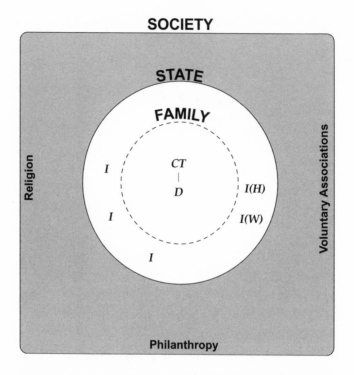

Diagram III. CT = Caretaker; D = Dependent. The categories of H and W, as well as C, are irrelevant Dependents can be children, the elderly, the disabled, or others in need of care. The Caretaker may be the person who is (was) a Wife and mother, or a Husband and father, or neither of these persons, rather someone outside of the old Family role models. The significant thing is that this person (or these persons, since the model is concerned with function, not form) is a Caretaker. I(H) and I(W) are those adults no longer distinguished by gendered Family roles based on sex. This would mean that the institution of the Family would no longer mediate those adult relationships. In interactions with each other, those adults would not be governed by special Family rules, but by the same rules that apply to all individuals in Society in defining their relationship with the state and with each other, i.e., contract, tort, criminal law, property law, and equity would be the bases for defining interactions with other individuals. Individual privacy would guard decisions from state interference in regard to sexual and reproductive matters.

family so it is able to perform those most important and fundamental tasks the family has historically been assigned. For example, it may be that the new family needs a different form or amount of societal assistance in undertaking responsibility for dependency. It may be that other societal institutions will have to adjust to the changes in the family in order to build a coherent policy. It is clear, however, that some simultaneous reconception of those other institutions must be compelled by the state in order to ensure that these institutions respond in ways that accommodate and facilitate the family in carrying out its societal responsibilities.

One final diagram is necessary, although as explained in the postscript it is not my preferred model of state/family organization. This model is one in which the individual exists unmediated by the concept of family as a separate, private, and privileged space within the state (see next page).

Diagram IV. I = Individual; I(H) = Husband; I(W) = Wife; I(C) = Child; I(CT) = Caretaker; I(D) = Dependent. This particular configuration of the family is a version of the state unmediated by family. Family is defined by a line of privacy or nonintervention. An example of this might be the ancient Spartan system or, a more recent example, the kibbutz system in Israel.

Chapter Three

The Family in the Rhetoric of Civil Society—Privileging Marriage

I. INTRODUCTION

In recent years, commentators concerned with the state of civil society ("communitarians" or civil societarians) have given their critique of what ails modern American civilization. The focus has been on the state of that part of the society defined by them as nongovernmental institutions and organizations. Mostly progressive and liberal thinkers, civil societarians have formed important institutions and act as commentators on policy matters. As well-positioned academics and political and policy advisers, they have been very politically influential at both the federal and state governmental levels. The publications of the civil societarians claim the family as one significant aspect of their policy domain, and set forth its rehabilitation as one of their missions. Rehabilitation is perceived to be achieved by the preservation and perpetuation of the family's marital form. Members generate and disseminate social scientific papers and reports on the status of the family as an institution in crisis.

On an ideological level (and along with much more conserva-tive commentators), civil societarians believe that the marital family is a foundational institution—the "cradle of citizen-ship"—that teaches "standards of personal conduct that cannot be enforced by law, but which are indispensable traits for demo-cratic citizenship." [1] Problems with the marital family, therefore, are clearly seen as problems for democracy, justifying legal and political responses.

In recent years, a number of civil societarian groups have met, held conferences and hearings, and generated position pa-pers and calls for action in an effort to engage the nation in a dis-cussion of civil society. [2] This chapter examines two reports that set forth the purported diminished state of civil society and that suggest proposals for civic renewal: "A Nation of Spectators: How Civic Disengagement Weakens America and What We Can Do About It," prepared by the National Commission on Civic Renewal [hereinafter Commission] and "A Call to Civil Society: Why Democracy Needs Moral Truths," prepared by the Council on Civil Society [hereinafter Council]. [3]

There is some significant membership overlap in the two bod-ies, which may explain the similarity in analysis and in policy recommendations. [4] Of particular interest is the fact that William Galston, an adviser to both former president William Jefferson Clinton and former presidential candidate Albert Gore, is both a member of the Council and the executive direc-tor of the Commission. Professor Galston has been an active and influential advocate from the liberal or progressive camp, arguing for policies that encourage the traditional two-parent family. The reports evidence that he has played a strong concep-tual role in both bodies.

Galston's position on the family exemplifies the civil societar-ian approach. Unfortunately, his emphasis on the decline of the two-parent family operates to eclipse concern about social and economic forces that are truly destructive to families, regardless of their form. Of particular concern in this process are the political implications of civic societarian discourse, which is replete with allusions to crisis and "family breakdown." The assertions of crisis and breakdown are supported by "evidence," such as opinion polls and academic studies.

Initially, from a purely academic perspective, civil societarian arguments' reliance on public opinion polls is troubling. These polls are often used as though the responses to certain questions by a majority of those polled represent some transcendent "truth" about the state of American society.[5] That "truth" then becomes the justification for recommendations for legal policy that would punish some families and privilege others.

Civil societarians justify coercive action based on opinion polls that show that "the American public" agrees with their dire observations about the family.[6] But as discussed in chapter four, the term "family" is susceptible to a variety of definitions. In addition to the "traditional" family, populated by formally married sexual affiliates and their biological children, family can be understood to include other types of couples, such as unmarried sexual affiliates, whether heterosexual or homosexual.

Family may come with or without children in coupled households. To some people, family may also mean collections of individuals not necessarily related by blood, but held together in kinship systems in which sexual affiliation is not the paramount tie. Slightly different is the sense of family associated with lines of descent; an extended and intergenerational concept of family. To many, particularly those who are living it, single parenthood does not preclude the designation of family. There are a myriad of possible meanings of family, but the point I want to emphasize is that it is by no means clear what definition respondents have in mind when replying to opinion polls inquiring about "the Family."

It is also unclear what respondents have in mind when asked to state their opinions on family functioning and moral decline. For example, agreement with the statement that "breakdown" in the family is a major indicator of "moral decline" *may* evidence concern with divorce and single motherhood on the part of some responding to the opinion poll. But to others, agreement may indicate concern with the breakdown of intergenerational ties, as illustrated by adult children's no longer caring for their aging parents at home. Breakdown in family discipline may be thought to have moral significance, evidenced by the fact that overworked parents (married as well as single) don't discipline their children into "civility."

The very use of the term "breakdown" to epitomize changes in family structure indicates that the civil societarians incorporate the premises of an ideologically driven analysis. They could have chosen another, less loaded word, such as "transformation" or "evolution," to talk about changes in family form. Using "breakdown" to describe changes in patterns of intimate behavior is manipulative—it generates in the minds of the respondents a sense that there is a societal crisis, which influences the response they give. In this way, the communitarians transform demographic information into a societal problem, a problem inherent in the image they initially conjured.

The civil societarians not only identify changing patterns of intimate behavior as an existing crisis for democracy and its political institutions; they also call for policy solutions directed at those entities. They have constructed a crisis in individual morality as well, turning the absence of marital status into an indication of individual moral failing. Marriage in the civil societarian's hands becomes much more than a legal category. It is reconfigured into the mantle of morality, from both a societal and an individual standpoint. Marriage is presented as the path to personal and familial (and therefore societal) salvation.

But as I argue in chapter four, marriage is primarily a legal category and does not have a well-defined practical definition that is consistently manifested across all couples who participate in the institution. Being married in itself does not indicate how individuals are living their lives, performing their societal functions, or expressing morality. And, for those civil societarians concerned with poll results, it is significant that the overwhelming majority of Americans surveyed in a recent poll do not want to see the government pushing marriage as social policy.

Columnist David S. Broder, reporting on a poll taken by Andrew Kohut from the Pew Research Center, remarked on the American people's concern with the "decline of moral character of the nation." Kohut found that three-fourths of those interviewed thought people were "not as honest and moral as they used to be and that young people lack the same sense of right and wrong their counterparts had a half century ago." Yet, Kohut also reported as "a real surprise to him" that when the same people were asked if they thought the government should develop programs such as those proposed by President Bush to encourage people to get and stay married, the answer was an "emphatic no." The margin indicating that the government should stay out of marriage promotion was 79 percent to 18 percent. "Even among 'highly committed' white evangelicals, Kohut found, the verdict was 60 percent to 35 percent against such programs." The speculation was that it would be just "too intrusive a role for even a well-intentioned bureaucracy." [7] Such reservation is consistent with the American version of individualism discussed in chapter one, a sense of autonomy that translates into a demand for freedom *from* governmental action.

Public opinion polls aside, it seems to me that the question should not be how we can resuscitate marriage and thus save society and the family, but how we can support all individuals who create intimate family relationships, regardless of their form. Of

particular importance are concerns for the caretaking tasks performed in families—whether children are being cared for and
whether the elderly and ill are being nurtured and loved. If there
are problems in our society for those members who are dependent, we must then ask what institutional and other adjustments
are warranted in order to address their needs. By exclusively focusing on marriage and deviant family form, the civic societarians seem to ignore these questions.

II. DEFINING THE PROBLEM—
THE CIVIL SOCIETARIAN PERSPECTIVE

Upon reading civil societarian literature, one is confronted with
a mass of assertions, assumptions, and accusations concerning
the declining state of the nation, many of them unfootnoted, as
though beyond dispute.[8] Consider the following statement from
the Commission's report:

> During the past generation, our families have come under intense
> pressure, and many have crumbled. Neighborhood and commu-
> nity ties have frayed. Many of our streets and public spaces have
> become unsafe. Our public schools are mediocre for most stu-
> dents, and catastrophic failures for many. Our character-forming
> institutions are enfeebled. Much of our popular culture is vulgar,
> violent, and mindless. Much of our public square is coarse and
> uncivil. Political participation is at depressed levels last seen in the
> 1920's. Public trust in our leaders and institutions has plunged.[9]

The report of the Commission suggests that the state of
morality in American society is "suppressing satisfaction with
the state of the nation . . . weighing down American attitudes as
Vietnam, Watergate, double-digit inflation and unemployment
once did."[10] This is reflected in the passivity and disengagement

of the average person, who is seen as lacking the confidence "to make basic moral and civic judgments, to join with [their] neighbors to do the work of community, to make a difference." [11] In seeking to strengthen the forces of civic renewal, the Commission asserts that there are roles for "[i]ndividuals, families, neighborhood and community groups, voluntary associations, faith-based institutions, foundations, corporations, [and] public institutions." [12]

As is perhaps appropriate in a report of "civic" health, most of the attention in the report that follows focuses on the individual responsibility of citizens. As citizens, we are certainly seen to be a much diminished group that "place[s] less value on what we owe others as a matter of moral obligation and common citizenship; less value on personal sacrifice as a moral good; less value on the social importance of respectability and observing the rules; less value on restraint in matters of pleasure and sexuality; and correspondingly greater value on self-expression, self-realization and personal choice." [13] The Commission's final report concludes where it began, with a "call to [more responsible, old-fashioned] citizenship." [14]

The family, labeled "the seedbed of virtue," is seen to produce citizens. [15] Families are "crucial sites for shaping character and virtue, they provide vivid models of how to behave in the world, and they help connect both children and adults to their neighborhoods and communities." [16] One need not dispute the importance of family to individuals and to the future of the nation to find fault with the Commission's perspective. Chapter two of this book, which focuses on dependency, recognizes the essential role that the caretaking family performs for the society and its institutions. The point is that many strong supporters of family are nonetheless more tolerant or accepting of diversity in family form than is the Commission.

In fact, the report states that a major failing of the self-indulgent citizen is the rejection of the institution of marriage.

This behavior is particularly significant since marriage is central to the civil societarian's concept of "the family." The Commission's report is very clear that the family at the center of civil society is a traditionally populated one—a nuclear or marital family. The Commission's conclusion about the decline of the family is evidenced solely through measuring the incidence of divorce and nonmarital births.[17] The report is full of assertions about the inferiority of the nonmarital family's child-raising ability. The authors recommend that the nation make a commitment to the proposition that "every child should be raised in an intact two-parent family whenever possible."[18] This focus on form, to the exclusion of other aspects of family, assumes that form determines function. Its effect is to provoke law reform proposals that seek to make divorce more difficult and to deter single parenthood.

The report narrowly focuses on the institution of marriage as being essential to the success and future of the family without discussing some of the problems inherent in that position. For example, it totally fails to recognize that marriage is and always has been an exclusionary institution. Until the Civil War, African Americans who were enslaved were not allowed to marry. Until well into the second half of the twentieth century, white Americans were prohibited from marrying members of a different race in many states.[19] In spite of a few court and legislative victories, gay men and lesbians are still precluded from marrying partners of the same sex in all states and in federal law.[20] In addition, marriage is reserved for those couples in which the partners are unrelated to each other, are not married to others, and conform to certain state mandates in regard to their capacity to contract.

The report is also narrow in its focus on individuals and individual lack of moral direction as the source of the problems we face. There is virtually no demand for societal engagement with the problems the report associates with the decline in marriage. The report is further limited by its lack of attention to how changes in nonfamily societal institutions have affected the family and civic health in general. At one point the commissioners recognize that "[a]lthough civil society is independent of the state and market, it is not unaffected by them." [21] This insight is limited to a concession that the norms expressed in public law "inevitably shape and temper the values and goals" of voluntary associations.[22] There is no recognition that the policies and practices of both the state and the market also shape the material circumstances and well-being of citizens and families, and thereby have a potentially profound effect on the development of civil society.[23] Nor is there recognition that the moral state of the family and individuals within it are profoundly affected by the moral state of the nation and its other institutions.

III. FAMILY FUNCTION AND FAMILY FORM—
COLLAPSING THE DISTINCTION

The Commission constructed an "Index of National Civic Health." [24] This index, perhaps devised to suggest that there was some scientific nature to their inquiry and fact-finding process, purports to measure changes in civic health in the period between 1974 and 1996. The Commission established five equally weighted categories as being relevant to the assessment of civic health: political participation, political and social trust, associational membership, family integrity and stability, and crime. The Family Component contained only two variables or subcategories within it: divorce and nonmarital births, which are each equally weighted at 10 percent.

This narrow and exclusive focus on family form, when addressing the family within civil society, is consistent with other polemical writing on the topic. In its "Report to the Nation," the Council on Civil Society expressed concern with the moral state of the nation and identified as the first of three proposed goals "to increase the likelihood that more children will grow up with their two married parents." [25] The Council found proof of declining morality primarily in the "steady spread of behavior that weakens family life, promotes disrespect for authority and for others, and insults the practice of personal responsibility." [26] The Council's report drew the civil societarian's typical causal link between nontraditional family forms and social harm. [27] Whether in the language of the Council or of the Commission, the "disintegration" [28] or "breakdown" [29] of the family [30] evidences, as well as further causes, civic decline.

It is important to note that this perception of breakdown is viewed as serious enough to justify exceptional treatment of the family, in that the intervention recommended is outside the general paradigm for civil society. Both the Council and the Commission express an image or concept of civil society that focuses on its *voluntary* nature; the groupings and associations of concern to the civil societarian are defined as standing outside the state. [31] Nonetheless, as is clear from the Council's recommendations, their conception of the family within civil society is that it should be a coerced institution, coerced through state regulation of marriage. Hence, they suggest that no-fault divorce laws be reformed for the purposes of both "lowering the divorce rate and improving the quality of marriage." [32]

Thus, the family is not to be treated as a voluntary or unregulated institution. Quite the contrary: regulation would be manifested not only at entry into marriage, but also at exit, with requirements of fault reimposed in some instances, such as through the establishment of a covenant marriage model. [33] Marriage is the only civil institution for which the Council recommends a system of coercive laws and regulations over formation and dissolution. In addition to reinstituting fault as the basis for divorce, the Council recommends repealing federal regulations that prevent school districts from discouraging unwed teen childbearing, so that schools are free to adopt disincentives to such behavior.[34] It is also suggested that preferences in public benefits, such as public housing, be established for married couples.

By contrast, when considering what actions might be appropriate for other civic institutions, the Council reflects the American preference for limited governmental intervention by recommending less governmental control (e.g., passing legislation to allow the media to develop a *voluntary* "Family Hour" policy without fear of litigation by the government).[35] Other institutions are not viewed as being in need of coercive legislation or ongoing supervision in order to perform their civic responsibilities. Business, labor, and economic institutions are "urged" to, or cajoled into, reconsidering priorities.[36] Communitarians suggest no rules or restrictions for monitoring the operational decisions of economic institutions.

IV. REGULATING THE FAMILY—
MORAL JUSTIFICATION AND BEYOND

In considering the justification for regulation of the family, it is helpful to untangle moral objections to the non-nuclear family from arguments asserting that there are harmful consequences to children's being raised in such families.[37] Morality is prominent in the discourse of those concerned with civil society, but most commentators supplement moral concerns with secular ones. For example, Galston made "a liberal-democratic case for the two-parent family" in a widely quoted article in *The Responsive Community.*[38] He begins his argument by positing the family as a moral unit that makes an "irreplaceable contribution to the creation of citizens possessing the virtues necessary for liberal democracy." [39] His tying together of morality and family is followed by a reference to a *Washington Post* article that reports the results of a nationwide inquiry into the public mood. [40] Galston uses the poll data and the article to conclude, "the public believes that America is in the grip of 'moral decay.' " [41] Further, the explanation for moral decay is reported to be the "breakdown" of the family. [42]

Galston, apparently buoyed by what he took to be the public's endorsement of his analysis, deemed their characterization "hardly the product of an overheated public imagination." [43] At this point, he cited statistics on divorce and nonmarital motherhood, presumably considering them hard evidence of public perceptions. There seems to be something counterintuitive and confusing about this turn in Galston's argument. He has imposed upon his reader the definition of what constitutes "breakdown" for the public responding to the poll—divorce and single motherhood. [44] But if his assertion that these statistics illustrate the problem is true, and if it is also true that the divorce rate continues to hover around 50 percent [45] and never-married motherhood is on the rise, [46] then a significant number of those responding to this, and other, polls about the state of American moral health must be agreeing that *their own behavior* is an indication of moral decline—that they themselves, or at least their behavior, are immoral.

I am not convinced that this poll indicates anything about the nature of the public's opinions. [47] The map of the public mind that Galston seeks to draw is too uncharted to support his construction of the moral family as exclusively the marital family. In addition, poll information based on public perception and opinion should not be presented as evidence of the "truth" of moral decay.

As a liberal political theorist, however, Galston does not rest his argument for regulation of the family on morality alone. He recognizes that coercive rules have the potential to jeopardize a liberal democracy's dedication to "a wide sphere of individual freedom."[48] He concludes that "[s]tate action must therefore be justified in light of widely shared public purposes, and the line separating such public purposes from personal moral preferences must be vigilantly safeguarded."[49] Galston then undertakes a search for non–morality based public purposes for his preference for intact two-parent families, such as economic consequences and nonmonetary or noneconomic consequences of single parenting.[50]

Galston identifies the consequences of family breakdown in both economic and noneconomic terms, arguing that the effects on children are particularly serious.[51] The economic effects are well documented—single-parent families are generally poorer than two-parent families.[52] Galston suggests that "it is no exaggeration to say that the best anti-poverty program for children is a stable, intact family."[53] One must wonder if he is unaware of the many poor working two-parent families in the United States. While having two parents may increase the likelihood that a child will not starve, it certainly does not guarantee it. Therefore, to label the intact family as "the best" program to prevent childhood poverty seems glib and insufficient.

Of course, if the problems confronting children were only economic, the solution would be obvious—transfer monetary resources to the child-rearing unit (from one parent to the other, or from the state to the caretaking parent). Galston identifies other consequences for children living in one-parent homes that are less susceptible to economic measures, however.[54] Quoting Karl Zinsmeister, he asserts that there is an emerging consensus on the noneconomic consequences of divorce: "There is a mountain of scientific evidence showing that when families disintegrate, children often end up with intellectual, physical, and emotional scars that persist for life . . . We talk about the drug crisis, the education crisis, and the problems of teen pregnancy and juvenile crime. But all these ills trace back predominantly to one source: broken families." [55]

Galston further elaborates by describing the conclusions of a few studies to support his assertion that "*the disintegrating American family is at the root of America's declining educational achievement.*" [56] According to Galston, one study's lead investigator indicated that children "need authoritative rules and stable schedules, which harried single parents often have a hard time supplying." [57] Quoting the investigator, Galston writes: " 'One of the things we found is that children who had regular bedtimes, less TV, hobbies and after-school activities—children who are in households that are orderly and predictable—do better than children who [are] not. I don't think we can escape the conclusion that children need structure and oftentimes the divorced household is a chaotic scene.' " [58]

Galston explicitly recognizes that his preference for an intact two-parent family does not mean that this is always true or that all single-parent families are "dysfunctional." [59] I presume he would also recognize that quite often, two-parent families are chaotic. His is a statistical argument directed at shaping social policy. It is also explicitly a moral or "frankly normative" argument, whose building blocks are not only scholarly evidence, but also "the moral sentiments of most Americans." [62]

Speaking for "most Americans," Galston asserts that "[a] primary purpose of the family is to raise children, and for this purpose families with stably married parents are best. *Sharply rising rates of divorce, unwed mothers, and runaway fathers represent abuses of individual freedom,* for they are patterns of adult behavior with profoundly negative effects on children." [61] With this intriguing choice of emphasis, Galston joins the moral with the statistical, labeling as "abuses" parental martial behavior that he posits has a negative effect on children.[62]

To combat the abuses he has constructed, Galston advocates changes in law and policy, including a braking mechanism on divorce and serious efforts at collection of child support.[63] As mundane as those suggestions seem in light of current policies, the logic of his argument is to lay the groundwork for more coercive rules.

In Galston's rendition of reality, not only is family form a predictor of economic well-being, but unmarried motherhood is a proxy for poor organizational skills and individual immorality.[64] Many other commentators have clarified, elaborated upon, or challenged the empirical or "scientific" findings of the effects of family form on children that seem so persuasive to Galston and other two-parent-family proponents.[65] For example, Professor Judith Stacey commented on the process whereby the results of only some studies (those supporting the family disintegration thesis) get publicized and aggressively made part of public policy discourse through think tanks and advocates with access to media.[66]

Furthermore, new studies call into question civil society advocates' conclusions that single parenthood is harmful to children.[67] For example, a large, multiethnic study at Cornell University indicates that single motherhood does not necessarily compromise preparedness for school, suggesting that what matters most is the mothers' abilities and educational levels.[68]

In another large study, of nearly 1,400 families and more than 2,500 children conducted over three decades, Professor Mavis Hetherington concludes, "The negative long-term effects of divorce on children has been exaggerated to the point where we now have created a self-fulfilling prophecy."[69] Hetherington asserts that the reason divorce has been called harmful to children is that studies have failed to examine long-term effects, instead focusing only on the first year or two after divorce.[70] She asserts that over a longer time frame, the majority of children from divorced homes "looked a lot like their contemporaries from non-divorced homes." [71]

It may also be that younger scholars, not as tied to the institution of marriage as their elders, might look with a more critical eye on existing gloom-and-doom material.

In an interesting paper examining the causal basis of communitarian family values (and Galston's work in particular), Andrew Lister concludes that the connection between family structure and negative outcomes is far from clear and documents the obstacles that stand in the way of gathering evidence on this relationship.[72] For example, mere associations, such as that between single-parent families and poor school performance, do not tell us very much about causation.[73] Children in two-parent families may graduate from high school at a higher rate, but children living in one-parent households are less likely to have college-educated parents and are more likely to be black or Hispanic (hence subject to discrimination, language barriers, and relatively diminished pools of family resources available for education).[74] If such factors are not taken into account, it is impossible to determine how much of the difference in school achievement is due to family structure and how much to other parental characteristics.[75] Lister concludes that it is misleading to focus our debate on scientific evidence about the effects of family structure on children's well-being and suggests that we directly consider the moral balancing involved in setting family policy.[76]

In regard to moral issues, feminists raise additional points of contention that are normative in nature, reflecting concern for the historic role of marriage in the subordination of women. Professor Iris Marion Young has questioned Galston's exclusive focus on children, noting that a preference for marriage "amounts to calling for mothers to depend on men to keep them

out of poverty, and this entails subordination in many cases." [77]
Professor Pepper Schwartz expressed her disagreement with the
arguments favoring the two-parent families thus: "On what
grounds could I possibly dissent? How about gender? How
about man's inhumanity to woman? How about a thousand
years of female sacrifice unnoticed, almost unmentioned? And
how about the family as the primary institution of women's subordination?" [78]

It is important to see the extent of the difference in moral visions between Galston and such commentators. While the proponents of two-parent families seem to believe that parents
indulgently divorce with little concern for their children's welfare, feminist arguments, such as those I have described, indicate
that there are deeper social problems associated with the institution of marriage than the fact that some people divorce or that
some choose to have children without marrying.

I agree with the criticisms of the work on the inherent advantages of the marital family offered by both social scientists and
feminists. Those who are skeptical of the predictive value of the
"science" underlying claims for the superiority of the two-
parent family have a valid basis for that skepticism. Conflicting
evidence about the success of single-parent families, as well as
inconvenient evidence about the shortcomings of traditional
families, seems to get lost in the civil societarian's smooth transition from observations about the need for action to help children to laying blame on parents living in nontraditional family
forms.

However, *even if* civil societarians are correct in that divorce
produces harmful effects on children, their analysis fails to consider, let alone add to the equation, the costs suffered by women
(and, ultimately, the children they care for) if we deter divorce
and punish single motherhood through establishing economic
and normative disincentives. The children who today live within

the families we seek to discipline are punished along with their mothers in the effort to lessen the harms it is argued will be suffered by other children in the future. Commentators such as Galston fail to consider that harm to the primary caretaker will inevitably negatively affect those children for whom she cares. Professor Susan Moller Okin argues that women become vulnerable when they assume the role of primary caretaker, and that "their vulnerability peaks if their marriages dissolve and they become single parents."[79] She argues that women are made vulnerable at divorce by their responsibility for child rearing and dependence on the marital relationship.[80]

The feminist critics are also correct to point out that marriage remains a gendered institution—one in which wives, rather than husbands, carry the larger share of the burdens associated with intimacy and child care.[81] For some women, reproduction outside of the marital family may be easier than having to cope with the vestiges of patriarchal privilege's shaping the expectations and demands of their husbands, in addition to caring for children and working. Civil societarians should remember that their vision of the marriage relationship as being benign and beneficial is not always the experience of women. Abuse and violence within the institution remain a real concern for many.[82]

V. POVERTY AND WELL-BEING

Rather than reiterating and elaborating upon insights already eloquently presented by others, I want to turn to a different set of questions and concerns about the role of the family in civil society debates. Specifically, I want to question the lack of attention given to the effects of other societal institutions on the family. My perspective is that those concerned with the health of civil society and our nation should focus on the pressures placed on the institution of the family (however defined) by significant trends or changes in the nonfamily institutions of society, particularly those in the business or market sector. The pressures generated by uncontrolled market institutions are at least as relevant to the health and well-being of children and families as are uncontrolled mothers and fathers: the irresponsibility of the state in not regulating or mediating the excesses of market activities is at least as devastating to a child as the irresponsibility of any unwed or divorced parent. We must count the costs to the family and, hence, to civil society of increased income disparity,[83] wage stagnation for middle- and lower-income wage earners,[84] and persistent impoverishment for too many of our nation's children.[85]

One interesting study by two leading researchers suggests that it is the government's failings regarding poverty that are responsible for the problems seen in today's families.[86] The study notes that the United States has a 21.5 percent child poverty rate, which is almost double the rate found in Western Europe.[87] The authors attribute this phenomenon to a relative lack of government tax and money transfer benefits to families below the poverty line in the United States as compared with European countries. For example, in Europe there is a guaranteed minimum level of child support to single parents when the absent parent cannot or will not pay child support.[88] They further note that attempts to relieve child poverty in the United States have failed. For example, the recent $400-per-child tax credit does nothing to aid families who already have no federal income liability because of their low annual incomes.[89] The authors suggest that these two solutions—guaranteed child support and child allowances for every family—would produce better results in fighting child poverty in the United States.

A. The Uncontrolled Market and the Unresponsive State
Interestingly, the Council on Civil Society initially identified "growing inequality" as a primary condition endangering "the

very possibility of continuing self-government." [90] The nation's current predicament was cast as "growing inequality, surrounded and partly driven by moral meltdown." [91] The recognition that there is growing inequality, and that it is relevant to assessing the decline in civil society, was ultimately and quickly overshadowed by the council's identification of morality as the paramount concern. Once again, gross public data proved valuable in shifting the discussion to morality. The Council cited an opinion poll finding that "[b]y a margin of 59 percent to 27 percent, Americans believe that 'lack of morality' is a greater problem in the United States than 'lack of economic opportunity.' " [92] Whatever the Americans answering the survey might have meant in giving their responses, the Council on Civil Society followed the civil societarian's traditional litany—that the problem is moral meltdown and that it can be traced to the broken "cradle of citizenship," the family. [93] The implications and effects of inequality were left unexplored.

I think there is a strong argument to be made, however, that growing inequality does have implications for civil society and that it should be central in the debates. In order to begin that argument, it is productive to map the growth in inequality on the same grid that the Commission on Civic Renewal used in constructing its "Index of National Civic Health." The Commission selected the period from 1974 to 1996 to measure those things it considered relevant—falling political participation, decline of political and social trust, a decrease in membership in organizations, and youth crime rates. [94]

During that same time period, there has been significant, growing inequality in income distribution in the United States, as well as a general decline in wages for many Americans. [95] There also has been a contraction of responsibility for the provision of basic social goods, such as insurance, by market institutions, and a withdrawal of the federal government's entitlement to welfare benefits. [96] These changes and others detailed in chap-

ter nine, such as declining real wages, increased economic inequality, and more tenuous connections to the labor force, have
had a tremendous impact on the well-being of families and children. In fact, these inequalities may be more central to understanding the other designated indicators of decline than either
the rising divorce rate or the increase in never-married motherhood (factors that the Commission identified as the relevant
variables in the Family Component of its index).[97]

B. Inequality and the Family

What happens to families (regardless of form) whose economic
well-being is threatened? Families are entering poverty at larger
rates. In 1977, 7.7 percent of families lived below the poverty
line.[98] In 1993, 11.4 percent of families were below the poverty
line.[99] Even in an era of strong economic growth, poverty persists. For example, in a recent article in the *New York Times,* Nina
Bernstein detailed how the poverty rate in New York City per-
sisted in spite of the strongest economy in years. Nearly one in
four New York City residents had incomes below the poverty
threshold in 1998.[100]

Of particular concern are children; in recent years, about one
in five American children (12 to 14 million) has lived in a family
with income below the poverty line.[101] The United States is the
only Western industrialized nation that does not have some
form of universal cash benefit for families raising children.[102] In
addition, child poverty rates are higher in the United States than
in sixteen other industrialized countries.[103] Poverty has both
short- and long-term consequences for children. Evidence supports the conclusion that family income can substantially influence child and adolescent well-being, specifically physical
health, cognitive ability, school achievement, emotional and behavioral outcomes, and teenage out-of-wedlock childbearing.[104]

Even in families well above the poverty line, falling economic
fortunes create a scramble to stay ahead. Certainly wage and job

instability produces stress, encourages longer work hours, and necessitates the participation of more family members in the workplace. In this regard, it is interesting that although families are entering poverty at increasing rates, more married women with young children are entering the labor force.[105] In 1970, 30 percent of married women with young children were in the labor force.[106] In 1987, 57 percent of married women with young children were in the labor force, and that number has continued to rise.[107]

Reporting on a study by Ellen Galinsky of the Families and Work Institute, the *Washington Post* indicates that children's inter-action with their parents is affected by parental job-related stress.[108] Further, economic necessity means that both parents are working longer hours—over the last two decades, Ameri-can fathers' time at work increased by 3.1 hours per week, while mothers added 5.2 hours.[109] Employed fathers with children younger than eighteen now work an average of 50.9 hours per week, and working mothers average 41.4 hours per week.[110]

Americans surpass citizens of every other industrialized na-tion in time spent on the job, putting in the equivalent of two weeks more per year than the Japanese.[111] In addition to having a negative effect on parent-child interaction, this increase in hours and the stress it generates affects the marriage relation-ship[112] and leaves little time or energy for indulgence in volun-tary civic activities. Perhaps the real danger to civic society is the runaway nature of contemporary American capitalism and the inequities it has generated.

C. Economics and Civil Society

Stagnant wages and income inequality are major factors con-tributing to a diminished American dream.[113] The experience of inequality must certainly contribute to suspicion and mistrust on the part of those who see others getting further and further ahead. Inability to provide one's children with minimal goods and services can lead to frustration and despair. John Ehrenberg, in his new book on civil society, comments on the series of articles by Sara Rimer in the *New York Times* in which she investigated the effects of the "downsizing of America" on community life.[114] Rimer found people too exhausted and busy to participate in their communities.[115] Ehrenberg, referencing William Julius Wilson, further notes that there seems to be an association between lack of work and the disappearing civil society.[116]

The real danger of the civil societarian's narrow focus on family form is that it will deflect attention away from the more serious problems that the current political and economic contexts present for the family. Many different types of families succeed at their assigned societal tasks. It seems clear that a certain level of resources is necessary to accomplish those tasks, and in recent years, these resources have become less available to many families. This is not the fault of the families, but rather the result of changes in attitude and in the scope of governmental safeguards and market practices. How should society respond to these changes? Focusing on family form will not help us begin making coherent policy to help our families. To consider what appropriate family policy might be, we might begin with the following questions:

- How should the need for resources for caretaking be satisfied so caretakers can act independently, make decisions, and fulfill societal expectations in ways that best respond to their individual circumstances?
- Should caretakers be primarily dependent on the family for such resources?
- Given the uncertain status of marriage, in which the divorce rate remains around 50 percent[117] and women are expected to be wage earners as well as wives and mothers, how can we

continue to have the traditional model of the family offered by
politicians as the solution for poverty?

- Shouldn't the richest country in the history of the world have
  a family policy that goes beyond marriage as the solution for
  dependency?
- Specifically, doesn't the family, as it exists today, require substantial assistance from other societal institutions?
- Is it fair that the market and the state (which are totally dependent on caretaking labor and in no way self-sufficient or
  independent from caretaking) escape responsibility for dependency, *and* continue to be freeloaders (or free riders) on the
  backs of caretakers and families?
- Isn't it time to redistribute some responsibility for dependency,
  to mandate that the state and the market bear their fair share
  of the burden?

These are the questions to which I would urge the civil societarians to turn their attention. The problem with society is *not*
that marriage is in trouble. The real crisis is that we expect marriage to be able to compensate for the inequality created by and
within our other institutions.

Chapter Four

Why Marriage?

I. INTRODUCTION

As I argued in chapter two, the marital family has designated functions within a society. It also has significant meaning to many individuals. But what exactly is that marital family? What does it mean to society and to individuals as a set of practices as well as a politics? This chapter explores the many potential individual and societal meanings that may be ascribed to marriage, and the ways in which those meanings can inform and influence our thinking about laws and policies that relate to marriage. I also examine the history of changes that have occurred, both within marriage as an institution with assigned and assumed societal functions, and in our expectations about the roles that individuals will play within this institution.

When thinking about what marriage means, both to society and to individuals, we need to remember that marriage is an institution susceptible to societal pressure and change. This means that marriage has a history of transformation and reconstitution that may be relevant to contemporary consideration of the relationship. Certainly, marriage as both practice and aspiration is not the same institution today as it was in our grandparents' youth in the mid-twentieth century.

Consider how we, as a contemporary, modern, and secular society, might imagine the legal institution of marriage if we were able to work upon a "clean slate," freed from the religious and common-law history of the institution. What would be our sense of the appropriate content, purpose, and function of this legal institution of modern marriage? One way to begin to answer that question is to look at what marriage does mean today on a cultural and social level, looking to see how people are "living marriage" in their everyday lives.

This line of inquiry might be pursued along two separate paths: First, what does the word "marriage" convey to us as individuals? In addressing this question, we look at marriage from a personal perspective—as a cultural and social practice in which we engage. Second, what does marriage convey to us collectively—as a society? From this perspective, we look at the functions that marriage performs on political, ideological, and structural levels—its construction as an institution in law and policy.

Related questions that might also be asked include: how is it possible to have only one legal definition of marriage in a diverse, pluralistic, and secular society such as ours? Further, is marriage about behavior and functioning, or is it about legality and form? What does the legal designation of marriage foster, reform, facilitate, support, preserve, or protect? Real and constructive debate about these issues is often obscured or obstructed by marriage's potentially infinite number of meanings.

II. THE MANY MEANINGS OF MARRIAGE

A. *Individual Meanings*

Of course, today both individuals and society know that marriage constitutes a legal relationship. The law defines some meanings of marriage for individuals. It is also an exclusive, and excluding, institution—not everyone can enter. Through law, the state establishes uniform standards for marriage, specifying who may marry whom and what formalities must be observed. In addition, law sets out the consequences of marriage at the dissolution of the relationship, be it by death or divorce. These consequences have become clear and predictable to lawyers and others administering the system.[1]

However, making predictions about the ultimate content and conduct of any given ongoing marriage is far from a clear-cut task. Within the boundaries establishing entry into and exit from the institution, individuals are free to create a variety of meanings of marriage for themselves. This is because society, through its laws, has historically covered existing marriage relationships with a shroud of "privacy," shielding them from direct state micromanagement and supervision, and thus allowing the conduct of individual marriages to vary widely. This concept of privacy still affects the way we think about the relationship between the state and the marital family.

For ongoing marriages, the norms for state/family relations are those of nonintervention and minimal regulation. There are exceptions to this norm of privacy, but most of them are fairly recent innovations, such as increased legal recognition of and response to domestic abuse and neglect, and removal of the common-law interspousal tort immunity, which precluded one spouse from recovering from the other for negligently inflicted injuries.[2] Other regulatory interventions into ongoing family relationships, such as the rules that preclude spousal testimony in criminal cases, are trivial from the perspective of concern with institutional dynamics.[3]

Because the law governing marriage leaves the day-to-day implementation of marriage to the individual spouses, it is the conduct of the parties that actually defines their marriage, giving it content and meaning, not the mandates of the state. Ongoing marriages are individualized, idiosyncratic arrangements. Even if cultural institutions, such as the media, or religious imagery might influence how some understand marriage norms, these norms are not mandated on individuals by law.

The doctrine of "marital privacy," which is discussed in detail in the postscript to this book, facilitates and reinforces the individualized nature of ongoing marriage. For purposes of the discussion here it is only necessary to know that the doctrine provides that, except in extreme situations, there are no mechanisms of legal enforcement available to resolve disputes in an ongoing marital relationship. This is true even when the terms sought to be enforced are those established by the state—imposed by its "marital contract." So, while a wife might have a "right" to support under family law, she cannot enforce that right against her husband in a court of law.[4] The doctrine of marital privacy mandates that the marital relationship first be ruptured through some form of dissolution proceeding, such as the divorce process.[5]

In other ongoing formal and legal relationships—the relationship between shareholders and corporations, for example—there is no expectation of privacy. Rights and obligations are defined, limited, and structured so that the range and nature of interactions are predictable. They are also potentially publicly enforceable even without dissolution. By contrast, the issuance of a marriage certificate does not require any specific legally mandated conduct on the part of the partners its issuance joins. Modern marriage does not come with or require a charter of incorporation, bylaws, or an oversight body such as the Securities and Exchange Commission to interpret what the union means to its participants and to monitor how those participants fulfill their designated responsibilities and duties within the relationship.

Therefore, in both practice and form, marriage is as diverse as the inhabitants of our contemporary, secular state. Our legal doctrine and structures create a vacuum—an absence of legally mandated meaning—leaving open for negotiation the content of every individual marriage. Couples fill this vacuum with various nonlegal and sometimes conflicting aspirations, expectations, fears, and longings. Reflection on the prospect of varied possibilities for the meaning of marriage suggests the institution's individualized and malleable nature.

Marriage, to those involved in one, can mean a legal tie, a symbol of commitment, a privileged sexual affiliation, a relationship of hierarchy and subordination, a means of self-fulfillment, a social construct, a cultural phenomenon, a religious mandate, an economic relationship, the preferred unit for reproduction, a way to ensure against poverty and dependence on the state, a way out of the birth family, the realization of a romantic ideal, a natural or divine connection, a commitment to traditional notions of morality, a desired status that communicates one's sexual desirability to the world, or a purely contractual relationship in which each term is based on bargaining. Of course, this is not an exhaustive list—there are many additional potential meanings for marriage, perhaps as many meanings as there are individuals entering, or *not* entering, the relationship.

B. Societal Meanings

The contemporary meaning of marriage is no easier to pin down and ascertain if we look at it from a societal, rather than an individual, perspective. While it is true that societal expectations of marriage are more publicly articulated, there are multiple expressed institutional meanings for marriage within the society that constructs and contains it. In fact, despite profound changes in the practice of marriage over the past decades, the explicit reasons articulated for the institution from society's perspective have not changed all that much. Some rationales are mundane, such as the need for formal record keeping and for assigning responsibilities and rights among persons (e.g., to facilitate property transfers at death or identify persons responsible for payment of household debts).

There are also claims that society benefits by regulating marriage in regard to traditional public health objectives. The application for a marriage license can also be the occasion for mandatory health screening or counseling on genetics. The process can be used for social engineering purposes, such as to supply information on the importance of marriage or to educate couples about the purported negative impact on their children, should they have any, of any future decision to separate and divorce.

Other societal justifications for marriage are more global in nature and, therefore, also more questionable. Marriage, it has been argued, is an effective method of containing and harnessing (male) sexuality in the interests of the larger society.[6] Sociobiologists (and some legal and policy analysts) view men as naturally polygamous and aggressive when it comes to sexual conquest. The expression of such "innate" qualities would result in violence toward other males and ultimate abandonment of women and their children by a mate in pursuit of new conquests.[7] In assigning responsibility for a woman and her children to one man, marriage channels his socially acceptable sexual expression and frees the energy he might otherwise expend in sexual activity for socially productive work.

Such assertions present complex theoretical and empirical issues. Do men in *this* society, at *this* time in history, given our *existing* sets of cultural, economic, and social relationships, desire and need intimate connections with women and children? If so, is their need for such connection with women different from and more complicated than mere sexual desire? Can men care about children independent of those children's role as carriers of genes into the next generation? If the answer to such questions is "yes," the next question is whether male need and desire for intimate connections is such so as to shape their behavior *even without* the loose and tenuous bonds modern marriage supplies?

In addition, it may be noted that even if men do not need intimate connections and the sociobiologists are right, it is not the end of the matter. The so-called "male problematic"—men's abandonment of women and children—need not be problematic if there is social and economic support for those women and children from other sources. If women and children do not need physical protection from predators in modern American society and have access to material and other goods, it may not matter if men leave them, at least not to their ultimate survival.

This mention of the needs of children brings to the fore an important and historic state interest in marriage. The institution of the marital family has been the traditional site for the socially essential reproductive process. Reproduction clearly entails important societal interests: society must reproduce itself and often creates policies that encourage women to have children. Society is also rightly concerned with the ways in which children are educated and disciplined into productive workers, voters, and citizens, tasks traditionally undertaken by the marital family.

In fact, the state interest in children continues to be used to justify state regulatory interest in the marital family.[8] However, as more and more nonmarital families perform these important tasks (and perform them well), it becomes increasingly difficult to use marital status as a basis for distinction in the allocation of social goods to children and parents.

Of course, if there is some demonstrable harm to children or others—clear links between cause and effect—associated with the absence of marriage or its replacement with an alternative relationship, then that might justify some state-provided incentives for marriage. However, the harm alleged should be something more concrete than an affront to an abstract sense of morality or to the symbolic order preferred by some officials. In any case, even if there were some harm, that would not necessarily support negative regulation and prohibition of alternatives. Quite the contrary. If our concern is really with the well-being of children, then we should have policies in place that seek to put alternatives to marriage on an equal footing with that relationship in regard to social subsidy and support. We should strive to see that children are not disadvantaged merely by the form of the family in which they find themselves.

One reason increasingly offered for maintaining marriage in its privileged position is that the weakening of that institution is potentially harmful to society itself. Marriage is argued to be an essential institution for our democracy. This argument, based in political theory, is supported by "evidence" that is largely historical in nature. Proponents of the position that marriage provides the "seedbed" of democracy bolster their arguments with ringing declarations about its position as the "most important relation in life," statements that are for the most part traceable back to nineteenth-century Supreme Court decisions, such as *Maynard v. Hill* and *Reynolds v. United States*.[10] They also resort to and wax eloquent upon statements made by various Founding Fathers about the need for a "moral" nation in order to have democracy flourish.[11]

Offered as the *coup de grâce* of nineteenth-century sentiments about marriage is the work of Alexis de Tocqueville. His writings from 1835 that there was "no other country in the world where the tie of marriage is more highly or worthily appreciated" and that "the American derives from his own home that love or order which he afterwards carries with him into public affairs" are used to bolster the connection between marriage and freedom.[12]

These arguments conflate marriage and family (and also virtue, morality, and marriage). Having done so, they fail to recognize that even if marriage was central in the nineteenth century, it may not be so today. Perhaps in the nineteenth century, the institution of marriage was considered central in discussions about the nature of "domestic habits" as a " 'necessary precondition' for maintaining the constitutional Republic,"[13] but those who merely reiterate ancient platitudes do not adequately respond to today's critics of the institution.

Those who urge that marriage is essential to democracy are using nineteenth-century arguments based on nineteenth-century institutions—historic notions of what constitutes democracy, virtue, marriage, and family. In this regard, it is important to remember that the version of our democracy in operation during the nineteenth century denied all women and a good number of men the right to vote and otherwise participate in political life. Our virtuous nation and its Constitution legitimated slavery. So, too, the marriage invoked was the common-law version that reflected a very different sort of sensibilities than ours today—lifelong, patriarchal, and hierarchical. Even if called by the same name, the institution of the nineteenth century is certainly not the vision of marriage we have today. Neither marriage nor democracy has remained constant in definition over time and across changes in our culture.

Finally (and I believe this is the real issue for many advocating its centrality), marriage can have important expressive meaning for a society, reflecting its moral or religious conventions. This role, however, seems problematic for a diverse and secular state such as the United States, with a constitutional system mandating separation of church and state. This separation between religion and the state is particularly significant and important when marriage is the means whereby the state distributes significant economic benefits. And it is not only the economic relationship between husband and wife that the state shapes through marriage. Marriage also structures the relationship between the state and its citizens (as husbands or wives). For example, in considering the legal significance of marriage, the Supreme Court of Vermont listed a variety of interests or relations affected by marriage:

> the right to receive a portion of the estate of a spouse who dies intestate and protection against disinheritance through elective share provisions; preference in being appointed as the personal representative of a spouse who dies intestate; the right to bring a lawsuit for the wrongful death of a spouse; the right to bring an action for loss of consortium; the right to workers' compensation survivor benefits; the right to spousal benefits statutorily guaranteed to public employees, including health, life, disability, and accident insurance; the opportunity to be covered as a spouse under group life insurance policies issued to an employee; the opportunity to be covered as the insured's spouse under an individual health insurance policy; the right to claim an evidentiary privilege for marital communications; homestead rights and protections; the presumption of joint ownership of property and the concomitant right of survivorship, hospital visitation and other rights incident to the medical treatment of a family member; and the right to receive, and the obligation to provide, spousal support, maintenance, and property division in the event of separation or divorce.[14]

The list encompasses not only the reciprocal economic relationship between spouses, but also the significance of the couple's relationship in regard to claims they can make on third parties, such as landlords and tortfeasors. In addition, the list demonstrates that marriage conveys access to benefits and subsidies from the state for spouses. Marriage plays a significant role in the delivery of social goods from state to individuals.

Considering the role of the institution of the family in the allocation of these and other economic goods,[15] it becomes particularly important to ask why one religious group's sense of what is moral or divinely ordained should act to limit the options and possibilities for us all. Why should marriage be the price of entry into state support and subsidy? Why define the family through this connection?

C. Arguing Meanings

People are not always clear about which of the many ways of thinking about marriage inform the arguments that they make. It is legitimate to demand that our policymakers and politicians be specific about the roles or functions they ascribe to marriage as they tinker with the institution. How do they understand marriage from a societal perspective, and how are they filling the marriage-meaning void as the institution relates to individuals?

It may be the case that some advocates of privileging marriage are substituting an *individualized* meaning for a societal rationale in their support for the institution. I argue that only societally based rationales should be considered legitimate in fashioning society-wide regulations and rules associated with the institution of marriage. So long as we leave the infusion of meaning into marriage to the individuals engaged in the institution one couple at a time, the state should maintain a neutral stance. State privileging is only justified when there is a corresponding legitimate state interest in the institution. Therefore, society must justify the expression of its interest in marriage through regulation and subsidy. What exactly is the state interest should be the first question—the second is, why is this particular intervention necessary to preserve or manifest it?

In regard to the historic, societally based rationales for state involvement with marriage, some, perhaps most, may no longer seem appropriate in our changing world. For example, a couple may want to marry because marriage means access to state subsidy in the form of economic and social benefits not available to other forms of sexual affiliation. The same couple may also want to marry because of the institution's meaning to them as individuals: a symbolic, cultural, or religious manifestation of their relationship that will affirm their commitment to each other.

If they are a same-sex couple, however, some religious leaders and politicians will oppose such a marriage. They may do so because they regard marriage as a natural, divinely ordained relationship (an individualized, religious meaning). On the other hand, they may do so because they view the subsidies of marriage as appropriately confined to heterosexual couples that form reproductive units (a moral or tradition-based societal meaning).[16] It is at this point that the debate should begin. Individual meaning should not remove the need for the state to articulate a societal reason for exclusion of same-sex couples from the economic benefits the state confers through the institution of marriage.

I would argue that if we are to keep marriage as a legal and privileged tie in our secular state, the state may appropriately allow religious leaders to deny the ceremonial blessings to a union of which they disapprove, but it may not correspondingly deny the secular legal and economic consequences of that status. Thus it is illegitimate for the state to discriminate against same-sex couples merely because they fail to fit within the traditional, religious definition of marriage.

Given the recognition and openness of same-sex relationships, as well as the rise of other alternatives, and the general decline of the traditional family, the issue is whether the historic role of marriage as the exclusive mechanism to provide certain economic benefits and protections can be appropriately maintained. This was the question that set off the line of reasoning used in Hawaii and Vermont cases in which the Supreme Courts of those states mandated that same-sex couples be entitled to all the privileges and benefits conferred on marital couples.[17] Looking at the current state of both marriage and patterns of intimate behavior, the majorities in those cases concluded that the state must either open up that institution to same-sex couples or create a nonmarriage category that confers all the economic benefits of that status. The allocation of state economic benefits was not to be limited by the moral or historical and traditional meanings of marriage.

The questions faced by the courts in those cases—the questions the rest of us have been avoiding thus far—included a consideration of when history and tradition should give way to new patterns of behavior (such as nonmarital and same-sex cohabitation), as well as a reflection on the broader issue of when laws should mirror a purely moral condemnation. This consideration is particularly compelling when there is no societal consensus as to whether the conduct in question is immoral. As the Hawaii majority in *Baehr* noted, "constitutional law may mandate, like it or not, that customs change with an evolving social order." [18]

As illustrated in this chapter, the questions associated with a modern consideration of marriage might become more complicated and difficult to answer if we must first reveal the meaning (or meanings) we assign to the institution of marriage. This type of consideration forces our focus away from the historic, symbolic nature or form of the marital relationship to the role or function we want the institution of the family to serve in our society. It also reveals that we are making certain assumptions about the capabilities and capacities of marriage as distinguished from other types of family relationships in society—assumptions that may no longer be warranted—and about its unique ability to accomplish certain societal functions.

Further, if we are clear about our expectations for and assumptions about marriage, it may become apparent that in today's world marriage is not the intimate family tie that should warrant our concern. If we are concerned with dependency and want to ensure caretaking through social and economic subsidy of the family, then why not focus on the direct relationship of caretaker/dependent? It is not necessary to support this unit indirectly through marriage when we can do so directly with caretaker/dependent directed policies.

III. THE LAW OF MARRIAGE

Of course, as the Hawaii and Vermont cases indicate, when it comes to marriage, we do not have a clean slate. Nor do we have an institution consistent in nature and form over time. There is a lot of writing on the walls, much of it in legalese in the form of the special rules of "family law." Not surprisingly, given the way we have historically divided up the world into public and private, the law also reflects the notion of separate spheres. This legal division complements the political and theoretical tendencies to distinguish the rules that apply to the family from those that structure the state and the market. Law has conformed to the assumption that each of these distinct spheres demands specialized rules focused on the unique issues and institutional arrangements contained within. While the market and state are concerned with the law of contract and property, mediated by notions of due process and equity, the law of the family is rooted in the status of marriage.

The special laws that apply to the family are consistent with the idea that it is an autonomous, separate, and self-sufficient entity. The unique nature of these rules has been justified by reference to the family's relational aspects and its intimate nature.

In fact, "family law" can be thought of as a system of exemptions from the everyday rules that would apply to legal interactions among people in a nonfamily context, such as the law of contract and tort, as well as criminal law, property law, and rules of equity. These exemptions are complemented by the imposition of a set of special family obligations. Law defines the responsibilities of family members toward one another and the claims or rights they have, placing more duties on them vis-à-vis one another than would apply were they strangers.[19] It is not surprising, therefore, that one common subject of family law literature has been how to use law to redefine, reform, or regulate intrafamily dynamics.

But family law does more than confer rights, duties, and obligations within the family. It also assumes and reflects a certain type of relationship between family and state. As diagrammed in the introduction to this section, during the nineteenth century this relationship was typically cast as one of "separate spheres." Family (the private sphere) and state (the public sphere) were perceived as largely independent of one another. This metaphor of separation reflected an ethic or ideology of family privacy in which state intervention was the exception.

The characterization of the family as autonomous—distinct and separate from the state—still resonates in our rhetoric about families. The family is designated the quintessentially "private" institution. Family is distinguished from both the market and the state (the quintessentially public institution) by its privateness. In a sense, privacy is what defines the family, sets it apart from other societal entities, and gives it coherence as a concept. For the modern private family, protection from public interference remains the articulated norm—state intervention continues to be cast as exceptional, requiring some justification.[20]

However, privacy has not been awarded to just any group considering itself a family. The contour of the family entitled to protection through privacy has historically been defined as the reproductive unit of husband and wife, giving primacy to the marital tie. It was anticipated that this basic pairing would eventually be complemented by the addition of children. In earlier times, others, such as apprentices or servants, might "join" the family.[21] Extended-family members, such as elderly parents or unmarried siblings, may also have been incorporated into the family once its basic tie was forged. The legitimate family—the one entitled to privacy and protection—however, was defined in the first instance through marriage.

IV. DEFINING THE FAMILY

While there might have been some consensus about the superiority of the marital family over other forms at some point in our nation's history (at least among political and economic elites), today there is much disagreement about just who should be considered "family." The traditional core of husband and wife (with or without children) seems to qualify under all definitions of family. In fact, this reproductive unit is considered by many people to represent the "natural" and essential form of the family. Some people argue that it should also be considered an exclusive vision of family in terms of policy and law.[22] In spite of the tendency of traditionalists to continue to equate *the* family with the marital family, on an empirical level, family-like intimate entities come in many different forms.

The most recent census data for the United States reveal that for the first time in our nation's history, less than a quarter of households are made up of married couples with their children.[23] This is the form of family labeled by the Census Bureau as "traditional." The number of married-couple families with children grew by just under 6 percent in the 1990s. By contrast, families with children headed by single mothers increased by 25 percent during the same period.[24] These families are not centered around sexual affiliations. They are caretaking units and reflect increases in nonmarital births and the continued relatively high divorce rate in the United States.

Empirically, it also seems that marriage is a less-dominant form of intimate connection for heterosexual couples than in the past. The number of heterosexual unmarried couples has increased geometrically over the past few decades. The recent census figures indicate that in 2000, 4.9 million households were classified as opposite-sex unmarried-partner households.[25] In 1970, there were only 523,000 such households identified.[26] Many of these cohabiting couples are also caretaking units and have children. In fact, according to the census data, about half of the children living with cohabiting parents are living with both their biological parents.[27] Others live with one biological parent and his or her cohabitant, resembling a stepfamily situation.

The Census Bureau's special report, "Married-Couple and Unmarried-Partner Households: 2000," actually begins by making note of the ongoing changes in family form: "[a] reflection of changing life styles is mirrored in Census 2000's enumeration of 5.5 million couples who were living together but who were not married, up from 3.2 million in 1990."[28] Even the questionnaire used to gather information for the 2000 census reflects the potential complexity of the definition of a household. When determining how household members are related to the head of household, the questionnaire provides ten options for related household members, including "other relative—print exact relationship" and an additional five categories of unrelated household members.[29] The statistics on unmarried partners include both opposite-sex couples, which account for 4.9 million of the households in question, and same-sex couples, which account for 594,000 households, or about one in nine of the total unmarried-partner households.[30] Since my objective is to replace the marital family and its sexual and reproductive affiliation as the core tie, with the caretaking family and its relationship of care and dependency as central to the objective of social policy, the sexual orientation of the adults within the entity is irrelevant.[31]

In addition to married-couple and unmarried-partner households, the census also identifies a growing number of units designated as "nonfamily households," which consist of people living alone or with people to whom they are not affiliated or related in terms the Census Bureau recognizes. Growing at twice the rate of family households, these nonfamily households now make up about one-third of the total units.[32] Some of these households undoubtedly consist of unidentified same-sex partners who would obviously resent the label "nonfamily" being applied to their relationship. Of course, these other "nonfamily" units may have forms of intimate connection other than the sexual one—they may be families of choice forged through bonds of platonic affection. Such groupings may be constituted by nonsexual affiliates who are merely "friends" or household units composed of siblings or adult children and their elderly parents. These units may also be desirous of family status and the material and symbolic rewards it confers.

The census figures show us changed and changing forms of intimate connection, but as the discussion of the civil societarian position in chapter three indicates, understanding family is about more than awareness of the current demographics. The family has an institutional and cultural history, and for many, the term "family" represents a constellation of values and norms with far-reaching emotional and psychological significance.

It is the *marital* family that has historically been viewed as the foundation of society, as the "healthy" form of family essential for the well-being of the nation, as well as for individuals. Many in our society would not even count some of the units described in the census report under that category of families. Others might concede the designation, but modify "family" with terms such as "broken" or "nonmarital," even "illegitimate," signifying that those units deviate from the ideal marital norm. For them, it is the traditional unit alone—based on the marriage of one man and one woman—that is indisputably entitled to the label "family."

This notion of the marital family as foundational to society has resonated across centuries in our legal rhetoric—it is reflected in the very organization of our laws and the nature of legal subjects constructed under them. Compare Justice Field's 1887 opinion that marriage "is an institution, in the maintenance of which in its purity the public is deeply interested, for it is the foundation of the family and of society, without which there would be neither civilization nor progress"[33] with the language of a more recent court case. In *Feliciano v. Rosemar Silver Co.*, the court held "[m]arriage is not merely a contract between the parties. It is the foundation of the family. It is a social institution of the highest importance. The Commonwealth has a deep interest that its integrity is not jeopardized."[34]

We can also look to the privileged positioning of marriage in the welfare reform bill that came into effect in 1996 (the Personal Responsibility and Work Opportunity Reconciliation Act): "Congress makes the following findings: (1) Marriage is the foundation of a successful society. (2) Marriage is an essential institution of a successful society, which promotes the interests of children."[35]

In the twenty-first century, our president echoes this ancient mantra, linking it to more focused concerns about the relationship between marriage and child well-being. The presidential initiatives have resulted in the passage of new, marriage-oriented legislation: bringing the issue of marriage onto the national stage, George W. Bush in March 2002 opined that too many families were fragile and broken. The president proposed spending $300 million to promote marriage as part of the reconsideration of the 1996 welfare reform that was scheduled.[36] Bush proposed funding programs that help couples work out their problems before and during marriage. His analysis was based on the following assertion: "You see, strong marriages and stable families are incredibly good for children, and stable families should be the central goal of American welfare policy." Promoting marriage was also part of the 1996 law that ended welfare as an entitlement, but only five states actually ended up using federal dollars for this purpose. As Congress prepares to hash out the reauthorization of the welfare law, marriage is more central, and a debate looms over what role government-sanctioned marriage promotion should play in fighting poverty.

Some commentators argued we would do much better to fight poverty more directly. According to the 2000 census figures, 6 percent of families with two parents lived in poverty, compared to 33 percent of families headed by single mothers. Responding to such figures and asserting that marriage is not the answer to relieve the poverty of women and children, feminist groups such as the National Organization for Women point out that poor women would benefit more from higher-wage jobs with good benefits than from premarital counseling.

Stephanie Coontz, national co-chair of the Center for Contemporary Families, was also interviewed when the Bush proposals first surfaced. While not arguing against providing counseling for fragile families who cannot afford it, Coontz worried that marriage promotion would be stressed at the expense of what she considered "true anti-poverty programs."

Often, Coontz said, not being married is a symptom, not a root cause of poverty. Her own research shows that men who become unwed fathers are more than twice as likely as married fathers to be unemployed and to have physical or psychological problems that interfere with their ability to hold jobs. In addition, unemployed men are far less likely than employed men to form and sustain stable relationships, while men who have stable jobs tend to seek mates who also have higher educational levels and earnings potential.

Coontz and other researchers point out that pushing marriage while failing to give parents long-term support systems may do more harm than good. "Job education and training are what people need." Coontz said. "It makes them more marriageable and makes marriages more likely to be stable but doesn't penalize children in those families if the marriage breaks up or they don't get married." While good marriages may be positive, endorsing marriage at all costs could put children at risk of living in unhappy two-parent homes. Another potentially destructive consequence is setting children up for instability and disappointment when their parents' relationships fail. Statistics show that marriages and long-term relationships among poor adults are more at risk of breaking down than those of financially stable citizens.

V. MARRIAGE IN CONTEXT

The American marital entity has an interesting lineage as a legal category. It is directly tied to one religious set of concepts and beliefs. Looking back into its legal history, we see that marriage was not created *de novo* as an American institution. As a legal relationship, its content and terms were drawn from British institutions that had evolved rules exemplifying rigid relationships.[37]

In England there was a direct historic connection between the state religion and the legal treatment of intimate relationships. Marriage was a sacrament administered by the church and subject to its rules. Under the common-law system in effect in England until fairly recently (as legal institutions go), issues concerning the creation and dissolution of marriage and other aspects of family formation were left to the ecclesiastical courts. It was not until the passage of the Matrimonial Causes Act of 1857 that jurisdiction over marriage and divorce was transferred to civil courts.[38]

Consistent with the precepts of these courts' religious approach, marriage was viewed as a lifelong commitment. An annulment or, failing that, desertion were virtually the only routes out of an unhappy union.[39] The Church of England's ecclesiastical courts could grant a divorce "from bed and board," which allowed couples to live apart, but not to remarry.[40] Divorce was theoretically available, but only through a special act of Parliament, and between 1800 and 1836, an average of three such bills of divorce were granted each year.[41] Generally, access to divorce was limited until the late twentieth century.

This view of the presumed permanence of marriage was also evident in colonial America, where divorce could be granted by a secular judiciary, though this rarely happened.[42] In fact, prior to the mid-twentieth century in the United States, judicial divorce, although increasingly common over time, was available only for "cause."[43]

An "innocent" spouse could ask the state to sever the marital tie when she or he was successful in demonstrating the "fault" of her or his mate. Fault grounds indicated there had been some egregious offense to the very marital union. At that time, states such as New York only permitted divorce for very serious offenses that were considered to undermine the nature of the marital connection, such as adultery.[44] Other states considered the amorphous category of "cruelty" to be a sufficient basis for dissolution.[45] Colonial divorce laws varied considerably by region, and the northeastern states tended to be slightly more liberal than their southern neighbors.[46]

In the United States, there was no established state religion but the relationship between religious perceptions and beliefs about marriage and the construction of state principles regarding that connection was still evident, if attenuated. The individual states incorporated common-law concepts and definitions from the religiously shaped English rules into their laws governing family. American judges tracked the religious rhetoric of their English counterparts when considering issues involving the family.

Divine laws governed family relationships, setting out the natural order for the individuals who entered them.[47] The content of the marital relationship was also divinely structured. In what has become one of the most famous concurrences in the American legal tradition, in the 1873 Supreme Court case of *Bradwell v. Illinois,* Justice Bradley made what is still considered the classic statement regarding the common-law perception of the divinely determined distinct roles of husbands and wives:

> [T]he civil law, as well as nature herself, has always recognized a wide difference in the respective spheres and destinies of man and woman. Man is, or should be, woman's protector and defender. The natural and proper timidity and delicacy which belongs to the female sex evidently unfits it for many of the occupations of civil life. The constitution of the family organization, which is founded in the divine ordinance, as well as in the nature of things, indicates the domestic sphere as that which properly belongs to the domain and functions of womanhood. The harmony, not to say the identity, of interest and views, which belong, or should belong to the family institution is repugnant to the idea of a woman

> adopting a distinct and independent career from that of her husband. So firmly fixed was the sentiment in the founders of the common law that it became a maxim of that system of jurisprudence that a woman had no legal existence separate from her husband, who was regarded as her head and representative in the social state . . . [48]

As this quote so clearly illustrates, the marital family—the "traditional family" of the common law and the Church of England—was defined by distinct and hierarchical roles across gender.

The organization of the family in the British and American legal tradition was also patriarchal, with the husband—"head" of the family—owed obedience and the wife performing domestic and sexual services for him. In return, he was obligated to support her and their children. The husband's role conferred rights as well as responsibilities, including the right to punish family members. Since he bore responsibility for their actions, a husband had the right to reasonably chastise both wife and children. His support obligations gave him a corresponding right to the earnings of his wife and children, and to control over their property.[49]

Further, the view of marriage expressed by Justice Bradley on the divinely ordained respective positions of the spouses also limited the expectations and opportunities for married women in the larger society. The marital family's hierarchically organized and well-defined gender roles placed the spouses in different spheres. Women, excluded from many of the public aspects of life, were perceived as appropriately dependent. As the Bradley concurrence in *Bradwell* expressed, their true calling was considered to be the home and family.[50]

This ordering of domestic life was intuitive—responsive to the natural dependency of women. Common law–imposed disabilities on women supported this ordering of the world. Married women were not able to own property or to make contracts.[51] In some instances, they could not even be held responsible for their own torts or crimes. Their husbands, perceived as controlling them absolutely, were charged instead.[52]

The common law expressed a structure in which the distinct specialization of the spouses complemented each other—the wage earner and the housewife; the protector and the protected; the independent and the dependent. Each spouse needed his or her complement in order to attain and maintain a whole, complete family entity, an entity that provided for all its members' needs. This specialization, bringing together the head and the heart of the family in the form of husband and wife, allowed the marital family to function in a self-sufficient manner, providing both economic and domestic resources to the unit.

VI. CONCLUSION

This unequal, if complementary, positioning of men and women within the common-law family was revealed as problematic for women when divorce became more prevalent under no-fault statutes.[53] These statutes changed a fundamental aspect of marriage. Marriage in its common-law manifestation was considered a lifelong commitment, but no-fault divorces ushered in a revolution in our way of thinking about the permanence of the relationship of marriage. No-fault meant much easier access to divorce. In many states, divorce became available on unilateral demand of one spouse, even over the objection of the other that the relationship could be salvaged. Men who wanted to be free of their "faultless" wives (as determined under the previous fault divorce statutes) no longer had to bargain with those wives and buy their complicity in the divorce process through concession of property or other economic incentives.

Initiated by both wives and husbands, no-fault opened the divorce floodgate and exposed the economic vulnerability of the common-law assignment of ownership of all wages and property to the wage earner. Wives were not considered entitled to a share of property accumulated during the marriage, since they did not earn the money to buy it, and since typically title was in the husband's name. As a result, women found themselves and their children destitute at divorce.[54]

The discouragement of married women from participation in the workplace and investment in a career under the *Bradwell* system also had more general negative economic implications. After divorce, women found that they had to work in the marketplace as well as in the home, yet the old vision of marriage had discouraged them from honing those skills they needed to do so.

All of this has changed, of course. The no-fault revolution coincided with another revolution in the way we understand the world—the gender-equality movement, which ushered in massive changes in all phases of life, including marriage. These changes are examined more fully in the next chapter.

Chapter Five

The Future of Marriage

I. INTRODUCTION

This chapter asks the question: given changes in the legal regulation of marriage, coupled with changing patterns of intimate behavior, why should marriage continue to be the exclusive, preferred core or basic family connection? It is marriage that is asserted to be the tie that defines which families are legitimate.

For some critics of the status quo, the issue is the inclusion of alternatives to the husband/wife dyad within the category of marriage. For others, the question is marriage itself as a legal construct that carries with it significant societal benefits. Why should marriage be so privileged? Some proponents of abolishing marriage as a legal category argue that marriage should be replaced by contract, allowing couples to structure their relationships in the ways they want. According to this position, there is no reason for the state to be involved in the articulation and imposition of those terms any more than it would be involved in the enforcement of contracts in general.

Feminists might also point out that one of the state's historic interests in the institution was to use regulation of marriage and divorce to mediate relations of dependency between husbands and wives. Since wives are no longer dependent persons who are confined to home and hearth, there is no longer any appropriate rationale for the state's involvement in marriage. Given aspirations of gender equality, which posit that couples are capable of making their own marital terms and freely deciding when and for what reasons to dissolve their relationship, it should be they, not the state, who make such determinations. What is, and what should be, left of marriage as a status in modern American society? What societal purposes could state intervention and regulation of marriage serve in a no-fault, prenuptial-recognizing, gender-egalitarian world? Shouldn't private lives be left to private ordering—to contract?

Further indicating to many that it is time for a serious reassessment of marriage and its role in society is the fact that marriage drags along with it certain historic assumptions about the institution and its members that limit the coherent development of family policy. Marriage also impedes other policy formation: it is offered as the social policy resolution for poverty in welfare debates. Marriage may in fact be the only clear and consistent family policy idea developed in the United States. The existence of the institution and assumptions surrounding it distort our policy and politics. The theoretical availability of marriage interferes with the development of other solutions to social problems involving children and poverty.

As the various (and by no means exhaustive) meanings of marriage listed in the previous chapter indicate, marriage is expected to do a lot of work in our society. It is not to quibble that much of this work must be done. Children must be cared for and nurtured; dependency must be addressed; and individual happiness is of general concern. However, we should be asking ourselves as we consider each of these tasks, what does marriage have to do with it? Is the existence of the institution of marriage, in and of itself, essential to accomplishing any of the societal goals or objectives we seek to bring about?

In this chapter, I argue that for all relevant and appropriate societal purposes, we do not need marriage and we should abolish it as a legal category. I argue that we should transfer the social and economic subsidies and privilege that marriage now receives to a new family core connection—that of the caretaker-dependent. In making this proposal, I want to be very clear about two things. First, to state that we do not need legal marriage to accomplish many societal objectives is not the same thing as saying that we do not need a family to do so for some. However, family as a social and legal category should not be dependent on having marriage as its core relationship. Nor is family synonymous with marriage.

Family affiliations are expressed in different kinds of acts, only some of which are recognized by the law. Some affiliations are sexually based, as with marriage. Some are forged biologically, as with parenthood, although this tie can also be created legally through adoption. Other affiliations are more relational in nature, such as those based on nurturing or caretaking or those developed through affection and acceptance of interdependence.

Second, even if we conclude we don't need marriage as a legal category, this does not mean that marriage as a societal institution would disappear. The symbolic dimension of marriage—the coming-together of two individuals with vows of love and commitment—would most likely continue to exist as a social, cultural, and/or religious construct.[1] Without legal status, however, marriage would no longer be the privileged mechanism whereby the state distributes certain social goods.

II. "MAN AND WIFE"——FROM PROTECTED TO PARTNERED

The move to no-fault divorce might have altered our view of marriage, but the gender-equality revolution altered the way women perceive their societal, extrafamilial roles. It seems hard to believe that it was less than a century ago that women won important political and civil rights, such as the vote, which was achieved in 1920 with the passage of the Nineteenth Amendment.[2] Even after women achieved the right to vote, they were still excluded from service on juries. Although the first women were summoned to jury service in 1870, as a rule, women were systematically denied or exempted from jury service for the next century, usually for reasons that were considered "benign" and "practical."[3] It was not until 1994 that the Supreme Court declared that peremptory challenges based on sex do violate the Equal Protection Clause of the Fourteenth Amendment.[4]

Until recently, the common-law rule was that a woman's domicile (essentially her legal place of residence) was always the same as her husband's. This caused difficulty for many married women, as a person's domicile is used in determining marriage validity, the award of a divorce, custody, adoption, tax liability, probate, and guardianship, as well as the right to vote, to hold and run for public office, to receive state benefits, or to qualify for tuition benefits at state colleges and universities.[5] Because a woman's legal identity had traditionally been merged with that of her husband, her domicile was assigned based on her husband's place of residence, and a woman had no control over this determination. As divorce laws changed and women's destinies were less tied to the institution of marriage, the inappropriateness of this situation became more obvious. The common-law rule began to change in the 1970s, and the American Law Institute (ALI) finally ratified this change in 1988.[6]

An important part of the move to gender equality involved

women's seeking to (or being forced to) forge an attachment to the workplace independent of marriage and husband. Many younger and well-educated women began to think of self-fulfillment and careers as their due, but certainly the instability of marriage after the introduction of no-fault divorce also helped to build momentum, pushing and pulling women out of the private family sphere and into the world of wage work. But in addition to altering expectations for women about work and career, the gender-equality revolution also had profound implications for the way we as a society view marriage and divorce.

Further, other rules beyond those governing divorce reflect the idea that women and men are equal. Massive changes have occurred in the workplace and other aspects of public life that have had a profound impact on the way that women are perceived as actors, both in the family and in the larger society. Women are no longer seen as incapable of bargaining and conducting business. Women have effectively undermined the idea that they are "unfit for many of the occupations of civil life," to use Justice Bradley's terms.

The view that women are competent in regard to business-type transactions has had an impact within, as well as outside of, the family. This has been particularly evident in the courts' changing approach to the validity of prenuptial agreements. Historically, courts refused to recognize such agreements, asserting that they violated public policy by altering the essential aspects of marriage, specifically the support obligation.[7] Judges were also concerned with the unequal bargaining position of women relative to men. As women gained the presumption of equality in the work world, "paternalistic" notions in the context of family law were eroded. Today, such agreements are routinely enforced, providing there is disclosure of financial information and meaningful consent to the terms.[8]

When applying these ideas in the context of real divorces,

judges have explicitly recognized that women are equally capable of making valid contracts that alter the otherwise default legal rights and responsibilities of a marriage. In *Simeone v. Simeone* (1990), the court set aside the presumption that prenuptial agreements were invalid, acknowledging that society had changed in ways that required corresponding changes in the law:

> There is no longer validity in the implicit presumption that supplied the basis for . . . earlier decisions. Such decisions rested upon a belief that spouses are of unequal status and that women are not knowledgeable enough to understand the nature of contracts that they enter. Society has advanced, however, to the point where women are no longer regarded as the "weaker" party in marriage, or in society generally. . . . Nor is there viability in the presumption that women are uninformed, uneducated, and readily subjected to unfair advantage in marital agreements. Indeed, women nowadays quite often have substantial education, financial awareness, income, and assets. . . . Accordingly, the law has advanced to recognize the equal status of men and women in our society. . . . Further, [earlier decisions] embodied substantial departures from traditional rules of contract law. . . . Prenuptial agreements are contracts, and, as such, should be evaluated under the same criteria as are applicable to other types of contracts. Absent fraud, misrepresentation, or duress, spouses should be bound by the terms of their agreements.[9]

Prenuptial agreements came to enjoy a presumption of validity, as long as they were made voluntarily and with full disclosure of financial information. Some courts still maintain the additional requirement that an agreement be substantively "fair" to both parties. Even so, these courts typically recognize the changes in gender expectations. For example, while the Supreme Court of Kentucky maintained that the terms of prenuptial agreements must still be "fair, reasonable, just, equitable, and adequate in view of the conditions and circumstances of the parties," it also observed that "the legal status of marriage partners is vastly different today" and that earlier cases had been decided at a time when "the status of women in this society was decidedly second class." [10]

The more modern approach is exemplified by the case *In Re Marriage of Greenwald*, in which the Wisconsin Court of Appeals upheld a prenuptial agreement that resulted in a highly unequal division of property between the parties, despite the fact that Wisconsin law had previously required that the division of the property at divorce must be fair to each spouse. [11] The *Greenwald* court based its decision on the fact that at the time of contracting, both parties were fully aware of each other's financial situation, and that they had intentionally created an agreement that would keep their property separate and allow it to pass to their respective lineal heirs, rather than to each other. The court stated that if a person would have entered into the marriage anyway, and if the agreement was freely and voluntarily made, then "we see no sound reason why the law should later intervene and undo the parties' contract." [12] Rather than uphold the (newly) traditional presumption of equal property division, the court recognized that as equals, the parties had the right to make an agreement that was intended to have an unequal result in the event of a divorce.

Several uniform laws also explicitly recognize the ascendancy of a contractual view of marriage, based on the parties' equal status. The Uniform Premarital Agreement Act of 1983 states that premarital agreements should be enforced as long as they are voluntary, the terms are not unconscionable, there was fair and reasonable disclosure of the parties' property and financial obligations, and the agreement does not cause either party to become eligible for public assistance or support. Note the limited possibility of a fairness review in this model legislation. A court would retain the right to modify such agreements, even if otherwise valid, to the extent necessary to require a party to financially support a former spouse in order to prevent them from transferring their economic dependency onto the state.

The most recent statement on this issue from a national body is found in the Proposed Rules for Dissolution of Marriage, drafted by the American Law Institute (ALI), which is composed of lawyers, judges, and policymakers. The ALI recommends that married couples, as well as those in domestic partnerships, be allowed to "accommodate their particular needs and circumstances by contractually altering or confirming the legal rights and obligations that would otherwise arise."[13] This ability would be "subject to constraints that recognize competing policy concerns and limitations in the capacity of parties to appreciate adequately, at the time of the agreement, the impact of its terms under different life circumstances."[14] Like the Uniform Premarital Agreement Act and the majority of case law, the ALI recognizes that married couples, like unmarried domestic partners, are qualified to make agreements that modify the traditional obligations that attend such relationships.[15]

As the evolution in the rules governing the acceptance of premarital contracts indicates, marriage is becoming more and more like other legal relationships in regard to the individual's ability to create or limit responsibilities and risks through contract. With the recognition of equality between women and men, we assume parity in bargaining capacity on the part of individuals entering these relationships, and no longer see a need for the protective intervention of the state.

Meanwhile, as formal marriage and family are redefined, we now see nonmarital relationships between sexual affiliates being given marriage-like consequences. Equitable or implied contractual principles result in allocation of property or other economic adjustments at the termination of a nonmarital co-habitation relationship in ways similar to the rules that apply upon divorce in many states.[16] In its Proposed Rules, the American Law Institute recommends that when domestic partners terminate their partnership, their property be defined and divided by the same body of rules by which this process would occur if the parties were legally married.[17] Domestic partners are defined as "two persons of the same or opposite sex, not married to one another, who for a significant period of time share a primary residence and a life together as a couple."

Unlike the Vermont statute that recognizes civil unions for same-sex couples and grants them the "common benefits and protections that flow from marriage under Vermont law,"[18] the ALI's Proposed Rules include all domestic partnerships, whether the parties are same-sex or opposite-sex nonmarital couples.[19] The rules also do not require registration or any kind of formal affiliational act, which further distinguishes the ALI proposal from the Vermont statutory scheme.

In fact, the ALI proposal creates a presumption based on certain behavior that people who are living together are domestic partners: "Persons not related by blood or adoption are presumed to be domestic partners when they have maintained a common household . . . for a continuous period [of specified duration]. The presumption is rebuttable by evidence that the parties did not share life together as a couple . . ." "Sharing life as a couple" is determined by reference to such things as representations to others, intermingling of finances, the existence of a relationship that fostered economic interdependence or dependence of one partner upon the other, assumption of specialized or collaborative roles in furtherance of life together, emotional or physical intimacy, and other factors indicating commitment, even if there is no formal declaration of such.[20]

The point is that it is not the formal status of marriage, or even a certificate or registration process, that is being used to assess rights and responsibilities, but the nature and quality of the relationship that the partners have crafted. There is, at least on a theoretical level, less and less need for a well-established system of default rules imposed by the state.

III. BACKLASH

The move to a more liberal divorce process has generated a backlash that extends beyond the transformations in the institution of marriage to the whole concept of gender equality that undergirds many of those changes. Religious pockets of resistance are particularly visible, and what they seek to restore is not only the lifelong aspect of marriage, but also its patriarchal organization.

One of the most extreme expressions of this backlash is the growth of the Promise Keepers, a Christian men's group that claims to be "committed to building strong marriages and families through love, protection and biblical values."[21] The Promise Keepers believe that these changes will be accomplished by a return to the traditional family structure in which the husband is the head of the household and the wife is subservient and obedient to him in all ways.[22]

Southern Baptists have also demonstrated a growing commitment to the return to traditional marital roles. In the 1998 Southern Baptist Convention in Salt Lake City, a majority of the attendees declared their adherence to Paul's words to husbands and wives. The first advice was to wives, who are instructed to "[s]ubmit yourselves to your own husbands, as to the Lord."[23] This was interpreted by the delegates to the convention as calling for a *voluntary yielding in love* on the part of the wife. Husbands are not directed to subjugate wives; rather, wives are directed to "take submission into their own hands." [24] This state of affairs is viewed not as benefiting the husband, at least not primarily, but as consistent with God's natural order of things— "a mirror of the relationship between Christ and church." [25]

Feminist criticism was noted during discussions of this position, but was dismissed because, even though such objections may raise "sensitive and important issues . . . none of them is substantial enough to move Bible-believing Christians away from affirming the truths [that Paul teaches]." [26] Feminist theologians and others who favor a more egalitarian approach to marriage have been accused of taking a position that "assumes the egalitarian worldview and then 'hijacks' the Bible to make it fit. Texts are either accepted, rejected, ignored, revised according to the way they fit in with that motif . . . a mistake of the greatest gravity [because] it is plain that while the Bible teaches equality, it does *not* affirm egalitarianism or interchangeability in all things, but rather calls for distinguishable roles between men and women." [27]

The Promise Keepers treat feminists even more harshly. A prominent Promise Keepers leader has said: "I believe that feminists of the more aggressive persuasion are frustrated women unable to find the proper male leadership. If a woman were receiving the right kind of love and attention and leadership, she would not want to be liberated from that." [28] In this view, women, like children, are not equals, but dependents who must be guided and controlled.

Even if pro-traditional-marriage/antidivorce sentiments are not based in religion, as they are with the Promise Keepers, assertions about the significance of marriage abound. These ideas do not exist in isolation, but are an integral part of systems of belief about the appropriate ordering of the world. Some members of society believe that the no-fault divorce laws have gone too far, in that people can now marry without serious consideration of the consequences (since they know they can leave the relationship more easily than before) and can divorce too quickly, without trying to address solvable problems in their marriage.

Part of the political backlash against no-fault divorce has resulted in the introduction in Louisiana and a few other states of something called "covenant marriage," which has been described as "part of a larger effort to redefine and bolster traditional marriage in order to reduce divorce, unwed mothering and single parenthood."[29] Covenant marriage is an attempt to create a situation that is described as supporting the more "traditional" vision of marriage, in that it is more than just a return to the former fault-based requirements for divorce.

Couples who wish to enter a covenant marriage must attend premarital counseling, after which they must produce a notarized affidavit signed by them and their counselor indicating that they have discussed topics relating to the seriousness of marriage. They also must sign a "Declaration of Intent" that affirms the following principles: "[A] marriage is an agreement to live together as husband and wife forever; the partners chose each other carefully and disclosed to each other everything about their personal histories that might hurt the marriage; the couple received premarital counseling from a priest, minister, rabbi, or state-recognized marriage counselor; and the partners agree to take all reasonable efforts to preserve their marriage if they experience marital difficulties."[30]

Although the name evokes religious imagery, covenant marriage, proposed and passed by the legislature, is a legal entity rather than a religious construction. It is an alternative to the marriage in operation under the no-fault divorce system, and it is presumably more difficult to dissolve. While it is available to all Louisianans who apply for a marriage license, it appears that covenant marriage has not become widespread since its introduction in 1997. One survey, done in 1998, showed that only 1.5

percent of new marriages were covenant marriages, and that some people believed the entire idea was just "a cynical attempt by legislators to cater to pro-family constituencies without having a real effect." [31]

Despite backlash trends to the contrary, the liberalization of divorce rules is likely to remain. As statistics reveal, Americans freely take advantage of access to no-fault divorce, and the census figures show that nonmarital cohabitation continues to grow in popularity as an alternative to marriage. [32] It seems clear that marriage no longer represents the lifelong commitment it reflected in the common law. Nor do many women now expect that entering into marriage will be, for them, a relationship of domination and subordination.

IV. RETHINKING THE RELATIONSHIP OF STATE TO MARRIAGE—
A THOUGHT EXPERIMENT

The shift to a more individual and egalitarian form of marriage raises the question of whether the institution should continue to be given a preferred status by the state vis-à-vis other affiliative relationships. Marriage certainly does not have the same relevance as a societal institution that it did even fifty years ago, when it was the primary means of protecting and providing for the legal and structurally devised dependency of wives and children.

How should these changes affect our perceptions of marriage? Covenant marriage offers an instance in which the state establishes two legal forms of marriage from which couples can choose. Why stop with two? We could open up the category of marriage to the alternative arrangements that people are now practicing. On the other hand, we might take seriously the idea that adults should be free to fashion the terms of their own relationships and rely on contract as the means of so doing, effectively replacing the marital status with actual negotiation and bargaining, building on the increased acceptance of premarital agreements.

What are the advantages of abolishing marriage as a legal category? For one thing, it would make policy conform to our modern aspirations. On an individual level, abolishing legal marriage and the special rules associated with it would mean that we are taking gender equality seriously. If people want their relationships to have consequences, they should bargain for them, and this is as true with sexual affiliates as with others who interact in complex, ongoing interrelationships, such as employers and employees. This would mean that sexual affiliates (formerly labeled husband and wife) would be regulated by the terms of their individualized agreements, with no special rules governing fairness and no unique review or monitoring of the negotiation process.[33]

It is possible to view this call for the abolition of marriage as a demand for private ordering. But a proposal for the abolition of marriage as a legal category involves much more than just a simple preference for privatization of potential economic consequences. It is a step necessary for gender equality. Abolishing marriage as a legal category would not mean there would remain no protection for the economically weaker party.

For example, the interests of a cohabitant who contributed to the accumulation of wealth for the other, even if she did not have a contract, would be protected to some extent by default and equity rules. The general regulatory rules found in equity (such as unjust enrichment or constructive trust), partnership, and labor law could provide rules for decisions in disputes involving sexual affiliates. Constitutional and civil rights law offer some suggestive possible parameters for exploration of potential economic consequences of joint endeavors undertaken by those who formerly would have been exempt as family members.[34]

In other words, in addition to contract rules, I anticipate that ameliorating doctrines would fill the void left by the abolition of this aspect of family law. In fact, it seems apparent to me that a lot more regulation (protection) would occur once interactions between individuals within families were removed from behind the veil of privacy that now shields them. For example, without the defense of marriage, there would be no reason not to apply the regular rules of tort and criminal law to sexual affiliates.

Feminists have been pointing out for over a century that the institution of marriage is the location of a lot of abuse and violence. This is not surprising in an institution that is based on an unequal and hierarchical social arrangement in which men are considered the heads of households, with power and authority over wives and children. Once the institutional protection was removed, behavior would be judged by standards established to regulate interactions among all members of society.

What would be the practical implications of abolishing marriage from this perspective? Since it would no longer be available as a legal status, marriage would no longer be considered a defense to rape. It would also be more problematic to conceptually bracket off some assaults as "domestic" violence, rendering them somehow less serious than the nondomestic variety.[35] Perhaps we would even begin to develop theories of tort to compensate sexual affiliates for conduct endemic to family interactions but considered unacceptable among strangers. A tort for intentional infliction of emotional or psychological harm might emerge.[36] Norms that prohibit harassment (including stalking), verbal assault, and emotional abuse among strangers would be applied in defining appropriate conduct between sexual intimates.[37]

In a completely different vein, the end of marriage as a state-regulated and -defined institution would undermine, perhaps entirely erode, the state interest in controlling and regulating sexual affiliations. If no form of sexual affiliation were preferred, subsidized, and protected by the state, none would need to be prohibited. Same-sex partners and those forming other arrangements, such as multiple-partner sexual affiliations, would just be viewed as forms of privately chosen and individually preferred sexual connection. Such unions might be celebrated in religion or culture, but the state would have no regulatory interest.[38] The substantial economic and other societal benefits currently afforded to certain heterosexual units would no longer be justified, and punishment of "deviant" sexual connections would no longer be permitted.

In addition, some other types of family formation that are currently interpreted through norms of heterosexual marriage would be opened up with the abolition of marriage. Single motherhood, in particular, would be unregulated. Without marriage, motherhood would not be modified by the existence of a legal relationship between heterosexual partners. There would be no "single" mothers unfavorably differentiated in policy and politics from "married" mothers—only the unmodified category of "mothers." Women would be free to become pregnant without fear that a paternity proceeding would be mandatorily begun, even against the wishes of the parents and in disregard for their privacy, so that the state could fill in the blank under "father's name" on a birth certificate. Sperm banks and specialists in reproductive technologies, including artificial insemination and fertility treatments, would not feel that the marital status of their patients was an appropriate item for ethical or professional concern.[39]

In addition to freeing women from the heterosexual marriage paradigm in their reproductive lives, the abolition of marriage as a legal category would have other implications. While contract language is often used to discuss the family,[40] the rules seem more anchored in the role-defined, common-law concepts of status. The status of wife carries with it assumptions about what is owed—notions about obligations and duties that arise merely from a woman's occupation of that position.

It is interesting to note, from the perspective of contract as a metaphor for bargaining, that status encompasses and defines those human activities in which women might be considered either to have a "natural" monopoly or to possess more on the "supply" than the "demand" side of the equation. These activities have been written out of contract.[41] Paying women for reproduction, as in surrogacy contracting, is not allowed. Likewise, contracts or agreements to pay women for providing the sexual services that are assumed in the marriage contract are also not allowed.

Thus, sex and reproduction (certainly significant areas of barter and exchange) are not subject to negotiation and ordering through the private process of contract, unless we are talking about the marital contract. Sex and reproduction are historically considered central to that contract. For example, a marriage can be annulled—declared to have been void all along—if the parties never sexually consummate their marriage.[42] In addition, further illustrating the centrality of sex to marriage is the traditional common-law marital exemption for rape, which was based on the idea that husbands had a right to the sexual services of their wives.[43] Centuries ago, Lord Hale expressed the opinion that consent to marriage was consent to provide sexual services on demand.[44]

Why do we not allow enforceable individualized bargaining over sex outside of the marital contract? In fact, we have placed non-marital sexual interactions either as beyond the reach of the law, labeling them private (the modern position), or appropriately suppressed by law, labeling them deviant and subject to punishment (the historic position). Rules, both criminal and civil, such as sodomy laws or laws against fornication and adultery, bolster and reinforce the institution of marriage by penalizing or prohibiting other sexual affiliations.[45] There is no obvious reason why sex should be excluded from some contractual schemes (private bargaining) while it has been an explicit part of another contractual scheme (the services requirement in the marital contract).[46]

Of course, as this discussion of regulating sex and reproduction through contract indicates, significant questions would arise with the abolition of marriage as a legal category and the placement of the relationship between sexual affiliates within contract and other areas of law. What would happen to those other areas of law if sexual affiliation, like other significant areas of social interaction, were not treated differently—if there were no special category of rules regulating consensual, adult sex exchanges and if all were subject to contract?

There are a number of interesting legal process questions that are also raised by this set of speculations about abolishing marriage as a legal category and relying on other areas of law to address the problems that might arise between sexual affiliates. These questions have to do with the process of transformation of law and the ability of doctrine to adapt to accommodate new patterns of behavior. Ideological as well as structural forces would have to be considered.

For example, pouring disputes that arise between sexual affiliates into the arenas of contract, tort, and criminal law would not leave the doctrines that now govern those areas of law untransformed—but how would the content of contract, tort, and criminal law change? Would ideas about bargaining, consideration, and unconscionability be altered?[47] While this is an interesting area for speculation, it is beyond the scope of this book. My concern here is with the institution of the family and the role marriage serves in society.

V. OUTSIDE OF CONTRACT

Of course, what is revealed if we take the relationship of husband and wife—the institution of marriage—out of the special category of family law is the dependency of the child (or any other family member who is incapable of caring for her- or himself). Even advocates of a restructuring of the relationship between women and men do not necessarily believe that every family relationship should, or could, be reducible to contract. Family law historically recognizes that the state maintains a protective interest in the well-being of children, and that parental obligations in regard to them cannot be individualized and reduced to contract. This position is consistent with the arrangement in which the family is the repository of dependency, performing an important public function in which the state maintains a regulatory and supervisory interest. In addition, it seems that the state has not been deterred from defining—even reordering—relationships in order to preserve the family's role.

In regard to the state's maintaining a primary interest in the dependency component of the parent/child relationship, the cases and legislation are very clear. The essentials of the tie are for state determination. Husband and wife cannot negotiate child custody and support free from judicial scrutiny and approval.[48] The state retains an interest in these arrangements and the right to assess and alter any settlement the spouses may reach upon divorce, and even to modify existing arrangements in the "best interest of the child."

Economic or dependency issues concerning the ongoing needs of children that are addressed in the divorce context can be compared with the nonmarital situation. Historically, marriage defined the status of children in relation to their parents and the claims they could make upon or through them. The presence or absence of marriage determined which children were labeled "legitimate" or "illegitimate," and thus either granted or denied benefits accrued by their parents under state insurance and compensation schemes.

The Supreme Court of the United States has reduced the significance of marriage in regard to the parent-child connection.

It did so first in regard to mothers.[49] However, fathers' connection to children has also evolved so as to not require its mediation through the institution of marriage. Unmarried fathers now have rights and responsibilities for their children that were not part of the common-law scheme of things. Nonmarital children are entitled to benefits historically reserved for their marital counterparts, such as parental support, worker's compensation benefits, and the right to recovery in the event of a parent's wrongful death.[50] Such improvements recognize that the reality of dependency is more important than the status of the parents' relationship.

In fact, the Supreme Court considers illegitimacy to be a "suspect classification," which means that all distinctions made on this basis must be examined with a higher level of scrutiny than usual.[51] Clearly, the state can express its interest in protecting children independent of the marital relationship of the child's parents. The label "illegitimate" and many of the disadvantages associated with this status were substantially altered in the waning years of the twentieth century.

VI. CONCLUSION

The very existence of the marital family, as well as the ideology surrounding it as a societal structure, masks dependency. Marriage allows us to ignore dependency in our policy and politics because we can always safely refer that nasty subject to the waiting societal receptor.

This interaction between the institution of marriage and policy concerning dependency illustrates why it is important to clearly reject the idea that the marital family is a separate, private entity, and instead to focus on the role that this family has been assigned, and how that function can be best performed in the future. We have historically relied on the marital family to manage dependency. Yet changes in our expectations and aspirations for marriage have been profound. The institution does not have the same meaning to participants as it did decades ago.

Given that ongoing transition seems the current and likely future fate for marriage, we can no longer rest assured that the marital family alone can continue to adequately provide for the emotional, physical, and developmental needs of all those in society who may be dependent. Concurrently, it is simply inaccurate to assume that nonmarital family units cannot provide for the dependency needs of their members.

However, the dominance of the image of the marital family in our political rhetoric means that it remains the constant vision of the family that underlies debates about public regulation and market autonomy. In spite of empirical evidence to the contrary, we assume in our construction of social policy this family's existence and vitality, as a complement to the public institutions we explicitly address. There are substantial costs to our refusal to face the changes in intimate behavior and in patterns of family formation and function.

PART THREE

Feminist Critiques of the Family

Equality and Family

CAVEAT: In the introduction and chapters in this section, I will often use gendered terms, such as "motherhood," instead of gender-neutral terms, such as "parenthood." In an earlier book, *The Neutered Mother, the Sexual Family, and Other Twentieth Century Tragedies,* I argued that motherhood is a constructed social and cultural role, and that is exactly why it is important not to obscure the fact that it has specific meaning as a practice. That meaning incorporates a set of expectations for women in this society. I realize that not every woman becomes or wants to become a mother. I do assert that cultural constructs are powerful, however. They act in a coercive manner, imposing normative notions against which to measure behavior. I use the gender-neutral term "caretaking" in other sections of this book to refer to the social practice associated with the dependency work that is at the center of my concern. To use "caretaking" in this section, however, would be inappropriate because it does not convey the same cultural imagery as does motherhood as a practice. To say we need someone to take care of a child is not the same as saying that we want someone to mother that child. Nor is it equivalent to say we want someone to "parent" the child. As for "fathering" the child, while it does not have the same exclusive reproductive connotation that it might have had decades ago, fathering as a societal activity is understood more as the assumption of economic, rather than caretaking, responsibility in today's policy world. It is motherhood as a cultural and social practice that is burdened by our policies and politics. This is true even when it is men who mother or when individual mothers mother badly or not at all.

*   *   *

The chapters in part two looked at the position and privileging of the marital family in politics and policy discussions. The marital family is seen as being ideally self-sufficient and capable of handling the dependency needs of its members, and in this way, it is considered autonomous. The chapters in this section detail feminist struggles with the institution of the marital family. In this struggle, the autonomy sought is not that of the family within society, but that of women within the family and within society. Feminists realized that if women were to have a chance to achieve equality outside of the family, they must be liberated from the old gendered roles. Therefore, the marital relationship was an early target for feminist reform.

The story of twentieth-century family law in the United States is the transformation from a hierarchically organized marital relationship into a regime of marital partnership, in which spouses are conceived in gender-neutral terminology and each is equally responsible for her- or himself as well as for her or his spouse. Spousal equality in this context is consistent with the idea of spousal autonomy and independence.[1] The union is not one of domination and submission according to common-law differentiated family roles, but one of voluntary association between equals.

Our new legal and aspirational model for marriage is that of "partnership," an egalitarian concept that recognizes that both spouses make contributions, even if they differ in kind. The contribution of the wife might still be specialized and domestic, but the argument is that such a contribution, while different in form than that made by the wage earner, is nonetheless of presumptively equal value. Wives are not dependent and subservient. Rather they are equal contributors who have earned the property or support allocated to them at divorce.[2] The influential Uniform Marriage and Divorce Act (UMDA), which was the model for reform in most states, in Section 307(a)(1) recognized this fact by mandating that when disposing of property upon divorce, the court must consider the "contribution of each spouse to acquisition of the marital property, including [the] contribution of a spouse as homemaker."[3]

Further, this transformation in gender expectations encompasses more than just a change in the roles wives are expected to occupy. Wives and mothers may now be expected to participate in the workforce, as well as in their historic family roles, but fathers and husbands are correspondingly expected to share responsibility for domestic tasks and caretaking.

The equality imagery in marriage reflects a more generalized societal transformation associated with women's roles. The equality revolution has occasioned wide participation by women in the workforce. Young women expect to have equal access to education and workplace opportunities, and the law formally embodies these principles and aspirations. In fact, as revisions in welfare and divorce policy during the past several decades indicate, society has moved far from the historic idea that a married woman's place is in the home.

Yet, in this and all other societies of which I am aware, women have always been perceived as being tied to the family. Women's historic roles within the family anchor us to that institution in ways in which men's historic roles do not. Law and legal institutions reflect this pattern and have consistently considered family roles and responsibilities primary to definitions of women as explicit legal subjects.[4] The gender differences that are apparent in, and central to, the law's consideration of the family are reinforced in popular culture, as well as in more structured societal institutions, such as religion. It is here, within the family, that gender is manifest, and it is not surprising that one task feminists have taken upon themselves is the conceptual separation of women from family roles that have historically repressed their ability for autonomous action.

Given the continued inequality in our society, feminists are rightly concerned with the ways in which societal institutions such as the family incorporate, constitute, and replicate gender relationships. Feminists recognize the importance of gender in virtually all aspects of society. The relationship between the marital family and the perpetuation of gendered norms suggests that we can only successfully address the disadvantages that gender imposes on a systemic level. Individual resistance, while important, even necessary, is not adequate to the task of cultural and social transformation needed to achieve gender equality.

Marriage, gendered in its very foundation by its historic definition as a union between one man and one woman, has had particular relevance to the construction of the family as a legal and political category. As the preceding chapters demonstrate, in the United States, our dominant family ideology positions the core unit as the sexual and reproductive relationship of husband and wife.

From a feminist perspective, one must remember that marriage has not been a neutral social, cultural, or legal institution.[5] It has shaped the aspirations and experiences of women and men in ways that have historically disadvantaged women.[6] For that reason, I imagine that well before women first banded together under the label "feminist," at least some of us were concerned with marriage, the institution of family, and the content of family law. Women's concern with legal reform of the institution of marriage can be traced back to the first Women's Rights Convention held in Seneca Falls, New York, in 1848.[7]

Even given the general recognition of the family's importance to the construction of gender and to the maintenance of inequality, feminists have an ambivalent relationship to that institution. This ambivalence is manifested in part by the tendency to generally undertheorize the family as an entity. Of course, the economic or market and the political or public aspects of society have generated an extraordinary amount of critique and comment in which the family is implicated. For that reason, the family has not been forgotten in feminist scholarship. However, for the most part, feminist attention has focused on institutions and structures in the public sphere and typically skipped over the family, except to note its oppressive qualities. When feminists have focused on the family, they have tended to divide it up into competing interests, assessing the disadvantaged and adversarial position of women in their family roles vis-à-vis other family members—wife verses husband, mother verses father and/or child.

I argue that most feminist critiques of marriage and the articulation of aspirations for an egalitarian family do not go far enough. This is because the predominant feminist approach to the family has been to import concepts that have been successfully employed in career and other aspects of our nonfamily lives. In particular, the acceptance of a rather formalistic idea of equality and the reluctance to consider differences in the societal circumstances confronting women have resulted in a failure to develop a theory that confronts the issues inherent in the fact that the family has been a separate, differently organized entity.

Recognizing that the family is an integral part of the larger society and interacts within it, we need not and should not forget that it has historically been treated separately. In fact, it must, therefore, be approached with a set of analytic tools that reflect sensitivity to that fact. Even if our ultimate goal can be cast in a singular phrase, such as the implementation of equality across social institutions, that goal may have to be achieved through very different means within each differently constructed societal entity.

It is not surprising that feminists have criticized the family, given the significance of it as a perceived barrier to equality, as well as a site of inequity. Feminists have resisted the ideal of the family as a private institution, insulated from state intervention and supervision. This critique of the idea of a public/private divide has been an important foundation of feminist legal theory. There are two related aspects to the critique of public and private as constituting dichotomous, complementary spheres.

The first is the notion that everything is public, at least to the extent that everything is regulated and recognized in law, and therefore by the state. A corollary of this realization is that nothing is inherently "private" unless the state protects it as such. Intervention by the state is always a possibility. The state therefore actively defines what constitutes the private sphere by designating areas in which it will not intervene.

In an influential article written in 1985, Frances Olsen sets forth an extended analysis of the public/private divide and state intervention in which she argues that intervention does not accurately describe any intelligible policies or principles:

> [N]onintervention in the family [is a] false ideal. . . . As long as a state exists and enforces any laws at all, it makes political choices.

The state cannot be neutral or remain uninvolved, nor would anyone want the state to do so. The staunchest supporters of laissez
faire always insisted that the state protect their property interests
and that courts enforce contracts and adjudicate torts. They took
this state action for granted and chose not to consider such protection a form of state intervention.[8]

Crucial questions are raised in this metatheoretical approach:
What is the manner or nature of intervention? Whose interests
are being protected and advanced when intervention occurs
and when it does not? Who is rendered subservient and subordinate?

Feminists have successfully deconstructed the public/private
dichotomy in the context of the family. While the family may be
viewed as private in our rhetoric, it is highly regulated and controlled by the state. Law defines who may marry whom and what
formalities must be observed. Only some relationships are considered "legitimate" or legal ones that carry the weight of the
state behind them.[9] Law defines the consequences of marriage
and parenthood and implements significant policy directives in
the context of divorce.[10] Law also defines what responsibilities
are inherent in the family and what role the family plays within
the larger society.

The state also consistently acts in ways that affect individuals.
In significant part, it does so by shaping and regulating the family. Through shaping the family, the state contributes to the ways
individuals construct their identities within society. The state
also establishes mediated norms of citizenship and community.
Thus, the public state affects the very workings of private life. By
scooping out what is public, it also defines what remains private.

A second set of feminist critiques focuses more on the interactions between women and men within relationships that are afforded privacy by the state. The state is still seen as providing
structure, but the emphasis is on what transpires within the des-

ignated private space—in the operation of nonstate relationships. These critiques are exemplified by the contrasting analyses of Professors Catherine MacKinnon and Anita Allen.

Professor MacKinnon begins by asserting that privacy obscures private violence and abuse, which is often labeled "domestic."[11] For example, she is critical of liberal thinkers, as well as the majority of the Supreme Court, who adhere to notions of the private. Commenting on cases such as *Roe v. Wade,* in which the Supreme Court set aside a blanket prohibition on abortion based on privacy grounds, MacKinnon characterizes "the ideology of privacy" as "a right of men to be let alone to oppress women one at a time."[12] She understands privacy as a benefit to men, rooted in the concept of women's seclusion and separation from the protections that might otherwise be afforded them by the state.

Privacy is seen as a primary source of women's inequality—the private sphere is the location of her domination and subordination.[13] In fact, MacKinnon asserts that to even complain about inequality in the private arena is inconsistent with the whole idea of privacy. Privacy cannot be understood outside of its historic manifestation of female subordination.[14] MacKinnon asserts that for women, "the measure of the intimacy has been the measure of the oppression. When the law of privacy restricts intrusions into intimacy, it bars changes in control over that intimacy [through law]. . . . The existing distribution of power and resources within the private sphere are precisely what the law of privacy exists to protect—the subordination and domination of women."[15]

Professor Allen begins her discussion of relationships of privacy in the same place as MacKinnon—within the confines of the historic nuclear family home. Her major concern, however, is not with male violence against women, but with the exploitation inherent in family relationships—the sacrifices compelled by "[m]arriage, motherhood, housekeeping, dependence" and women's "own moral ideas of caretaking and belonging." [16]

It is a particular ideological manifestation of privacy, not the concept itself, that Allen critiques here. Allen disagrees with MacKinnon, disputing her assertion that privacy poses an inherent threat to women, and instead argues that after centuries of subordination, women finally find themselves in a position to "expect, experience and exploit real privacy within the home and within heterosexual relationships." [17]

Allen views privacy as a potential good for women, since it has multiple dimensions that relate to "family life within the home, and to the kinds of intimate personal relationships and activities commonly associated with them." [18] While recognizing that these relationships often were experienced as abusive in the past, Allen sees a need for "real" privacy for women. Privacy can provide seclusion and solitude for women, restrict access to information, preserve confidentiality, and secure decision-making autonomy. Allen makes an important argument for retaining the constitutional, individualized notion of privacy. Her concern is with making sure that the conditions for its use and enjoyment are afforded to women. [19]

Both MacKinnon's critique and Allen's defense of privacy assume there is danger for women in the domestic realm. The dangers are located in male excesses, on the one hand, and on operation of and expectations associated with heterosexuality and reproduction, on the other. In both approaches, women's interests are asserted as individual interests, independent of and in conflict with others in the family unit. For MacKinnon, this is played out as subordination of women by men who, with greater or lesser degrees of ill will, take advantage of them within intimate relationships.

Allen brings children into consideration, but maintains an individualized approach in her analysis: children boil down to caretaking, and caretaking interferes with, and may even preclude, "real" privacy.[20] For that reason, although I support some articulation of privacy rights, and thus more closely align with Allen than MacKinnon, Allen and I diverge in our analyses in that hers is an individualistic model imposed on the family, not a model that positively encompasses the demands of a caretaking entity. The demands of the home are seen as having robbed women of meaningful personal privacy. Allen is skeptical about any notion of "shared privacy" (described by her in terms of "love affairs") and terms it dangerous when "it replaces individual privacy."

Allen's objective is to articulate a personal, individual sense of entitlement to privacy, an entitlement that supports women's resistance to the imposition of the burdens of reproduction and caretaking. Her notion of privacy in this regard is as a tool to "put an end to the psychological predisposition of women to care themselves into oblivion"—a defense against intrafamily abuse.[21] As the subsequent chapters will show, in contrast I argue that we must develop a feminist theory that encompasses family obligations as a positive social and individual good, deserving of societal subsidy and support, including the protection of some form of entity privacy.

It is important to recognize that as essential as the debates concerning privacy have been to feminist legal theory, in other areas of law, the dichotomous world of public and private continues to have profound implications. For many legal theorists, although the private family recedes and the designated public remains the focus of concern and debate, the dichotomy between public and private is not challenged. As a result, not only are the family and dependency grossly undertheorized, but the very concepts of the "individual" and the institutions of market and state that are the focus of theory are distorted and skewed because the family is invisible, cast as quintessentially private and conceptually separate from market and state. Family is wrongly assumed to be unchanging, an essentialized institution, natural in form and function, that is the repository for dependency. The sorting into public and private, once struck, is not reconsidered.

Chapter Six

Feminism and the Family: Implementing Equality, Achieving Autonomy

I. INTRODUCTION

When addressing any topic from the position of "feminism," we need to clearly state that there are many differences in approach, emphasis, and aspiration contained within the general category.[1] Recognizing that there are many divergences in feminist theory, we can nonetheless make *some* generalizations. Primary among them would be the assertion that feminisms and feminists are concerned with "gender" and the many ways in which the genders, male and female, are shaped and defined within society and culture.

A. Gender

"Gender" is a term that refers to the cluster of characteristics deemed feminine or masculine in society, as distinguished from mere biological or genetic categories. Gender is socially constructed; it is imparted through socialization and culture rather than inherent. Part of the evidence for this is that characteristics that "define" the genders do not remain constant over time or across different cultures.[2] Feminists use the concept of gender to convey the idea that society contains cultural, symbolic, and ideological systems that generate and perpetuate dominant notions of masculinity and femininity.

The genders are constructed in a binary manner, created in contrast to one another,[3] with dichotomous and clearly value-laden pairings, such as strong/weak, hard/soft, and mind/body. Gender definition is not a "natural" or inevitable process, but is produced through a web of social relationships, constructed by and within societal institutions. Primary among those relationships are those found in the institution of the marital family, with its reproductive focus. Family gender roles have both a biological, reproductive component and a caretaking dimension, in which responsibility for dependency is assigned to women.

Notions about gender are also reflected through laws and other institutions that support, complement, and help define the family. In other words, gender does not operate solely on an individual level, or even a familial level: there are also institutional and structural forces that shape notions of gender. The construction of gender often operates as the conferral of power, opportunity, and benefits. This makes it difficult, if not impossible, for one to act outside of gender roles. One may "transgress" gender but the script is still imposed in the first instance, and the transgressor, as well as those who accept those imposed gender norms, are all reacting, not self-actuating in that regard.

B. Feminism and Legal Theory

Feminist thought came relatively late to legal institutions. When it did, most notably in the 1970s, the nature and history of legal institutions shaped the possible responses available to feminist law reformers. To a large extent, scholarship in the field of feminist legal theory was initially divided. Some feminists, using a domination or subordination model, focused attention on issues concerning sexual violence and/or reproductive rights. Other feminists, working with a discrimination model, confronted issues such as inequality in the workplace.

The antidiscrimination track was the most pronounced path that legal feminists trod. This is not surprising, given how the law had been developed under the Fourteenth Amendment to mandate equal protection for those in similar circumstances and forbid the states from discriminating based on certain classifications and characteristics. Under this amendment, groups that suffered disadvantages argued that they were not in any significant way different from those who were not disadvantaged. The strategy was to persuade the courts that there were no legally relevant differences and to therefore establish an entitlement to sameness of treatment.

The civil rights movement had built on this antidiscrimination principle, successfully attacking "separate but equal" education in *Brown v. Board of Education*,[4] as well as other exclusionary and discriminatory practices in a host of other subsequent cases. Legal feminists modeled their litigation tactics on the civil rights successes. One of the chief architects of gender discrimination law was (now Justice) Ruth Bader Ginsburg. She articulated the strategy thus:

> Laws ranking men as independent and women as dependent inhibit both from choosing the paths they will pursue in life based on their individual talents and preferences. And such lump classification of men and women is surely unnecessary, for neutral, functional description is an alternative plainly open to the legislature.[5]

In their efforts to reshape the world into a more egalitarian place through legislative reform, feminists were not primarily focused on the workings of the family. Concern with economics drew attention to the gendered and exclusionary nature of public institutions, particularly market institutions, which resulted in successfully tapping the regulatory potential of the state. Legislation was enacted that removed barriers and implemented equality measures, such as equal-pay legislation and other prohibitions against gendered forms of employment discrimination.

When intimate relationships did come under active feminist consideration, the issues most likely to be explored were associated with reproductive freedom, primarily access to abortion, and with violence against women, including sexual violence either by intimate partners or by strangers. Of course, coercive sex in the nonfamily world was also of concern to feminists, who generated public awareness about sexual harassment in the workplace. Rape laws were reformed, and extensive discussions focusing on a range of issues associated with giving women control over their own sexuality challenged old notions of female desire and resistance.

The treatment, if any, of the family as an institution in these discussions tended to be rather superficial, defining it as a subsidiary of the market, or as a bastion of male prerogative and privilege. The family was cast as another obstacle hindering full participation of women in the "public" sphere, because its arrangement left women subject to domination and victimization in the "private" sphere.[6] In focusing on adult female and male family members, feminists reached for the conceptual tool of equality, still close at hand from its successful employment in nonfamily contexts.

C. Implementing Equality in the Family

When early legal feminist theorists did consider the family, the concept of equality in its gender-neutral, nondiscriminatory form as developed in work and political contexts was imported into and imposed on their discussions. Under this conceptualization of equality, wives were to be more like husbands and were to pursue economic opportunities, and fathers were to be more like mothers and to participate in the care of children and in other domestic tasks. Wives were to be equally responsible for their own and their children's economic well-being, and husbands were entitled to alimony equally with wives, were they unable to support themselves postdivorce. Fathers were equally capable of caring for children and were not to be discriminated against in custody determinations by such antiquated and inappropriate doctrines as the "tender years" preference, which discriminated against them in favor of mothers.

When they turned to the situation of women within the family, feminists began from the perspective that these relationships were a subset of the larger gender-equality problem—the different and exclusionary treatment of women as contrasted with men in society and its institutions. In this regard, the focus on the relationship between husband and wife was predictable.

Women's traditional gendered roles within the family were considered problematic, primarily because they impeded women's realization of their role as equal participants in the economic and political aspects of life. Family and family roles, particularly that of mother, were often analyzed as oppressive and as impeding individual growth and independence. Feminists alleged that the family itself was often violent and dangerous. Of course, any feminist focus on the family found it in need of serious reform, in order to give women more autonomy.

In this regard, the aspect of marriage occupying feminist attention for the most part has been the legacy of the traditional, unequal gendered roles of husband and wife, as articulated in relation to religious and legal relationships. In accordance with the church's approach to marriage, legal and other texts analogized the relationship between husband and wife to other "natural" hierarchical arrangements. Thus, a man was enthroned as head of the family, just as Jesus reigned as the head of the church and the king was the head of the state. The respective positions of husband and wife were rigidly distinct and patriarchically ordered—the husband's role, as frail wife's protector, was deemed "divinely ordained." *Bradwell v. Illinois*,[7] a case discussed in chapter four, involved a prohibition on women's admission to the practice of law, indicating that this hierarchical thinking had implications well beyond the family and affected women's career and other opportunities. Women, whose primary calling was as wives and mothers, were considered unfit for the harshness of public life.

Common-law rules and regulations aided in the construction and maintenance of the subordinate gender roles in the family.[8] The structure of the common law mired married women, in particular, in family responsibility and left them on a legal plain far from access to independent and autonomous decision making. Given the power of the legal construct of the common-law family, in retrospect it seems naive of feminists to think they could just import concepts of equality developed in other contexts onto the existing inequality of the family. The prevalent understanding of equality that developed in the "public" sphere demanded an individualized notion of sameness of treatment and gender neutrality. Such notions seem singularly inappropriate in confronting what has historically been the most gendered institution in society.

D. Methods of Seeking Reform

One can see the embrace of equality in the activities of legal feminists who were involved in the movement for divorce reform. Autonomy (understood as independence) from historic family roles was the path to equality (and further, to individual autonomy) in the larger society. Feminists argued for both equality (as in sameness of treatment) and gender neutrality as the basis for reform of marriage, introducing a partnership notion to replace the old common-law hierarchy. This partnership model was more than a mere conceptual device conveniently borrowed from business in order to legitimate the transfer of funds from husbands to wives at divorce, however. Legal feminists were truly interested in the establishment of a broad egalitarian family ideal, and the partnership model of marriage reflected that aspiration. The idea was to make husbands and wives share *all* responsibilities and benefits of the institution of marriage—to androcentrize the family roles and facilitate sharing them.

The logic supporting this suggested reconceptualization of the family involved two primary justifications—one internal and one external to the institution of the family. The arguments for reform based on the internal family dynamic pointed to the unequal nature of historic gendered arrangements and interactions. There were inequalities within the hierarchical and patriarchal family, exemplified both by economic dependency and by labor force disadvantages, that became even more apparent with divorce reform, which revealed women's economic vulnerability.

The battered women's movement documented the prevalence of physical and psychological abuse of women. The dependency of wives was thought to contribute to and exacerbate the prevalence of these abuses within the family. Such abuse was largely shielded from public view. Legal protection was limited by the concept of family privacy, a noninterventionist doctrine that was applied to intact families. Legal feminists attacked this whole notion of family privacy, arguing that it concealed real and material psychological and physical injuries occurring within the hierarchical, patriarchal family.

The second impetus for reform was provided by those feminists concerned with women's position *outside* of the family. They argued that domestic responsibilities within the family, particularly motherhood, had profound negative implications for women's prospects in the larger society. Feminists realized that formal gains in equality of access and opportunity for women in education, politics, and the workplace could not be fully realized if there were not corresponding changes in family roles and the responsibilities women were expected to assume.

By and large, legal feminists agreed that women, both inside and outside the family, were primarily defined, and thus confined, by their family roles of wife, mother, and daughter. These family roles contained inherent economic dependency, self-sacrifice, and subservience. Further, family roles displaced other aspirations on an ideological level, with concrete implications for educational and career opportunities available to women. Expectations governing the private (family) sphere correspondingly defined aspirations and possibilities for women in the public (workplace) sphere. In other words, it was not necessary that cases such as *Bradwell v. Illinois* impose *de jure* exclusion of women from market institutions—acculturation and family expectations worked just as well at accomplishing that goal.

This agreement reflected the merger and conclusions from the two types of arguments for legal reform focused on the family. Both lines of argument ended with changes directed at responsibilities and roles within the family. Even those arguments that looked at social arrangements that disadvantaged women outside targeted the internal operations of the family as the primary site for reform and transformation.

In considering the focus on the internal workings of the family as a site for legal reform, we need to keep in mind that in real-world legal and political practice (outside the debates within feminist legal theory), the idea of family privacy is a coherent concept. Except in areas of extreme abuse, such as domestic violence, the popular and political idealization of the ongoing family mandates that it retain its private character. State intervention and monitoring is considered inappropriate absent some significant breakdown. This is important because these perceptions mean that state intervention into any specific family situation is improbable.

The practice of gender equality exists only to the extent that individual married couples choose to embrace it, unsupervised by the state. Yet, within the marital relationship, independent of any legal assurance of equality, the spouse with superior economic and social power can wield such power in ways that preserves the status quo. Therefore, it is not surprising that many couples continue to act out traditionally gendered scripts of behavior, mimicking the roles taught through unreformed socialization processes.

As a result, while equality in the context of the marital family might be imposed in a formal manner, each couple designs the actual terms of their marriage relationship. Their respective bargaining power will be influenced by the bargaining power they bring to that relationship, which is often the product of how much they can mobilize social resources outside of the family— how much autonomy they have. Unless the marital relationship dissolves and the courts are asked to intervene to allocate economic resources in the context of a divorce, equality is realizable only at the whim of the person with the most economic and cultural clout. The monitoring and implementation of equality for the intact marital family is left to the individual family and its members—it is a self-regulating system.

Self-regulation is not the primary assumption made in the context of imposing gender equality in the public sphere, however. In the workplace, equality is not only imposed, but also monitored. Laws structure working relationships in the first instance, and mandate that employers provide equal pay for equal work and otherwise treat women equally with men. If there is discrimination, individual and governmental actions are provided to remedy this, and unlike the case of the marital relationship, the benefits of equality are not withheld until the worker terminates the relationship.

Recently, some reformers have turned their attention to the relationship between the traditional demands of motherhood and the failure of women to achieve equality in the workplace in spite of legal dictates. It should be increasingly apparent that if we want to change the family, we must also transform the workplace to accommodate that change. A few feminist legal scholars are now focused on what has been labeled the "work-family conflict." The problem with this focus, from the perspective of American policymakers, who are saddled with an antiregulatory rhetoric and a free-market ideology, is that to resolve the conflict, it will be necessary to regulate the workplace, placing demands and obligations on employers. Undoubtedly, this will be perceived as interfering with the autonomy of those employers and the freedom of the marketplace—transgressions of considerable magnitude in today's political contexts.

However, it is exactly this type of reform that must occur. Feminists must confront the difficult issues and political pitfalls involved, and argue for a more humane workplace and a more responsive state to emphasize the democratic and egalitarian traditions in our capitalistic system. Until the structures that make it so difficult and costly to combine caretaking responsibilities with paid work are changed, the status quo of family dynamics and workplace demands will continue to place women in a relatively disadvantageous position.

What are needed are not more legal reforms of the family, but a restructuring of the conditions of the workplace, which will most likely require substantial state intervention. This is not a plea for more "mommy track" options or other minor adjustments that separate out women for different treatment and thus, in practice, work in a discriminatory manner. As discussed more fully in chapter eight, it is a claim that the workplace should be restructured, its demands structured and channeled in ways that are compatible with the no-less-legitimate demands made in other spheres of life upon all workers.

II. THE WAKE OF FEMINIST FAMILY LAW REFORM

Practical considerations aside, when assessing the value of family law reform, many would argue that the law has important functions beyond coercion—it can be aspirational, providing the articulation of a superior normative structure. If we focus solely on the rhetorical changes made in regard to expressing expectations for husbands and wives, it seems quite clear that the sameness-of-treatment equality model and antidiscrimination-based reform were successful. Family law scholars brought marriage under legal and theoretical scrutiny and made powerful and effective arguments that altered the way we think about gendered violence,[9] reproductive rights,[10] and the economic relationship between husband and wife.

In an important survey of feminism's effect on family law, Katherine Bartlett, dean of the Law School at Duke University, suggests that feminism's "principal" contribution to the law of the family "has been to open that institution to critical scrutiny and question the justice of a legal regime that has permitted, even reinforced, the subordination of some family members to others."[11] This rendition of reform defines the task of feminism as confronting inequality and subordination and effecting moves toward greater equality and autonomy within the family.

Bartlett casts the contributions of feminist family law scholars and practitioners in this manner as largely a "success story." Feminists challenged the public-private divide, making abuses within the family visible. They generated instability in, and subsequent reform of, "traditional" patriarchal family law. Feminist engagement with and use of powerful legal concepts such as "equality" led to recasting marriage as a relationship between equal partners. Divorce rules have changed to reflect the perception that wages and income are the product of family labor, not only of individual efforts. The legal relationship between husband and wife has been completely rewritten in gender-neutral, equality-aspiring terms. So-called domestic violence is now subjected to criminal and civil sanctions, and "marital rape" is no longer considered an oxymoron. Most women, whether they identify themselves as feminist or not, benefit from and generally approve of such manifestations of gender equality.

Yet Bartlett also concludes that the most "divisive issues" for feminists, as well as for larger society, "have been those that concern the preservation, or elimination, of traditional 'gender roles' in family or family-related areas of the law." [12] Her discussion of division implies that these differently gendered roles still exist. She further asserts that "[f]amily-related issues concerning gender roles have generated the most backlash against feminism in the popular culture." [13]

I think it unlikely that Bartlett is referring to the norms of gender equality that govern the relationship between husband and wife when she refers to the divisions among feminists, although that move has generated some backlash in certain circles. When considering the divisions within feminism, I think it much more likely that Bartlett's remarks were in response to an ongoing struggle about how we should view the roles of mothers and fathers in the newly constituted egalitarian family.

Bartlett's essay explores three areas of family law, all of which exemplify the gendered nature of family relationships between adult women and men. She addresses the relationships' reform in the contexts of divorce, reproduction, and domestic violence.[14] These are indeed areas of success for feminism. But there are other areas of inquiry that would show less success and more ambivalence on the part of feminists. Certain areas of law concerning families bring children and issues surrounding dependency into the picture in ways that divorce, reproduction, and domestic violence do not. Specifically, the maternal dilemmas presented by work-family conflicts and the recasting of state welfare systems raise issues concerning the role and responsibility of the state to provide for those in need because of caretaking responsibilities.[15]

It seems that many feminists are preoccupied with the relationship between women and men to the exclusion of a consideration of other intimate connections. However, the articulation of appropriate male-female interactions across a wide range of issues is "easy" for contemporary feminist thought. It is easy because in focusing on intimate relationships between adults, the goal of gender equality (however we get there) seems clearly and uncomplicatedly appropriate. This is why in many areas there is no longer much disagreement as to the need and desirability for reform, either among feminists or between feminists and the larger society. Laws governing divorce, sex and reproduction, and domestic violence address areas in which there is equilibrium, perhaps even close to societal consensus, forged in part through feminist sensibilities.

In making this claim about equilibrium or relative consensus, I am not forgetting about the religious right and the conservative backlash against gender equality. Nor am I ignoring the fact that within communities that generally support contemporary policy, there are nuanced debates that still exist, such as those concerning late-term abortion in pro-choice feminist circles. My assertion is merely that the majority of American society (feminist and not):

[1] seems to be settled on policies that allow relatively liberal divorce laws, coupled with a partnership model for doing economic justice between spouses;

[2] has settled into a "live-and-let-live" approach to sex, complemented by recognition of a woman's right to "choose"; and

[3] believes that perpetrators of domestic violence should be punished and that society should provide support and protection for their victims.

With so many old issues now successfully addressed, perceptions of just what social arrangements currently constitute "gender issues" ripe for the application of feminist legal thought has (or should have) been evolving. The gendered nature of women's relationship with men, now a much less pressing issue, allows concern with the tenacity of women's socially and culturally assigned role as caretaker to surface. The attendant material and other disadvantages that role brings should become central objects in feminist theory.

What are we feminists to do with motherhood, as both a practice and an ideological structure? In the family arena, it is not what we want for woman as "wife," but what we aspire to as "mother," that divides us and provokes dissension and debate in and outside of feminist communities. When we ask questions about motherhood, the focus moves from the male/female dyad to that of mother/child. Concepts such as equality, while useful in defining relations between adults, seem inadequate to address the dynamics inherent in what is considered by many to be a more primal tie.

There is no autonomy to be found in motherhood. Motherhood is mired in dependency—the dependency of the child, in the first instance, and the dependency of that person assigned responsibility for caretaking, in the second instance. Dependency seems incompatible with equality; it undermines the notion that women can achieve autonomy and be free from family disability. In this regard, legal feminists seem to have a much more ambiguous response to woman's role as mother than that generated in response to her traditional role as wife.

The assertion that motherhood is the real "gender issue" frames a conceptual and theoretical challenge in family law for contemporary legal feminism. This is particularly true since it has become increasingly obvious that the solutions to the dilemmas created by dependency and caretaking cannot be found within the family. The politics and policies surrounding work-family conflicts and welfare are among the most contentious issues in society today. These issues are divisive and generate controversy within feminism precisely because they reach beyond the family and the individuals within it to implicate other societal institutions. In doing so, these issues force us to confront the limitations of equality and gender neutrality. Yet, we have no readily accepted supplemental concepts with which to try to transform the practice in families and guide the responses of other societal institutions.

These areas are troubling for feminists and others concerned with the welfare of women and children because they reveal that many individuals and the families they form cannot live up to the ideals of our autonomy myth as it is expressed in terms of independence and self-sufficiency. Focusing on the pressures and stresses that arise in trying to combine work and family responsibilities, most starkly presented in the context of welfare policy, forces us to confront the realization that more than the family is in need of reform.

The stress suffered by all too many modern families brings to the forefront the incompatibility—given existing societal structures—between what we still aspire to as mothers and what we now aspire to as equals in the workplace. Further, we can predict that it will be feminists who are, and feminism that is, destined to be blamed for the failure of the family in this regard. After all (the argument will proceed), it is feminism that imposed the mandate of egalitarianism on the family, protected women's right to choose when and if to become mothers, and championed the image of single motherhood as an acceptable alternative. These families, because they fail to conform to the idealized traditional model, are unable to maintain the family's historic role in regard to dependency. It is the act of tampering with the traditional family model, not the unresponsiveness of the unaccommodating workplace and the reluctance of the state to regulate, that will be seen as responsible for the family's predicament.

How should feminists respond to such assertions? In the first instance, we must reject the notion that the problem of work/family conflict should be cast as the problem of a lack of equal sharing between women and men of domestic burdens within the family. We have gone down that road and it is a dead end. Our arguments for reform must now acknowledge that the societally constructed role of mother continues to exact unique costs for women. This is true in spite of decades of attempts to equalize family responsibility and to draft gender-neutral, equality-enhancing rules. The difficulty that women and men experience in trying to change their behavior as mothers and fathers and to equalize the costs of caretaking remains striking.

Feminist legal theorists anticipated that as women became more active in the workplace, men would become more involved in the family. However, although the former has occurred, the latter has not—the "revolution" has been accomplished. Statistics reflecting persistent gendered divisions of family labor stand in contrast with the aspiration to reconfigure women's relationship to the workforce. Norms of equality are firmly entrenched in the laws governing both areas, but are much less successfully implemented in the family realm.[16] While it is true that patterns of equality are manifested increasingly in regard to expectations for and behavior of men and women in their roles as wives and husbands, the quest for equality and gender neutrality has not produced the same sort of "progress" in affecting the actual practices of mothers and fathers. Generations after the formal articulation of gender-neutral parenting principles, the assumption of responsibilities for children and other dependents continues to be gender skewed.

As a result, the social, economic, and cultural implications of motherhood remain very different from those of fatherhood. Of course, within individual families we may see signs of successful struggle over sharing responsibility. Some men are actually attempting to redefine their own behavior and society's expectations for fathers. Studies show that when they do, they suffer some of the same disadvantages and negative consequences as mothers.[17] For example, in some cases, men who asked for parental leave were seen as not dedicated to their career.[18] Perhaps this illustrates why it is so difficult for women and men to try to equalize their behavior as mothers and fathers: the equalization is going to hurt, at least within the larger social system currently in place. Someone is going to suffer in the workplace if there is caretaking to be done in the home. Women have been in that position for generations, so the status quo prevails, but it is important to emphasize that it is the *task* of caretaking, not the sex of the caretaker, that operates as a disadvantage.

This last point brings up another limitation of feminists' tendency to be preoccupied with the interactions between women and men. This focus distracts us from some more fundamental manifestations of inequality. Because feminists have been uncomfortable confronting the implications of dependency, our law reform efforts, for the most part, have been limited in imagination and reach. We have been relentless in an exploration of internal inequities and injustices within the family, but have failed to consider that institution in its larger societal context.

Undertaking such an exploration would move the feminist perspective away from concern about family roles and gender equality (at least initially) and direct our attention to the place and meaning of marriage and the marital family in our cultural, social, and ideological systems. It also brings us into direct confrontation with the implications of economic ideology and practices of capitalism, which some argue have not been enough of a focus for feminists within the United States. However, until we undertake this kind of exploration, it will be impossible for us to consider what kinds of reforms are likely to make things better (more equal and just) within marriage, within the family, or within society in general. Real reform cannot proceed, or even be adequately theorized, until we understand and appreciate the way changes in the expectations for and functioning of the marital family in order to gain greater gender equality will challenge and threaten other social institutions. In the sense that they are built around the continuation of a gendered family structure, these institutions are actually dependent on it. If that structure is undermined, so are the institutions weakened. Feminists must respond to these threats with ideas for new structuring that will benefit us all.

In her article, Bartlett alluded to a backlash against existing feminist reform. Certainly that backlash is generated in part by the realization that feminism, insofar as it equalizes ambitions and opportunities, threatens the traditional family. If women really aspire to equality, the family will not be able to perform its historic task of being the repository for dependency. Those who lash back against feminist egalitarian aspirations realize something we should also take seriously: successfully transforming expectations and behavior within the family will necessitate profound corresponding transformations and accommodations on the part of other societal institutions.

Feminists must not replicate the same sort of mistakes that mar other theoretical and policy discussions, focusing only on one area of law and set of relationships and failing to consider how change there might reverberate throughout society. As we approach changes to the family, we cannot assume that other societal institutions either do not matter or will simply be transformed to conform to our specification about what is needed in the way of institutional support for a revised ideal family form or function. We must consider the constraints that will be placed on any transformation of the family, constraints that are inherent in the existing organization and structure of the market and our ideology about the state. Part of this process will be a consideration of the limits on possibilities for reform that may be built into existing theories of justice and law.

When considering these other societal institutions and how they impact and are impacted by the family, we cannot just critique the internal aspects of the marital family, focusing on the gendered nature of relationships. In order to achieve an egalitarian family, we must also confront the reality and timelessness of inevitable dependency and the burdens it entails, both for the family as an institution and for those individuals who take up its demands. Unless other societal institutions are restructured so as to assume some of those burdens for the family, the costs will continue to be borne primarily by women within the family. The implication of dependency, coupled with the fact that women are the primary caretakers in today's society, means that many women are also dependent. This reality belies the myth that autonomy, understood to be independence and self-sufficiency, is attainable for everyone in society.

What does this specific type of dependency mean for feminists? For one thing, it is clear that society has some interesting (and potentially divisive) issues in need of feminist consideration. Women who are mothers cannot function in the same way that women who are not mothers (and men who can and do choose not to mother) function in either the workplace or the family.

I argue that feminists cannot just walk away from dependency, ignoring the dilemmas presented by children and others in need of care, even if we ourselves are not caretakers and our theoretical interests are in less "mundane" issues. Dependency issues must be of central concern in feminist theory, but it will take some real effort to make them so. The language of legal feminism, developed through looking solely at women vis-à-vis men, was framed by the quest for equality, juxtaposing ideas of domination with antisubordination, victimhood with agency, and special treatment with equality. These are concepts developed to address the legal and structural burdens imposed on women in relation to men in society. They do not adequately capture the dilemmas confronting women in their role as mother, as someone derivatively dependent because she is taking responsibility for the inevitable dependency of others.[19] Feminists need to define the concepts and create a vocabulary to be employed in addressing the dependency of mothers.[20]

We also need a way to think about the inherently unequal and dependent relationship that children have with mothers and others who care for them. This area of concern is likely to be at least as contentious among feminists as is the assertion that we need theory infused with consideration of caretaking. In the postscript to this book, I argue for a reconfigured concept of entity privacy to shield the caretaker/dependent relationship from intervention and state scrutiny, a concept that is an essential part of developing a theory of dependency and an argument for collective responsibility. Some version of privacy will be necessary to address the assertion that collective responsibility carries with it the right to collective control over decisions such as who shall have children and under what circumstances.

III. THE FUTURE OF FAMILY REFORM

It is interesting to note that other disciplines also struggle with these ideas of dependency and the meaning of family, even if they do not explicitly cast the struggle in feminist terms. In his comprehensive law and economics reader *Foundations of the Economic Approach to Law,* Professor Avery Katz devotes the last section to "an application on the frontier: family law." Katz asserts: "Economic analysis can shed light on any sphere of human interaction in which individuals pursue their goals subject to constraint."[21] He describes family relations as

> externalities imposed by individual families on the rest of society and by individual family members on others in the household; incentives to invest in the family's material assets and in the human assets of its individual members; strategic behavior arising from family members' efforts to influence each other's conduct; insurance against the financial and emotional risks of disability, unemployment, and household dissolution; and the effects of limited information and bounded rationality on such crucial personal decisions as family formation and career choice.[22]

Katz speculates that among the reasons that economics has enjoyed "relatively less influence" in family law than other doctrinal fields have is the persistent tendency to conceptualize the market and family as separate realms.[23] Equally significant is his identification of the difficulty associated with the "fundamental issues of liberalism" raised by the "recurring need" (inherent in the whole idea of family) for some family members to make decisions for others who are incapable of protecting their own interests.[24] Katz thus labels the family "the archetypal paternalist institution."[25] An economic model that posits independent, rational individuals not only interacting with each other, but also seeking to maximize their own utility in that interaction, does not reflect what is assumed about family relationships.[26]

The "recurring need" for a "paternalist" family presents a dilemma not only for economists but also, as I have argued, for feminists. The feminist version of the dilemma arises because inequality and gender neutrality have defined the feminist family law project thus far, to the exclusion of an examination of this recurring need. Need and dependency mandate not only paternalism, but also maternalism—the family needs a wage earner and caretaker, roles historically separate from one another and imposed in a gendered manner.

Traditionally, men, as husbands and fathers, operated as the heads of families, with responsibilities to support and discipline wives and children. Women, as wives and mothers, provided domestic services—caretaking and sexual services—and owed the family head obedience and deferral. The traditional gendered roles complemented each other, father and mother providing the whole in fulfilling the economic and caretaking needs of the family.

But who or what is filling the caretaking void left behind as women abandon or refashion their roles as wives and mothers? Certainly not men; they continue to act primarily as economic actors. In fact, what we see emerge, as a result of women's move to expand their opportunities outside of the family, is a crisis of care. We have enough information from educational and employment patterns to know with some certainty that most women are no longer satisfied to act exclusively in the roles of wife and mother.

To the extent that the changes in family form reflect changing patterns of gendered behavior, in which women are rejecting their primary assignment to the family, many feminists view this as a cause for celebration. As women's roles are repositioned within society, however, the necessity of the traditional gender arrangement for the success of the family, as it has been historically understood, becomes apparent. By disrupting the gendered assumptions that confined women to the home, feminists also revealed the role or function of the family within society. In exploring this, feminists attacked the notion of public and private, and called into question the idea that the family was located outside of—separate from—society.

One erroneous assumption often manifest in feminist approaches to the family as an institution in need of reform was that the family and the gendered roles within were malleable, easily recast and reformed in ways that could facilitate women's equality in the nonfamily areas of life.[27] This profoundly affected the direction of the reform movement. While old gendered language has fallen to judicial and legislative gender-neutral zeal, there has to be much more feminist skepticism about the likelihood that changes in rhetoric might actually be incorporated into the interactions and working of real family relationships.

Complicating what has happened in the context of family law reform is the fact that the form of equality that is imposed in the workplace is assimilationist in nature. Ignoring that there have historically been different social and cultural contexts in which women operated, all that is required by this type of equality is that women be treated the same (equally) as the men who have preceded them.

There is little recognition, and almost no concession, that women and men may be differently situated, making equal rules operate inequitably in practice. Specifically, domestic and caretaking responsibilities are not distributed across the genders equally. Workplaces historically have been designed with the unencumbered worker in mind. The law only demands that women now have equal access to jobs and careers and be treated the same as that "autonomous," unencumbered individual. However, this autonomous worker can only exist when there is someone in the nonwork world doing the dependency work. Someone who in the past or in the present has done the dependency work necessary in the nonwork world subsidizes the autonomy of this actor.

These different social and cultural contexts have complicated feminists' search for equality through sameness of treatment. Familial responsibilities cause women to earn less in the workplace, even when policies guaranteeing equal treatment have been implemented.[28] But because of the way we understand equality (and refuse to examine our ideas of autonomy and dependency), we live in a world where gender neutrality is equated with equality. It seems futile to argue that attainment of equality (and the prospect of autonomy) may in fact require unequal treatment. However, parity, given different gendered realities, is only possible through different treatment, afforded with attention to the different contexts in which lives are lived.

Of course, accommodation could be made in a gender-neutral manner. We could urge that circumstances, such as caretaking, must be supported regardless of who undertakes them. It is the role of mother, not her sex, that is disadvantageous to a woman in a workplace that has been designed for a "breadwinner" who is supported by someone at home doing the dependency work. But neutral characterization aside, the existing circumstances of women and men means that accommodation would have gendered implications. Accommodation would tend to benefit women more than men, given the ongoing unequal investments made in domestic tasks between the sexes. This disparity in impact leads some to make strong objections to even a gender-neutral argument for accommodation.

Some feminists argue that a policy of accommodation serves only to emphasize the differences between men and women, using men as the "starting point for analysis."[29] Martha Minow argues, for example, that an "unstated male norm makes pregnancy and maternity leaves 'special treatment,' contrasted to the 'normal treatment' given to employees."[30] Others remain deeply skeptical about recognition of any differences, even biologically based ones, such as the respective roles of women and men in reproduction.

In the classic piece on equality as sameness of treatment, Professor Wendy Williams argues against any recognition of differences, no matter how they might actually affect opportunity.

> The same doctrinal approach that permits pregnancy to be treated worse than other disabilities is the same one that will allow the state constitutional freedom to create special benefits for pregnant women. The equality approach to pregnancy . . . necessarily creates not only the desired floor under the pregnant woman's rights but also the ceiling. . . . If we can't have it both ways, we need to think carefully about which way we want to have it. . . . My own feeling is that, for all its problems, the equality approach is the better one. The special treatment model has great costs. . . . At this point we need to think as deeply as we can about what we want the future of women and men to be. Do we want equality of the sexes—or do we want justice for two kinds of human beings who are fundamentally different?[31]

IV. CONCLUSION

The particular combination of 1) the impossibility of designing a means for the implementation of equality within the ongoing family and 2) the imposition of a formal version of equality as sameness of treatment in the workplace has meant in practice that mothers now are free to compete with unencumbered women and men in a workplace that continues to fail to take family needs into account. As a society, we remain relatively unresponsive to the contradictory and conflicting demands placed on caretakers who also are members of the paid workforce.

Additionally, many people perceive the gender revolution to be accomplished. For many, the workplace is seen as being successfully reformed, with the imposition of an equality mandate and the prohibition of discrimination based on sex. These measures do not address the reforms necessary because we have hidden the problems associated with caretaking within the family and have not explored their implications for opportunities at work. It is not a solution to this dilemma to deny the gendered aspects of this pattern of behavior, pretending we can substitute androgynous individuality for the differentiated, complementary roles within the traditional family without drastically transforming the workplace and expanding the role of the state. I return to these themes in chapters nine and ten.

Chapter Seven

Mothering in a Gender-Neutral World

I. INTRODUCTION

A. Egalitarian Family Law

Consistent with the way in which equality is understood in America to be sameness of treatment, the language of family law is now gender neutral.[1] Equality mandates that legal decisions be based on the character, and not the gender, of the individual. Respect for the rights of the individual demands case-by-case assessments and rejects rules based on gender "stereotypes." This is required even when those stereotypes have some empirical validity.

Gender neutrality has been applied in the law to the categories of "mother" and "father" and to the categories of "husband" and "wife." These categories have been collapsed into "parent," on the one hand, and "spouse" or "partner," on the other. What we see in family law is the imposition of an equality model onto an existing unequal distribution of labor and sacrifice. As argued in chapter six, this imposition of equality disadvantages women, at least to the extent that they are performing traditional domestic roles.[2]

This model of equality actually furthers inequality because it doesn't take into account the realities of "mothering" within the family, particularly the ability of a woman who is a mother to compete with an unfettered person in the workplace. In this chapter, I argue that these equality rules may also disadvantage children. Certainly, one effect of the equality revolution has been the undermining of the legal institution of motherhood. Caretaking has become a suspect category. The idea of mothering or nurturing as an activity entitled to rewards and warranting "special" treatment or consideration has been attacked by liberal legal feminists as well as by policymakers, politicians, and fathers' rights groups.

For feminists, the distrust of special treatment for motherhood often springs from an overarching commitment to equality for women, which also makes feminists attentive to all situations in which men are treated differently. Many legal feminists endorsed a presumption of joint custody following divorce. For these feminists, it is imperative that the law reflects society's *aspirations* for equality, rather than attempt to remedy inequality caused by existing (gendered) allocations of household labor.

Some equality feminists go so far as to suggest that there should be no ameliorating rules at divorce designed to compensate women for losses suffered as a result of their assumption of traditional domestic tasks. The rationale is that for their own good, all women must be directed toward paid work, even when they are married to a man who can more than adequately support them. The goal is for women to be economically self-sufficient, and so there should be no incentive for them to not pursue a career.[3] Of course, men are to be nudged into assuming their share of domestic tasks. The primary strategy, however, is determined by the belief that by refusing to compensate or reward women for choosing traditional domestic tasks over market work, society would influence women, and eventually men, to change their priorities and behavior.[4] The motivation of these feminists is one of social engineering, in which the goal of gender equality is clearly a paramount concern.

Liberal feminist equality motivations aside, a great deal of political discussion about legal reforms *is* explicitly punitive in nature. This is certainly the case with discussions about incorporating incentives against single motherhood into policy reforms, whether single motherhood results from divorce or from women's having children outside of marriage. Some commentators condemn single-mother families because they wish to restore the authority of the father and fear that women are raising children without appropriate paternal supervision and economic support.[5] For this group of equality advocates, the real goal is the restoration of historic inequality. Some of the proposals for driving women back into the institution of marriage or preventing them from leaving it seem overtly vindictive as well as punitive. For example, not too long ago, politicians were suggesting that children be taken from single mothers and placed in orphanages.[6]

Today, however, the backlash may be more subtly coercive. Recently, we have seen attempts to repeal no-fault divorce, which would impede on individuals' ability to exit marital relationships. There are efforts to create incentives to encourage marriage, incentives fueled by federal funding that set up a competition among the states for creation of such propaganda.[7] Surprisingly, harsh policies directed at single mothers, such as the recent gutting of programs designed to aid poor families with children, have received general approval.

B. More Focused Family Reforms

Whatever the motivation of reformers, the continued high divorce rates and the statistics on reproductive, workplace, and family behaviors show that general and wide-sweeping punitive measures enacted into law are unlikely to cause significant changes in behavior.[8] Powerful and compelling cultural and social forces drive evolving changes in norms concerning sexuality, reproduction, and family formation at the dawn of the new millennium. Law seems a feeble and inadequate tool compared to such forces for those who wish to challenge these emerging forms of family and norms of individual intimate behavior.

More focused and pragmatic are those reforms that accept the changes in behavior, but try to reconstitute the single-parent family, structuring it through law into an entity that resembles the traditional two-parent idea. Such reforms, while seemingly changing expectations, nonetheless ensure that old patterns prevail.

Specifically, some recently enacted family laws make it much more likely that traditional patterns of paternal right and responsibility will continue even in a world in which the form of many families will otherwise not be traditional. For example, joint custody and other shared-parenting measures are designed to equalize biological fathers' rights to children, regardless of their marital status and even without demonstration of the father's commitment to parenting. Such rules are justified as means to establish male ties to children that will increase the voluntary assumption of responsibility for those children.[9]

For those who do not assume responsibility voluntarily, increased efforts to collect child support, along with the introduction of more invasive schemes, accompany broadened use of paternity proceedings. The objective of such measures is to legally link men to their nonmarital children, in order to enforce the norm of primary male economic responsibility in regard to those children. The concept of responsibility that informs these and other efforts reflects the gendered norms of the traditional patriarchal family—the male is clearly viewed as the economic provider, and male ties to children are not only biological and legal, but also economic.[10]

In addition, and consistently with the norms of a traditional patriarchal model of the family, many argue that it is important to ensure paternal responsibility in the reconfigured family by establishing and reinforcing paternal control over the discipline of children. Paternal responsibility is equated with paternal authority. It is fascinating that this inherently patriarchal project is accomplished within the framework of gender equality.[11] In fact, paternal responsibility and its corollary, paternal right, have both reemerged in the context of equality rhetoric in family law reform.

The equality rhetoric applied to the family has its roots in the mid-century women's movement for legal or civil equality.[12] As discussed in chapter six, one significant feminist law reform effort sought to discourage formal gender classifications and different treatment for women and men in the workplace and the political arena, as well as in families. This movement was successful, and family law is now formally gender neutral. In custody cases, this means that reference to or explicit use of a preference for maternal custody for younger children is no longer acceptable. Neither parent is to be advantaged (or disadvantaged) as a result of her or his gender.[13]

In and of itself, a reform that removes explicit gender designations from statutes and decision making is not objectionable. It can even be viewed as desirable on a symbolic level, particularly if removal of gender has no negative effect in terms of ultimate results in actual cases. In fact, it might be beneficial not to use gender as shorthand, but to be clear about social policy in this important area. Laws would then have to specifically detail the desirable characteristics or expectations about caretaking and nurturing norms that historically underlie the maternal preference.[14] Those characteristics would have to be expressed in contemporary gender-neutral terms. If the primary factor in custody determinations is the ability to care for and nurture the child, instead of a stated maternal preference, we could create a preference for the parent who has undertaken the responsibility for the ongoing day-to-day care of the child, or has demonstrated a willingness to put the child's interest ahead of career demands.[15]

Gender neutrality had the potential for the articulation of caretaking expectations outside of the cultural shorthand of "mother." Reforming the law in favor of gender neutrality in this manner would have been productive and encouraging of genuine reform. Yet the course of reform has been quite different. The quest for gender neutrality in custody decision making has proven to be too ambitious and too singularly focused on equality to be satisfied with the mere imposition of gender-neutral language. In custody decision making, in particular, reform has led to the search for standards or decisional factors that are neutral in *result* as well in expression. Of particular concern are legal rules and standards that are deemed to favor mothers disproportionately, such as a preference for custody with the primary caretaker.

The argument is that since in practice mothers are typically primary caretakers, the preference for primary caretakers in custody decisions is unacceptably gender biased in favor of women. This is a classic disparate-impact legal argument: the primary-caretaker standard would be said to have an adverse disparate impact on the custody prospects of men. Thus, a nurturing standard cannot be used. In its place are substituted what are deemed more "neutral" considerations, such as the quality of the respective school districts of the parents or general assessments about which parent is more likely to facilitate and support visitation by the other parent postdivorce. As one court succinctly stated, custody determinations must be "born of gender-neutral precepts in both result and expression."[16]

II. VALUING CARE

Our fetish for gender neutrality is inappropriate, particularly in that it imports disparate-impact concepts from wholly unrelated areas of discrimination law. More is at stake in custody rules than an objective assessment of the relationships and roles of women and men. Custody decision making occurs within the context of a legal system that has, as its stated objective, custody determinations that are in the best interest of the child. Given this mandate, it seems clear that the needs and welfare of the child, not the equality of the parents, should be the central inquiry, the measure with which to judge general rules and specific cases.[17] It seems that gender neutrality as it is implemented—requiring neutrality as to nurturing—is likely to actually prove harmful to children.

The obvious question is, how can we apply the "best interest" test without considering and heavily valuing those things that mothers overwhelmingly (even if stereotypically) do with and for children? Nurturing and caretaking—practices that are of primary importance to the rearing of children—are heavily identified in our society with the practice of responsible mothering. The imposition of this cultural expectation on women complements and is distinguishable from the economic expectations that primarily define responsible fathering. What is the logic or the justice in the position that women who live up to the expectations of motherhood (as well as the men who mother) should be denied the reward and responsibility of continued custody and care of their children? To do so devalues both nurturing and care.

Why this obsession with gender neutrality? Many feminists paradoxically justify their own tendency to undermine the identification of women with mothering and nurturing by pointing to the need to use gender neutrality to secure women's equality with men in areas of life outside the family. Such logic presents equality as the overriding consideration, regardless of what area of life is under discussion. If we are to have gender neutrality in one area, it must be mandated in all others, not only for consistency's sake, but because otherwise there will be equality nowhere. The desire for equality outside the family is not only the backdrop, but also the driving impulse mandating the legal system's reassessment of the fairness or justice of rules favoring mothers and maternal behavior in determining custody for children.

The absence of changed paternal behavior by those feminist legal reformers who have taken us in the direction of gender neutrality is not considered problematic. In fact, contemporary discussions about the unfairness of rules that favor mothering often assume that there have been extensive changes in parenting patterns that make fathering and mothering more alike. There is little empirical evidence to support this assumption, and some to refute it. The rhetoric of equality in this regard is rhetoric of assertion, aspiration, and accusation.

According to this idealized notion of the new, egalitarian family, because mothers are no longer formally assigned to the separate sphere of family, they must be considered as equal to men in their inclination and capacity to earn money. Fathers must be considered equal to women in their desire and ability to provide nurturance.[18] If this ideal is to be made real, it is argued that the law should facilitate and institutionalize egalitarian social transformations. One way to do this is by insisting on the gender-neutral ideal—an ungendered parenthood standard. This argument concludes with a basic appeal to justice: the claim that fathers, as a group, are unjustly discriminated against in the family court system.

The fact that only a small percentage of fathers get custody of their children at divorce is offered as proof of this claim. These statistics have been fleshed out by harrowing horror stories—accounts of men prevented from seeing their children and unjustly treated by courts, lawyers, and vindictive custodial mothers.[19] Testimonials to the unfairness of the entire process, some more scholarly in nature and ambition than others, are offered by the extensive and prolific fathers' rights network. The message is that men have lived up to their paternal responsibilities, even changed their parenting behavior, yet are unjustly treated as second-class parents. They deserve equal status with mothers and protection from the excesses historically perpetuated by the custody-and-control monopoly over children that courts have given to mothers.

Such anecdotal and undocumented assertions have changed the way fatherhood is approached and articulated in the rules governing custody at divorce. Fathers are increasingly seen as victims of an outmoded system of stereotypes, justifying a call for restructuring of the custodial process in the direction of conferring full equality upon fathers.[20] Equality is best encouraged through the implementation of a shared parenting model after divorce, and men are now more likely to get custody if they engage in a real contest. The real gain for fathers, however, is in their ability to maintain significant postdivorce control over day-to-day decisions regarding their children, even when they do not have primary responsibility for those children and can therefore evade the consequences of such decisions.[21] What happens is that fathers are given an option, the right to intercede and require that primary caretakers consult and negotiate with them, but they are not required to participate in the harder realities of parenthood.

In an interesting rhetorical maneuver, this restructuring on behalf of fathers is justified as being in the best interest of the child. It is argued that extensive contact with both parents postdivorce is essential to child development. As a result, the rights of the noncustodian are aligned with the needs of the child, and thus given ascendancy. The rules reflect a preference for custody not in the most nurturing parent, but the most generous parent. This is the parent who is most likely to facilitate extensive contact with the other parent postdivorce. Further, generosity is accomplished and ensured by extensive monitoring and supervision of the primary caretaking parent. For many advocates of paternal equality, the new ideal can only be realized in a preference for joint custody.

Rather than justice and egalitarianism, the degendered custody rules represent a perverse affirmative action scheme. Male parenting behavior during marriage is excused from assessment under otherwise-imposed nurturing and caretaking norms. Men will thus be permitted under laxer standards to continue to devote primary attention to their careers and extrafamilial activities. They can do so without risking adverse consequences when they decide they want to assert claims to control their children postdivorce. A mere basic biological connection to the child justifies a claim for shared custody and control rights that equalize the postdivorce relationships between both parents and their child. Nurturing is devalued, ignored, and unrewarded in such a scheme.

Of course, part of the logic behind this approach to custody is that fathers contribute in different ways to the well-being of their children. They provide economically. Some argue that a man should not be penalized postdivorce merely because he was the prime economic provider for his children, rather than the primary caretaker or nurturer. And, the argument continues, of course the wage earner role often decreases the time and energy available for caretaking. To overvalue the time and energy expended in caretaking in assigning postdivorce responsibility and authority would provide an inequitable windfall for the caretaker, unfairly advantaging her in the custody determination.

The asymmetry of this logic should make it clear why it is problematic (though it is not apparent to those making the argument). First, any system disregarding caretaking because of a desire to avoid penalizing the primary wage earner (equalizing his chances to gain custody and/or retain control over children) risks ignoring the penalties already suffered by the parent who has been the primary caretaker. The time and energy devoted to caretaking does, in fact, decrease and detract from opportunities to invest in individual market skills and participate in market activity.

In fact, the very argument offered by fathers' rights proponents to explain why fathers do not engage in primary caretaking—they are working—concedes that such caretaking demands the sacrifice of market skills and career development. Should custody law further deprive the caretaker, robbing her of the benefits of her nonmarket work? At divorce, she has already invested her time and energy in caretaking. Should that sacrifice be compounded by the infliction of a further harm—denial of that work by not counting it positively when considering who should have future custody and control over her children? Even if primary custody remains with the caretaker, the imposition of a sharing ideal postdivorce through joint custody–like arrangements burdens the custodian by forcing her to negotiate, cajole, and console the noncaretaking parent after divorce because she continues to be tied to him in a shared parenting scheme.

Provision of economic benefits to the family just does not have the same negative implications and consequences for the provider in the postdivorce world as does the provision of caretaking. A caretaker may compromise or forgo altogether skill

development that would add to her résumé, culminate in enhanced marketable skills, and improve her economic position.
Economic contribution to children's welfare, by contrast, is the
result of market activity that also improves the provider's owns
skills and stature in the market. This self-investment is not the
equivalent of the sacrificial investment in others involved in
caretaking. The trade-offs are not the same.

The adverse effects on the development of market skills that
result from an investment in children also occur when the primary caretaker engages in paid work in addition to caretaking.[22]
An employed caretaker compromises her market position by assuming primary responsibility for her children. There are risks
associated with everyday events, such as illness or failures in
childcare arrangements, that necessitate missing work or establishing more flexible (therefore more tangential) connections
with the workplace. These responsibilities are typically assigned
within a family to only one parent, usually the one with the
lower wage-earning potential (generally the woman).[23] Of
course, more attention to the demands of the workplace might
compromise her caretaking. It is a dilemma expressed in the
term "work-family conflict."

And, lest the anti-essentialist rhetoric totally obscure appreciation for elementary biology, we must take into account that
pregnancy and childbirth, as well as breast-feeding, are female
functions that may temporarily affect the physical and emotional resources available for other endeavors. These are gendered factors that have serious economic implications.
Nonetheless, custody debates do not explicitly address these implications and, through the imposition of the equality model,
treat caretaking and economic support as equivalent sacrifices
and contributions to the family.

In addition to the basic justice argument for valuing and re-
warding caretaking as something distinct, there is a social engi-

neering argument that should also be made. Equating care and economic contribution perpetuates the very behavior that equality advocates seek to change. If caretaking is devalued, men have no reason to change their behavior since they can leave the marriage relationship with the future benefits gained by their investment in themselves intact, as well as realize the benefits of their wives' investment in the marital children. They are not penalized for failing to sacrifice personal development or advancement to care for children.[24] Through the assertion of neutrality and equality, they are set free to continue the traditional male preoccupation[25] with the workplace and marketplace. Further, someone else's labor makes it possible for them to also have children without risking loss of control or paternal authority should divorce occur.

Why have the arguments evolved in this way? Certainly, as has already been stated, the power of equality ideology is crucial, but who actually wields the rhetoric also matters. It is certainly not the case that policymakers and legislators typically adopt feminist perspectives. Fathers' rights advocates, however, seem more successful with the equality language they have appropriated.

Less-symbolic justifications have also been at work on the fathers' rights side of the debates. One very effective argument for increasing the rights and control of noncustodial fathers has been that this will ensure compliance with child-support orders. The fact that child support enters into the picture as an influential factor in the context of divorce is not unexpected in a society in which payment of child support is the exception and not the norm.[26] But the nature and source of these arguments are curious. Economic irresponsibility is excused and justified by fathers' rights advocates, who argue that men's widespread failure to pay child support is attributable to the frustration and pain they experience as a result of their unjust treatment as second-class parents. Overwhelmingly, male policy bodies have accepted this argument and assume that divorced fathers have a basic goodwill and a natural inclination toward responsible behavior.[27] They believe this despite substantial statistical evidence that this is not how many divorced fathers respond postdivorce.

III. FATHERHOOD

What has been missing from policy and reform discussions thus far is a debate about the nature of fatherhood and the transformation of the role of the father in response to changing expectations, norms, and practices. How does the desire for gender neutrality and the ideal of egalitarianism play a role in the creation of a new set of norms for fatherhood? Men should be engaged in this type of rhetorical and conceptual exercise, following the consciousness-raising and conversational models of the last few decades through which women successfully transformed their roles.

Much of contemporary fathers' rights discourse, however, has concentrated almost exclusively on the perceived failings of mothers and their alleged vindictiveness and irresponsibility. The strategy is successful, and as a result, the failures of fathers are turned back on mothers. Male foibles are cast as merely responsive to women's actions and as understandably defensive. A sense of crisis for fathers has been generated concerning visitation rights, for example. The assertion of fathers' rights groups is that mothers typically persist in interfering with fathers' access to children. There are suggestions that in retaliation, these mothers should be subject to fines and/or imprisonment or should lose custody of the children.

It is also alleged that mothers are at fault for misuse of child-support payments. Fathers' rights advocates speculate that mothers use their meager and sporadic child-support awards to support vile habits or indulge new lovers.[28] These undocumented accusations receive media and legislative attention and have prompted suggestions for invasive reforms, such as mandatory yearly accounting.[29]

A substantial amount of fathers' rights discourse characterizes mothers using negative and malicious stereotypes, arguing for monitoring, punishment, containment, and control over mothers. Such rhetoric is premised on the assumption that mothers can exercise rights over their children only at the expense of others. Every step to benefit custodial mothers is perceived as causing potential harm to someone else, fathers in particular, but often also to those same children.

Another strain of fathers' rights rhetoric, not as overtly hostile to mothers, is associated with the historical exclusion of some men from many of society's rewards and privileges because of their race, class, or ethnicity. Even though sympathetic to women, this discourse is paternalistic and patriarchal.[30] Its practitioners do not conceptualize the problem as a loss of men's traditional privileged position in the family, but still indulge in the assumption that it is imperative to restore fathers to their mythic position as "head" of the household.[31]

In this line of argument, fatherhood represents a window into the "real" or hard issues of unemployment. Fathers must have access to jobs and training programs, it is argued, in order to be fathers. Once again, the essential nature of fatherhood is not found in caretaking, but rather in economic provision. These arguments resort to images of traditional patriarchy in an attempt to persuade the dominant culture of the need for economic justice for this class of fathers. In fact, it is considered problematic if mothers are economically independent of fathers, either through provision of state resources to single mothers or because the mothers themselves earn wages. Economically independent women are seen as taking over the male role.

Some of the rhetoric of civil rights organizations has gone so

far as to suggest that black women, particularly as single mothers, emasculate black men,[32] and that women in general are incapable of raising sons. Both strains of fathers' rights discourse
are based on notions of traditional fathers' rights and position.
Neither has any conceptual difficulty with the reactionary assertion that the welfare of children is primarily and largely dependent upon society's treating men better and reining in women
who have exceeded their family authority. The emerging social
reality of single mother–and-child units is either ignored or provokes punitive measures that we justify as necessary so that men
can assume their appropriate roles and actually perform as the
heads of families.

Many of the arguments about paternal right and responsibility in regard to children that have been made in the context of
divorce are also made in nonmarital contexts. In recent years,
unwed fathers' claims to custody and visitation have strength-
ened significantly. In contrast to the patina of parental nurturing equality in the discourse concerning divorce, however,
fatherhood in the welfare context is almost exclusively and most
explicitly about how to enforce male economic responsibility.[33]

While conservatives and fathers' rights advocates are most
vocal, the desire to ensure the dominance of marriage is also dis-
coverable in the work of more liberal commentators. They, too,
evidence a belief in the essential incompleteness, and hence
necessary complementariness, of the distinct social roles of
mother and father.

Political theorist Iris Marion Young astutely identified the patriarchal dimensions in the policy arguments of William Galston, the civil societarian discussed in chapter three. Galston
served as an influential adviser to former president Clinton during the 1996 welfare reform. He has asserted that the state
should not be value neutral but rather should pursue policies
that validate and strengthen traditional marriage.[34]

Young admonished Galston by asserting that society's interest in rais-ing good citizens can be accomplished in a variety of family forms. Galston's suggestion that the state create incentives to strengthen marriage wrongly assumes that only one kind of family form can nurture a strong society. Galston makes his assertions on the basis of ambiguous and inconclusive studies[35] that purport to show that "children in divorced families tend to suffer the kinds of economic and psychological damage that reduce their capacity to become independent and contributing members of the community."[36]

As Young points out, Galston equates poverty with single-parent status (although many of the poor are married) and recommends marriage as the cure for poverty.[37] She addresses and refutes these assertions, in part by pointing out that Galston ignores the fact that a "stable marriage means that women are often dependent on men and suffer power inequality and various degrees of domination by men both in and outside the home."[38]

Perhaps the most interesting feature of the liberal and conservative arguments against single motherhood and for reestablishing a marriage-based family ethic in the welfare context is the conflation of family form with economic consequences. The likelihood of any family, traditional or not, successfully escaping poverty and raising law-abiding citizens is related to the economic, social, and community resources it has available.

To refute the idea that only the traditional family provides mechanisms for avoiding poverty and other social ills, one need only look to the condition of children in other countries that provide such social goods as health care, day care, child allowances, housing, and guaranteed basic income.

In the United States, we ignore the fact that European countries, which provide such guarantees even if they have high rates of nonmarital births, historically have far less crime and poverty than we do.[39] In Sweden, for example, where the typical child is born in a nonmarital family, social status and economic destiny are not determined by the marital status of one's mother.[40]

In the United States, by contrast, there has never been a real welfare state, a structure in which the collective national community ensures basic entitlements for all its members as individual citizens, independent of the form of family in which they live. It is the private family, not the public state, that is primarily responsible for the welfare of children, the ill, and the elderly, eclipsing the need to consider collective responsibility for their dependency.

As discussed in chapter two, this private family is assumed ideally to operate independent of the state and of the market in fulfilling its caretaking responsibilities.[41] This independence, however, is not accomplished unless the family is able to produce both economic support and caretaking labor, tasks historically allocated among family members along gendered lines. Men's role as economic providers serves an essential function in an ideological system in which dependency is privatized and will not be readily displaced until there is some greater public responsibility for the provision of essential goods.

Historically, it was the male breadwinner who, acting in both the public and private spheres, brought from the workplace the economic resources to provide for the family. These resources were not only a paycheck, however. They also included what in other countries are social goods ensured by the government to its citizens—essential items such as health insurance and economic security in the form of pension benefits and social security. In the United States, these essential goods are delivered through the combination of marriage and workplace, not through the state as a result of its responsibility to guarantee all citizens basic human needs. Family and workplace serve as mediating institutions—structures through which social goods are distributed—and those who stand outside of one or the other risk poverty.

Coupled with this privatized structure is the failure of the state to assume responsibility for child care or to provide a child allowance, as other countries do in order to assist in caretaking. This means that the historic role of wives as caretakers anchored primarily in the family continues also. Today it may be that women work outside of the home, but this should not obscure the fact that the role of caretaker within the private family remains central to our thinking about the relationship between that family and the public institutions of state and market.

As these last insights indicate, changing the historic division of labor within the family will be difficult. Such change will necessitate recasting our societal expectations for fatherhood so that it is more than just an economic relationship with the family. However, expectations that fathers (or breadwinners generally) also engage in caretaking will cause as many complications as has the expectation that caretakers engage in market work.

In order to achieve either objective beyond a mere rhetorical level, it will be necessary to transform the workplace and revision the role of the state so as to ensure family-friendly public institutions that do not require compromise between the demands of the workplace and the demands of dependents.[42]

The lack of adjustment in market and governmental structures in the decades since the ascendancy of the egalitarian family is disheartening. Adjustment in these institutions is necessary to support and facilitate the attempts to make the family a more just social structure. If our society were interested in real reform, there are a few areas in which substantial reassessment and reevaluation might be undertaken.

Given how the roles of men as husbands and fathers would have to be altered in pursuit of a more egalitarian family, it is essential to tear down the ideological walls that separate family,

state, and market, and to realize that all are mutually contingent. We now limit and confine obligations and responsibilities
to one institution and ignore the responsibility of others by constructing independent spheres. What is needed is integration. If
we want to recognize that people have a right to work, but that
workers are also family members who may have responsibility
for the dependency of others, then we will have to develop po-
lices directing workplaces to accommodate caretaking responsibility.

It is naive to think that transformation in the family will not
necessitate some complementary restructuring of the workplace
and increased participation on the part of government.[43] Government and market in combination must remove the obstacles
and burdens associated with combining caretaking and paid
work that have developed around an antiquated, unrealistic
model of the family in which there was a caretaker who complemented the wage earner.

The new workplace norm should be that of the dually responsible worker. The question would then become: how can we
ensure the caretaker's right to work—her right to earn while not
sacrificing the well-being of her children or other dependents?

The market must be transformed. If it does not do so on its
own, the government must structure family-friendly policies in
the workplace. This can be accomplished by regulation or by incentives offered through the tax system. The list of proposals
may be long and details will be vexing, but at a minimum, paid
family leave for all workers, flexible workweeks, and subsidized
child-care facilities in which the workers are decently paid
would be foundational.

By making nurturing and caretaking a central responsibility
of the nonfamily arenas of life, we structure an equal opportunity to engage in nurturing and caretaking. Under these circumstances, men may actually be more likely to take time and

energy from their market careers to invest in nurturing their families. If they don't, at least it will be clear that they have made a free choice to forgo nurturing—a choice unfettered by institutional constraints. These men can then be justly held to the consequences of that choice when it comes time to decide who has earned the custody of children or the right to demand social subsidy for caretaking work. In this way, establishment of a dually responsible worker norm will lessen the cases in which women are punished in the market for caretaking responsibilities in the home.

IV. CONCLUSION

Women's roles within families and in relation to the marketplace have undergone tremendous changes over the past several decades. There is now an expectation that women will work in the market and continue to perform in the home. This expectation is enforced through gender-neutral family laws and an accompanying explicit set of expectations that women are responsible for their own and their children's economic well-being either postdivorce or if they do not marry. On the other hand, perhaps unsurprisingly, expectations about men have not been so transformed. In part, this is because we value economic advancement over nurturing. There are no corresponding sets of individually applicable rules mandating that men be responsible for nurturing to complement our expectations that women be economically self-sufficient. And families bear the burdens of dependency, while market institutions are free to operate as though the domestic tasks that reproduce the society were some other institution's responsibility. Instead of making more and more concessions to the unequal state of affairs that has resulted from this explicit ordering of priorities, we should forgo attempts to coax men into caretaking and instead require that all social institutions assume some responsibility for the needs of caretakers.[44]

Instead of structuring incentives for men to act responsibly, we should worry about the double burden that has been foisted on mothers, and seek to make it possible for them to meet the conflicting demands society is imposing. This will require substantial societal reordering, but when caretakers have the means to meet the demands of those for whom they have assumed responsibility, the entire society, including our children, will benefit.

Child support is not a viable solution to the problems of child care and dependency. In fact, the theoretical development of child support stands as a diversion to the development of effective policy.[45] On an ideological level, primarily because it is based on the traditional notion of a nuclear family, child support furthers the assumption that dependency is a private matter.[46] Indeed, insistence on child-support policy is an attempt to reconstruct the gendered complementarity of the traditional family through the imposition of the economically viable male.[47]

On a practical level, child support will not end child poverty. Even when it is paid, the typical amounts are woefully inadequate to actually support a child.[48] Many of the fathers who are under an obligation do not pay the child support they are required to, either because they are unwilling (deadbeat dads) or unable (dead-broke dads).[49] The Institute for Women's Policy Research, in a report prepared in 1999 on the relationship between child poverty and child support, concluded that

> . . . overall, child support constitutes only a small proportion of the total family income of single-mother families. For single mothers who are most disadvantaged in getting a stable job and

becoming self-sufficient, the same factors—low education, being
a minority, having young children, and weak attachment to the
labor force—are also associated with the chances of obtaining a
child support agreement, the amount of child support awarded in
these agreements, and the actual amount of child support collected. This points to the limitation of using child support as a
safety net or replacement of government transfers for single-
mother families on welfare, because those single mothers who are
disadvantaged in the labor market are also disadvantaged in obtaining child support.[50]

It may be that we want to establish and collect child-support
orders for reasons other than that they can in fact substitute for
governmental or collective assistance to children in poverty, but
in doing so, we should not delude ourselves that we are solving
the larger problem.

PART FOUR

The Autonomous Individual and the Autonomous Family Within the Social Contract

Mainstream treatment of law and jurisprudence typically fails to take into account the institution of the family and the problems of intimacy and dependency. Discussions focusing on the market, for example, typically treat the family as separate, governed by an independent set of expectations and rules. The family may be viewed as a unit of consumption, even as a unit of production, but it is analytically detachable from the essential structure of the market.

Similarly, jurisprudential work reflecting on theories of justice, autonomy, and construction of the individual assume the availability and competency of the family as the societal institution that takes care of dependency. As chapter six indicates, even many feminist works often proceed on the assumption that the family can be easily manipulated and transformed so as to serve the interests of gender equality.

The neglect of the family in legal and other theory is not an indication that it is a theoretically unimportant institution. In fact, as earlier chapters indicate, the family's importance is revealed in its very segregation from other areas of human endeavor. In setting it up as separate and distinct, we accommodate the otherwise messy problem of dependency. Earlier chapters review the doctrinal implications of this dual characterization of the family as both separate and essential, which is reflected in the conceptual division of the world (and law) into the realms of "the public" and "the private."[1] The family embodies the private sphere of human experience—a sphere in opposition to the public world of market and economic efforts. Furthermore, the characterization of the family as the preeminent private space carries with it sets of assumptions about family relationships. These are cast as different in formation, function, and form than relationships existing in the public world. Families are assumed to be altruistic institutions held together by affectional bonds.

Instead of being cloaked with the mantle of privacy, the family must be brought to the center of legal and jurisprudential theory and made an explicit part of that theory. In the chapters in this section, I further articulate the nature of the family as a sociolegal institution and explain why I feel it is essential to reconceptualize and transform our notions about the family and its relationship to the state and other societal institutions. This analysis is based on the insight that the family is not separate and should not be segregated into the "private" sphere. The family is an interactive and dynamic public institution that has been assigned an historic role that is essential to society. That role, as well as the aspirational and empirical dimensions of the family, must be explicit considerations in the development of any worthwhile social theory.

In recent debates over social policy related to family, caretaking, and dependency, there is little attention paid to figuring out what might be the optimal or appropriate distribution of responsibility for dependency across societal institutions. Nor is there consideration of how we might structure the corresponding relationships among government, market, and family in regard to dependency.

Of course, we do debate and theorize about structuring responsibilities in regard to some institutional arrangements. It is just the family that seems to be left out of debates as an explicit unit of analysis. For example, there is a great deal of attention paid to what might be the appropriate institutional interrelationship between state and market. Scholars and politicians set forth and defend competing positions on how to define the appropriate balance between freedom and responsibility; between subsidy and self-sufficiency, in regard to economic and regulatory matters involving state and market institutions.

My task in the chapters in this section is to lay the foundation for similar arguments about the family and its interrelationship with other societal institutions. How should the work associated with dependency be distributed? Should caretaking be publicly subsidized and supported or kept within the private family? How can we justly allocate the costs of caretaking? Of course, my goal in developing these arguments is ultimately to show how compelling is the case for the state and the market to assume more (or some) primary responsibility for dependency.

In developing my arguments about the need for adjustment in our basic social structures in chapter seven, I use the concept of contract. Specifically, I resort to the metaphor of "social contract" as a way to think about how institutions and relationships are thought to embody norms of justice asserted to be widely shared by members of a society. I do not intend to engage in the extensive, abstract (often turgid) debates about social contract theory undertaken by political theorists. My modest objective is to use the very modern concept of contract to question the justice of contemporary institutional relationships and arrangements.

Contract is a useful tool with which to examine family relationships—relationships that have their roots in the more ancient realms of status and hierarchy.[2] It is a useful rhetorical device precisely because it implies a process whereby individuals are seemingly given the means to voluntarily and willingly assume obligations and gain entitlements, thus expressing their autonomy. Although contract as an ordering mechanism is generally thought to bring stability and enforceability to relationships, contract theory also takes into account the possibility of change. In using the concept of contract I am particularly interested in exploring the tensions in the relationship between the social contract and societal change.

Change can destabilize existing relationships. In this regard, the idea that contracts are made in the context of "background" conditions—conditions essential to the continued viability of ongoing contractual relations—supports my argument that our social contract needs to be reworked. Once the background conditions have shifted precariously in ways that make existing relations impossible or unjust, the terms of the initial covenant must be reassessed. Specifically, profound changes in society and other institutions should provoke us to reconsider the role of the family—to explore whether its historic role in regard to responsibility for dependency has become unjust and unworkable on either societal or individual family levels, or both.

Social contract theory has a tradition in liberal political thought dating back to the seventeenth century, but it has only recently been revived and reworked into a modern theory of justice.[3] In its modern form, social contract theory does not purport to be an account of the historic origins of our political system, but a framework for thinking about legitimacy and political obligation.[4] Concepts of social contract theory are used to justify certain principles or political positions.

There are two arguments typically made in favor of using social contract as a device. First is the idea that social contract theory provides a means for resolving disputes in a diverse and democratic society in that it posits a prior commitment to shared themes and premises that can assist in resolving those disputes.[5] The second is "because of the moral significance of autonomy."[6] Christina Boswell states:

> . . . what is important about the contract is not so much that it ensures a stable outcome, but that it enables participants to exercise their individual freedom in choosing the terms of their interaction. The significance of the contract is in the exercise of autonomy in choosing terms, rather than the guarantee of cooperation.[7]

Social contract theory engages the concept of individual autonomy at two fundamental levels. Paradoxically, individual autonomy is viewed in the first instance as ceded to the state in order to confer upon it the authority to preserve order. Order is preserved so that the individuals initially giving up their autonomy may enjoy future full autonomy in their interactions with each other. David de Carvalho states the relationship thus:

> [T]he social contract [is] an agreement between individuals, by which they give to the state power to enforce the rule of law so that they can, to the greatest extent possible, exercise their liberty in the pursuit of their own interests, in particular through the operations of the free market.[8]

This statement reflects what has been termed the most "pervasive" and "indispensable" principle of contract theory generally—that the will of the parties sets their legal relationship. This is recognition of private autonomy's primacy in contract theory and the basis for the formal requirements of contract law, particularly the idea that there must be a "meeting of the minds" and "consent."[9]

Of course, the social contract is not a "real" contract, reduced to writing and signed by the parties, as private contracts typically are. The idea of the social contract is a way of approaching the relationship between the individual and the systems of coercion and authority within which she or he lives. The exact nature of this symbolic contract and its specific contours have been the subjects of political theory and legal debate for decades.

The works of Professors Robert Nozick and John Rawls illustrate two positions often named as contrasting models of social organization. Nozick's position is that basic social relationships are found in the interaction among autonomous and independent individuals, ideally unencumbered and unburdened by legal regulation and state interventions.[10] Nozick begins with the speculative assumption that in the state of nature, an individual owns himself, his own labor, and any property it produces or procures.

In this regard, the state appropriately assumes responsibility for the mechanism whereby a free market (for individual transactions) might be facilitated and maintained. But beyond providing police protection and institutions such as courts for the maintenance of order, enforcement of contract, and transmission of property, the state maintains a minimal role. Individuals owe little to the collective and have no moral or legal responsibility to others except that fashioned through criminal or contract law.

Under this view, the market is the basic social institution, distributing goods and values in a manner that is both just and efficient. If individuals fail, it is their own responsibility and reflects their lack of ambition, motivation, or talent. This position defines the basic parameters of the economic "conservative" argument today. Market relations are viewed as the most efficient way to create individual wealth and order society. Government intervention is condemned as fostering poverty and undermining family and other "private" institutional relations, ultimately leading to crime, social disintegration, and disorder. Correspondingly, the solution for existing social problems (caused by governmental intervention) is to return to the private sector—the market—allowing it to perform the collective function of efficient distribution.[11]

In contrast to Nozick, Rawls posits that the collective does have legitimate claims on the individual and that the state may appropriately work to perpetuate the "collective good," a social resource to which individuals may be required to contribute through taxation and other tithes.[12] Distribution of property is potentially problematic and susceptible to challenges based on injustice. Rawls is the intellectual descendant of John Locke, who, in 1690, asserted:

> It is true governments cannot be supported without great charge, and it is fit every one who enjoys his share of the protection should pay out of his estate his proportion for the maintenance of it. But still it must be with his own consent—i.e., the consent of the majority, giving it either by themselves or their representatives chosen by them; for if any one shall claim a power to lay and levy taxes on the people by his own authority, and without such consent of the people, he thereby invades the fundamental law of property, and subverts the end of government. For what property have I in that which another may by right take when he pleases to himself?[13]

Rawls likewise bases his theory on the premises that (1) in the original "state of nature"—the base by which to judge the justice of our current system—each person was in possession of his or her own labor; (2) there were resources that were held in common prior to their appropriation by individuals; and (3) justice demands that an individual is only able to appropriate a limited amount of property without violating principles of just entitlement. Waste and spoilage, as well as greed, are to be avoided. In the Lockean scheme, property is said to be commonly owned, and distribution is a social or political act that can provoke questions of distributive justice.

Rawls introduces into this formulation a construct that is useful in arguing that wealth redistribution should take place. In essence, he asserts that justice demands that the principles governing society should be those that citizens would invent from the perspective of the "original position." Citizens engaged in this thought experiment must imagine that they have all the information they need about society and its functioning, but are prevented by a "veil of ignorance" from knowing what individual characteristics they will possess in such a society. From this vantage (or disadvantage), the members of this hypothetical society can most disinterestedly and fairly bargain and deliberate about what general rules should govern them all. Because they are ignorant of the class, social position, and individual characteristics they will attain in the "real" world, there is no incentive to bargain for special advantages for one group. Justice will thus be free to emerge because considerations are disassociated from the individual characteristics and identities of the arbiters of fairness.

As part of his theoretical framework, Rawls presents two principles of justice: the difference principle and equal basic liberty. The difference principle posits that there are potential differences in social goods such as power, authority, wealth, or leisure. Equal liberty (or justice) requires a distribution that benefits most the most disadvantaged members of society. Furthermore, differences in the distribution of social goods are acceptable only if they are attached to positions open to all under the principle of equal liberty (opportunity).

It seems hard to refute the argument that one's perception of justice might be altered if one were not sure what set of individual and group characteristics one might have. These characteristics have attendant entitlements and social advantages in a world where poverty, illness, prejudice, and catastrophe are facts of many people's everyday lives.

Relevant to our consideration of autonomy and dependency, however, is the criticism of feminist theorists, most notably Professor Susan Moller Okin. Okin has criticized mainstream philosophers such as Nozick and Rawls for their failure to specifically theorize the family when articulating ideas about justice.[14] Okin is mainly concerned with the omission from the mainstream discussions of a sense of what would constitute justice within the family. Although she does not cast it in exactly these terms, Okin's focus is on the existing gender system, implemented in the family through dependency work.

Professor Eva Kittay also criticizes Rawls for failing to include a discussion of dependency in his theory.[15] Consistently with the arguments I have developed here and elsewhere,[16] Kittay argues that a society based upon a theory of the political cannot exclude dependency. If we exclude such concerns, we will end up exploiting caretakers and/or neglecting the dependents themselves.

Perhaps in response to such criticism, Rawls in his last book explicitly addressed the family, but in limited terms. He discussed the family in two places: in part I, "Fundamental Ideas," he observed that the family is one of many societal institutions that form the basic structure of a well-ordered society[17]:

> [T]o establish equality between men and women in sharing the
> work of society, in preserving its culture and in reproducing itself
> over time, special provisions are needed in family law (and no
> doubt elsewhere) so that the burden of bearing, raising, and edu-
> cating children does not fall more heavily on women, thereby un-
> dermining their fair equality of opportunity.[18]

Although he focused on fairness and justice, however, Rawls
did not elaborate on the problem of unequal distribution of
women's and men's contributions to society, nor did he suggest
any strategies to address this problem, other than the vague reference to "special provisions."

Rawls also mentions the family in part IV, "Institutions of a
Just Basic Structure," in a section entitled "The Family as a
Basic Institution." He opens with the caveat, however, that his
aims are "modest"—he intends to indicate why the principles of
justice apply to the family, but not to explain what reorganiza-
tion is required by these principles. He suggests that the family
performs a socially necessary function—the care and education
of children, who must develop a "sense of justice" so they can be
effective citizens.[19]

According to Rawls, the principles of justice and fairness
apply *to* the family, but not *within* the family. Principles of justice
can promote equality by guaranteeing the "the basic claims [to
rights and liberties] of equal citizens who are members of families."[20] Rawls does not seem to believe that the unequal distribution of labor between women and men is a pervasive problem,
as he asserts that "[s]ince wives are equally citizens with their
husbands, they have all the same basic rights and liberties and
fair opportunities as their husbands; and this, together with the
correct application of the other principles of justice, should suffice to secure their equality and independence."[21]

This concession to the family is not enough, and I therefore
agree with Okin's and Kittay's general criticisms of Rawls.

However, I would go even further. In the first instance, I find the Rawlsian position to be incomplete and unsatisfying because it proceeds from the wrong set of assumptions. Rawls's theory (and those that are conceptually compatible) is based on arguments appealing to empathy—to the idea that inevitably there are going to be victims in any form of social organization. If someone is operating from a position of ignorance, he will not know in advance what social disadvantages he will possess and will, thus, be fair in devising (or consenting to) a system of distribution.

Rawls does address many of the characteristics that are typically designated as disadvantages, such as race, class, and gender, but leaves the interfamily institutional arrangements outside of his theory. In failing to confront family position (or status) as conferring advantage or disadvantage, Rawls leaves an empirically significant source of actual social and economic injustice beyond his consideration.

This is important because it does more than obscure injustice within the family. It seems to me that relationships within the family are not only a source of inequality in need of correction, but also essential to understanding arrangements *outside* of the family. If family were a central part of a justice analysis, and family roles were also assessed behind the "veil of ignorance," the structural position of the family in society and the attendant appropriation of domestic labor by the state and the market would become apparent.

Thus, the injustice that would be revealed would be not only that between the genders, but also what results through the ordering of our social institutions. The family interacts with, shapes, and is shaped by those institutions, and its structure and functioning affect abilities and capabilities in those other arenas. Therefore, an appreciation of inequities in the family is essential to understanding the justice of other institutional arrangements.

Chapter Eight

Recasting the Social Contract

I. The Metaphoric Social Contract: Ordering the Public, Defining the Private

Chapter one, which sets out the concept of foundational myths, referred to the foundational documents that inform American political consciousness. The first few words of the Constitution of the United States capture the idea of the social contract: that the legitimacy of government is based on the consent of the people. The renewed interest in social contract theory since the 1970s[1] may have been generated by the public diversity of viewpoints and perspectives that began to emerge at that time, and that challenged the very idea of "we the people."

In the sprawling, secular, contemporary American context, appeals to social cohesion based on religious principles or on shared geographic boundaries are of limited usefulness. Voluntary participation in societal institutions may generate identification with a group, but this, too, is limited. A national identity can be based on acceptance of a shared or common language, culture, or history, but in pluralistic and diverse societies, citizens are often fragmented along exactly these lines.

The concept of foundational myths provides a way to begin to understand how some lines of social cohesion are forged and transmitted over time. One way to conceive of national community is through the establishment and transmission of myths or fundamental principles that address the way society is ordered and define the desirable traits of its citizens. Set out in mythic terms and reiterated through the generations, these can also be presented as coherent and binding principles—more than just aspirational, they can be asserted as symbolizing the existence of a social compact or contract that embodies consensus and community among those who would otherwise remain strangers.

The social contract is a legal or theoretical fiction—a metaphoric or symbolic idea that connotes a sense of connectedness and unity in purpose and belief among members of a society. Such members are envisioned as being united by agreement, in the same way that contracts between individuals reflect binding relationships around agreed-to conditions.[2] Contract is an appealing metaphor with which to consider social and political arrangements. It imagines autonomous adults, capable and equal individuals engaged in a process employing wit, knowledge, and skill, rightly held to the terms they hash out in the process.

In fact, in the modern context, the concept of contract is one of the primary devices for understanding individual and institutional relationships. Contract is the term we apply to all sorts of relationships, be they implied or formally established. Contract is viewed as displacing older, less democratic ways of understanding relationships, such as status and hierarchy, which impose structured relationships that are usually beyond individual alteration. The underlying and essential elements in a contractual relationship are [1] that two or more autonomous individuals with capacity [2] voluntarily agree (consent) to be bound by [3] some mutually bargained for benefit or trade (exchange). This process of exchange of agreement provides the basis for establishing a contractual (reciprocal) legal relationship between individuals.[3]

The actual reduction of agreements and understandings to formal written contracts is the way that many private relationships are ordered in the realm of the market and related arenas.[4] Formal contracts in business and commercial transactions are typically the product of actual bargaining encounters and are reduced to writing and signed, often in the presence of witnesses. By contrast, average people in their roles as consumers or tenants routinely sign standard form contracts, which are sometimes referred to as "contracts of adhesion."[5] These contracts have terms that are set out by only one party and are imposed in a take-it-or-leave-it manner. These sorts of contracts may be regulated by the government or through legal doctrines that make certain terms unenforceable in an effort to protect the consumer from overreaching or gross unfairness.[6] These exceptions aside, even with standard form contracts the process is generally thought to be appropriately outside of such supervision and restriction. The ideas of individual autonomy and freedom to contract mandate that people be justly held to the bargains they have struck.[7]

The metaphor of contract in political theory operates on several levels. It may be used to talk about the imposition of coercive rules (law). In this regard, the social contract is articulated as a justification for considering individual citizens to be bound by established societal norms and conventions and for justifying state sanctioning of deviations.[8] Looking at lawmaking as an occasion during which we articulate specific terms of the social contract should mean that this process places a heavy responsibility on the elected representatives of average citizens. They must ensure that their deliberations maintain integrity in regard to the spirit of the overall social compact, as it is understood by those whom it binds.

As a rhetorical and ideological construct, the social contract functions like the foundational myths discussed in chapter one, except that its terms are potentially coercive, rather than merely inspirational. The idea that we as individuals are parties to the social contract carries with it the threat that our breach of its terms may end in the application of sanctions. The idea of a social contract is the foundation for the application of law. As such, it is one of the ways we might make sense of the existing institutional arrangements in which rights and responsibilities are generated and imposed in our society. In this way, the idea of a social contract can be seen as an ordering mechanism whereby our own and others' actions may be judged. The perceived provisions of the social contract set up reciprocal and integrally related expectations and aspirations for individuals, institutions, and the state.

In utilizing the concept of contract as a tool to interrogate the justice of existing social arrangements, I hope to call into question those principles that Professor James Boyle suggested several years ago are foundational to liberal state theory. Boyle states, "[m]any flavors of liberal state theory hail it as definitionally true that abuses of public power are more to be feared than abuses of private power, that rules constrain governments more than standards and—perhaps most significantly of all—that autonomy is more legitimately the concern of the state than equality."[9]

A. The Social Contract

Just as reference to contract in the private [public] market context carries with it the understanding that the agreement it embodies is fair because it was bargained for and agreed to by the parties, a reference to the social contract is an implicit claim about the justice of the set of expectations, obligations, rights, and entitlements afforded an individual with regard to societal arrangements.[10] Of course, in considering the social contract, we encounter an arrangement that is not the product of individual bargaining or agreement. One is born into the social contract. Perhaps, for this reason alone, some social contractarian scholars have argued that we must be more attentive to its fairness, with the state assuming a more active role in monitoring the terms of the imposed social contract, as compared to bargained-for, private contracts.[11]

B. Social Contract and Status Quo

As a rhetorical and ideological construct, the terms of the social contract are up for contestation and struggle. Appeals to the social contract can serve as a justification for a society's current structuring, legitimating and explaining existing relationships. In this way, the concept of a social contract can bolster the status quo. It may be a stabilizing device and can even be wielded to justify unequal financial and power distributions produced by market institutions. In fact, it is the idea of a social contract that makes intelligible (and defensible) for some the fact that a modern, egalitarian-oriented, democratic state can accept, even condone, some degree and some forms of inequality.

The social contract varies across nations, even those with common legal heritages or similar cultural attributes. Roland Benabou, writing about unequal societies and the social contract, begins one article with the following statement:

> Some [countries] have low tax rates, others a steeply progressive fiscal system. Many countries have made the financing of education and health insurance the responsibility of the state; some, notably the United States, have left them in large part to families,

local communities and employers. The extent of implicit redistribution through labor market policies or the mix of public goods
also shows persistent differences.[12]

In this article, Professor Benabou is attempting to analyze the
differences among countries with similar technologies and
equally democratic political systems. Of particular interest to
my objective of spreading responsibility for dependency to societal institutions in addition to the family are the differences between the United States and European countries. Benabou
observes that European voters "choose to sacrifice more employment and growth to social insurance than their American
counterparts, even though both populations have the same basic
preferences."[13]

Europeans simply believe that the social welfare of individual
citizens is a more public responsibility than do those in power in
the United States. We tend to turn to the private sector when
seeking solutions to problems in society. In fact, one of the primary ordering mechanisms of the American social contract is
the creation of categories such as public and private, into which
social institutions, people, and problems are distributed, with
significant policy implications. In particular, the categories of
public and private structure the relationships between the state
and the market (the public category) and the state and the family (the private category).

This distribution is a political exercise. The family and the
market are inherently neutral social institutions that can be considered to be either private or public. The designation as private
carries with it a presumption that public supervision and control
is inappropriate. Within the social contract, a private societal
arrangement evidences a historically agreed-upon restraint on
governmental regulatory zeal. By contrast, there remains substantial debate about the scope of appropriate governmental re-

straint on institutions designated as public. This is reflected in the rather chameleonlike nature of market institutions, which are characterized as public vis-à-vis the family, but private (and beyond strict regulation) vis-à-vis the state.

One's position on the issue of governmental restraint in regard to public institutions can reflect an ideological predisposition on a number of important policy and legal debates. For example, economic libertarians and other "free market" proponents assert social contractarian terms that would leave most things, aside from military matters, to the "private sector"—to individuals acting in markets or within families or, if absolutely necessary, to small units of government.[14] Individuals thus freed from governmental restraints can work out mutually beneficial, particularized agreements among themselves within social institutions that are considered private, distinguished, and protected from the public sphere, as exemplified by the state or government.

In contrast, the terms of the social contract advocated by those with a more social welfare–oriented perspective define a more active role for public supervision and regulation. Someone with a politically liberal perspective might suggest that families and markets can also fail individuals and that existing disparities in wealth and power may be unjust, warranting some corrective measures by the government. Some perceived injustices must be considered of a public nature, a concession that some situations are beyond individual power to alter. Gross inequality and inattention to the "victims" of the free market are perceived to be public concerns, justifying governmental intervention and regulatory responses.[15] This position, while more liberal in regard to supervision, still concedes the fundamental distinction between public and private.

C. Contract and Consent

We can view the social contract as a fictitious, symbolic idea embodying the notion that social arrangements are legitimated through the norm of consent. Consent is through action (or inaction), indicating complicity with society in its present form. Social contract theory assumes an individual's actions, freely undertaken, to mean acceptance of the current social organization, norms, and institutions. In this way, the social contract represents an ideological or rhetorical map, defining the political landscape upon which to place existing and emerging social relationships.

A different type of consent is central to the concept of private contract. In private contract theory, one is legitimately bound because one has agreed to be bound by the terms of the contract. Consent to terms usually is expressed, but may sometimes be implied from one's actions.[16] Implied consent in the social contract sense, however, is a more ephemeral concept and is related to the social norm and expectation that autonomous individuals assume responsibility for the consequences of their freely taken actions. In the social contract setting, this idea has been the basis for arguments for withholding aid from those in a disadvantaged position, such as women on public assistance.[17]

Intentional indulgence in certain behavior results in predictable consequences, so the unsympathetic social contractarian would say. Consent in this context is tied to the idea that a person is getting what she or he "asked for"—our idea that there is justice in having to "lie in the bed" that one has "made." The idea is that individual circumstances are the result of individual choice, freely made, and that the consequences, even if negative, are therefore justified. Like its private counterpart, this notion of consent also implies that there is the option to not consent.

Within the rhetoric of public and private, contract and consent, existing institutional arrangements allow us to avoid general collective responsibility for inequity and to justify the maintenance of the status quo by reference to an abstract notion of individual "choice" or "personal responsibility" for the life circumstances in which one finds oneself.[18] In this way, we can often ignore the implications of the fact that individual choice occurs within the constraints of social conditions (including ideological constraints) that funnel decisions into prescribed channels and often operate in a practical and symbolic manner to limit or virtually eliminate options.

As discussed in chapter two, the idea of consent is problematic in examinations of existing social oppression. Using notions of individual choice or responsibility as justification for existing conditions fails to recognize that quite often a choice carries with it consequences not anticipated or imagined at the time of the initial decision. For example, in assessing who should bear the burdens or costs associated with dependency and child care, we may believe (cultural, familial, and societal imperatives aside) that a woman chose to become a mother, but does this choice mean she has also consented to the societal conditions attendant to that role and the many ways in which that status will negatively affect her economic prospects? Did she even realize what those costs might be? Is it possible that the society and culture might even have led her astray on the issue of costs, and misled her about the returns and rewards of caretaking?

It is worth repeating that social conditions, particularly conditions of oppression, are of far more than individual concern. They are of public concern in a society that has established norms of justice, incorporating ideals of equality and inclusion. These norms have been fashioned in ways that allow us (perhaps even encourage us) to measure individual circumstances independent of the idea of consent, at least initially. In taking this measure, individual situations can inform a discussion about the underlying fairness of the existing social contract.[19] There are instances in which we do not enforce private contracts, even those to which the parties have consented, such as when they are unconscionable, based on mistake, or impossible to perform.[20]

Of course, the traditional contractual requirement of consent is even more problematic in the context of an established *social contract*. The very concept of a social contract assumes that there is an agreement or arrangement that preexists and transcends the independent negotiations of any individual citizen. Individual bargaining and specific consent are neither provided for nor required. As discussed earlier, social contract theory legitimates compelling the individual to conform to certain existing interactions, expectations, and relationships with societal institutions. Consent by members of society to the social contract is predetermined—more accurately described as a concession on their part, based on the idea that they gain a collective good or benefits through such consent, and that societal consent is necessary for justice, reciprocity, and abstract equality. Consent or concession is presumed by virtue of the advantages and benefits conferred by the particular current organization of society.[21]

In our system, government has only limited authority to assess the underlying fairness of distribution systems developed in the market (or in the family). The government is not generally assigned remedial or protective tasks, such as promoting equality or redistributing wealth in order to counter the excesses of market institutions. The state is structured so as to be protective of private as well as social contractual arrangements.

However, sometimes an argument must be made that existing arrangements are unjust—so unjust that consent or ongoing concurrence should no longer be assumed. The historic social contract may be broken, or its conditions may have become impossible to perform or enforce in view of changed circumstances. Further, if given such change, and reconsideration is warranted, the state is the only institution that has any arguable mandate and capability to negotiate a reconsideration of the basic terms of our historic societal understanding.

II. THE SOCIAL CONTRACT—
THE (MIS)USE OF THE PRIVATE FAMILY

As discussed in chapter two, in our political ideology, dependency is considered to be a private matter. It is the family, not the state or the market, that assumes responsibility for both the inevitable dependent—the child or other biologically or developmentally dependent person—and the derivative dependent—the caretaker. The institution of the family operates structurally and ideologically to free markets from considering or accommodating dependency. The state is cast as a default institution, providing minimal, grudging, and stigmatized assistance should families fail. Ideally, each individual family is responsible for its own members' dependency, and to resort to collective resources is considered failure and deserving of condemnation. In fact, as is true with families on "welfare," the failure to adequately provide for its members can move a family from the private to the public category, where it is, therefore, appropriately regulated and disciplined.[22]

This set of institutional arrangements reflects the restricted nature of our social contract. These three institutions—family, market, and state—are the foci of politics and the objects of debates over public policy. Unlike more voluntarily organized segments of society, such as the religious, philanthropic, or charitable communities, these core institutions and the rights and responsibilities of individuals participating within them are heavily defined and regulated by law. For these reasons, it is compelling to consider them within the reach and rhetoric of social contract theory.

A. Contract in Context—Background Rules
A number of commentators, from the legal realists to the feminist theorists introduced in part three, have argued that the pub-

lic/private dichotomy is a false one and that most things are *both* public *and* private.[23] Questioning the public/private compartmentalization to some extent also involves questioning the structure of the debates associated with the idea of a social contract. If everything is both public and private simultaneously, then the labels will not resolve important questions concerning the current allocation of authority and responsibility among family, market, and state.

Feminists are not the only ones to have deconstructed the public/private divide. Others have made similar observations. Even though the market may be posited as private in social contract debates, how it functions and what it produces are of public concern and can generate a lot of political attention. Market institutions do not exist in a void—their actions have economic and other implications for the society in which they are located. Decisions about whether or not to provide "incentives" to businesses seeking to relocate, for example, can be as provocative to politicians and their electorate as decisions about who may marry whom or what should be the economic ramifications of single parenthood. Concern over certain practices, such as sloppy safety measures in a workplace, can generate as much will to regulate as can violations of an explicit criminal code.

Beyond the arguments based on public concern about the social goods and services produced by private transactions, however, is another realization about the nature of the market and its transactions within society. Economists and others have noted in the first instance that markets need law in order to function—they require enforcement by the public sector.[24] Private agreements rely on legal (state) structures, as the following discussion further details. Private contracting is ultimately a public activity because those who would rely on contract must also rely on law, courts, and police power as the default enforcement mechanisms. It seems sound public policy to allow some public monitoring to determine which private arrangements (whether in or outside the family) should be enforceable, entitled to legal protection and recognition, and which should not. In fact, this is why the law sometimes intervenes to regulate private contractual bargains and imposes on contracting parties duties such as that of good faith and fair dealing.[25] Contracts are not always enforced, and sometimes they are altered by practices, such as custom, that are independent of the individual parties to the contract.[26]

In addition, contract jurisprudence suggests there are always "background conditions" to the practice of contracting.[27] Often these background conditions are the assumed existence of other societal institutions, such as courts and law, which are clearly in the public realm. Commentators have argued that the traditional market paradigm, which views law as primarily a response to market failure, is wrong.[28] To such writers, law is also seen as a precondition to the very development of the market. The existence of background rules—law—is necessary so that actors can bargain and contract. This approach is distinct from the typical law and economics analysis in that law is posited as constitutive as well as reactive. From this perspective, law is viewed as having a significant and positive role in creating and sustaining the market. As a social and legal institution, the market does not exist independent of law. Even more fundamentally, the market relies on law, which is necessary in order for markets to function. A system of background or default rules is required in order that competitive and voluntary transactions— contracting—can take place.[29]

The notion of background conditions is simply the realization that all agreements are made in an historic context in which certain preexisting structures and institutional arrangements are assumed. Background conditions are essential to the process of bargaining and contract. Established, predictable relationships and rules facilitate the formation of new alignments since contracting parties are aware of what will happen should the agreement not work out. In other words, the parameters of any covenant are as influenced by the external arrangements as they are by specific terms set forth.

There are interesting and exciting questions presented by the application of this idea of background rules to intimacy and the family. If our focus is the family, one basic question we could ask might be, if we perceive marriage (at least partly) as a contract, are there background rules that facilitate the agreement to marry? There has been some interesting work in applying the concept of background rules to the marriage context. Professor Jeremy Waldron, defending Kant's conception of marriage as contractual, uses the idea of "rights" in ways that resonate with the idea of background rules.[30] Waldron states:

> [The] function of matrimonial law . . . is to provide a basis on which ties of love can be converted into legal responsibilities in the unhappy situation where affection can no longer be guaranteed. . . . The structure of impersonal rules and rights not only provides a background guarantee; it also furnishes a basis on which people can initiate new relations with other people even from a position of alienation. . . . [31]

Waldron asserts "the importance of a structure of rights that people can count on for organizing their lives, a structure which stands somewhat apart from communal or affective attachments and which can be relied on to survive as a basis for action no matter what happens to those attachments."[32] This example illustrates the significance of the concept of background rules to individual decision making. Knowledge of and reliance upon the integrity of background conditions facilitates action.

B. Background Conditions and the Social Contract

My concern with background conditions goes beyond speculation as to the structural assumptions underlying marriage. I am
interested in what is essential to the social contract. Even if it is a
metaphoric construct, and particularly if it is an ideological construct, the social contract is built upon background assumptions
and beliefs. What are the background conditions for the social
contract? Certainly they include the law (as do Waldron's background conditions to marriage). But what version of law informs the social contract and, additionally, what beyond law
shapes our understanding of it?

One would expect that a consideration of what constitutes essential background conditions to the social contract would produce a rather limited number of factors. This is because
background conditions are those things that are so routine and
normal that they can truly be said to have faded into the societal
background—the necessity of their existence is not even questioned—and in their ubiquitousness and normality they exist
outside of critical scrutiny. They are considered so foundational
and inevitable as to also be considered "natural" and organic in
nature.

Law partly operates in this manner—as background—because we cannot imagine a society without law and legal institutions. It is not necessarily the substantive content of specific law
that we take for granted, but the existence of law as a structure
through which disputes are processed and general dominant expectations and desires are enforced. Just as Waldron's family in
operation reflects the dominant family organization's reliance
on and ordering by law, so too the operations of the workplace
and the polity need the dominant understandings of those social
relations embodied in law.

Among the essential background conditions to the social contract, therefore, are those institutions upon which it inevitably

depends. Institutions, such as the family, structure, as they are structured by, other relationships and expectations. And it is the traditional marital family, with its gendered division of labor, that constitutes the necessary and essential background condition to the social contract in its present form. In the structuring and ordering of all our institutions, we assume that the family will function to absorb the costs of dependency.

Making the family visible as a background condition may call into question the idea that the social contract purely reflects relationships between autonomous individuals and the state. It also reveals that other institutions are important mechanisms whereby we achieve and maintain autonomy. The autonomy we attach to individuals in social contract theory is as much a product of the caretaking that takes place within the family as it is of individual action. It is that caretaking that sees us through our periods of dependency and (hopefully) provides us with the tools we need to operate in other parts of the world.

In addition to the family, other primary societal institutions form a background to the social contract. Certainly the market is also structured by social arrangements, and as with the family, we should think of the market as a necessary background condition. Furthermore, the public or political terms of the social contract reflect the expectations and norms of entitlement that individuals as citizens may legitimately assert vis-à-vis the state. Correspondingly, the relationship between the individual and market institutions is governed by customary norms associated with the (unwritten) employment contract between workers and workplace. The expectations of fiduciary responsibility and ethical dealing between market institutions and investors are reflected in regulatory law, but also in norms and customs of professionalism and in general ideas about fairness and trust.[33] The law, after all, is largely a written compendium of such societal arrangements.

C. Instability and Change

If we take this idea of background conditions and apply it to the covenant we call the social contract in light of some of the themes developed earlier in this book, we encounter some interesting theoretical questions. Paramount among them are the questions associated with the process of societal change. How does a change in the fundamental nature of an essential background condition affect the contractual relationship that is built upon it?

In considering the question of background conditions, it is striking to realize how stable they are assumed to be. Perhaps change was not a typical problem when the theory of background conditions was devised, because the contracts to which it was applied were individual in nature and were therefore relatively fleeting in duration. If change was a problem, doctrines such as impossibility or frustration of purpose could fill in the theoretical holes on a case-by-exceptional-case basis.[34] When thinking about background conditions and the social contract, however, we deal with more enduring relationships and must confront this issue of possible change. How should societal change affect our assumptions about the legitimacy and fairness of existing societal arrangements?

Specifically in regard to social contract and change in background conditions, we must ask, how should we think about existing long-term institutional expectations and aspirations for the individual, the market, and the state when they are built upon something as inherently unstable as today's marital family? What happens to these societal institutions when one of the background institutions upon which they are premised is under contest—when family arrangements are shifting and becoming uncertain and unpredictable?[35]

In addition, when should societal change signify the end of any pretensions to a societal consensus and necessitate that existing institutional arrangements be publicly and politically renegotiated? If the existence of a certain type of family is a prerequisite for the coherent development of our concepts of the "public" market and state, what happens when we are forced to concede that there have been widespread and not easily reversible changes in the way we think about and practice family in the United States?[36]

Changes in the family are visible and undeniable. The law has responded to these changes on one level by altering the set of expectations, obligations, and entitlements governing the intrafamily relationship between the spouses—by changing family law.[37] What we have not done, however, is to consider the required restructuring of extrafamily relationships given the changes within the family—the alteration of the state, the market, and the individual that must correspond to and complement our "new" family. In this context, it is not the obligations and rights of "husbands" and "wives" that need restatement, but the relationships among the state, the market, the family, and individuals who are now freed from their historic family expectations and roles and are in the process of redefining new patterns of intimate behavior.

What social expectations apply to the relationships among the state, market, and man (outside his former category as "husband") or woman (outside her former category as "wife")? How do we begin to decide what is the appropriate set of social relations and expectations to address the child's claim upon society and its institutions for provision of the goods necessary to meet her or his material, social, and emotional needs? If the family that would have provided the historic answer to this latter question no longer exists, our old reliable background begins to crumble. Further complicating this confrontation is the fact that the family is not isolated in its changes. Transformations in the family were provoked by (and further provoke) changes in other institutions.[38] Therefore, our existing ideology about such matters as the appropriateness of state intervention and regulatory action must also be reconsidered, perhaps shifted, in the context of change.

III. TAKING CHANGE INTO ACCOUNT: RETHINKING THE SOCIAL CONTRACT

The questions raised in regard to the ideas of background conditions and change are significant in light of the fundamental alterations over the past several decades to the basic societal institutions of family and workplace.[39] Both institutions have been designated by the terms of our social contract to be implicated in the delivery of social goods to individuals. Families "voluntarily" take care of us, provide for our needs throughout our lifetimes and through our periods of dependency. Through "custom," "contract," and "bargaining," the workplace, in addition to providing wages, supplies insurance against catastrophe to those families through such programs as health care coverage and pension plans.[40] Ours is a system in which there are no "rights" or claims to social goods that can be enforced by citizens against the government.[41]

Over the past several decades, however, the family has changed fundamentally, and furthermore the workplace is less likely to deliver social goods to families. The historic premises of the social contract have changed, and it would be unjust to consider these institutions, as they now exist, adequate to their historically assigned tasks. The argument that we must reconsider the terms of the social contract is made stronger by the fact that the state has participated in and facilitated these changes, particularly in the family.[42]

Of course, not all changes are good, and not all changes

should be accepted and facilitated in law or through policy. Change should be judged based on whether it represents progress for society, as measured by its fundamental aspirations. Changes in the family that have resulted in more women's joining the workplace and the decreasing influence of separate-spheres ideology push us as a society toward equality and inclusion. Women's position in law is no longer inferior or formally burdened with family disadvantages, and this represents progress.[43] By contrast, many of the changes in the market have operated in a manner that actually threatens inclusion and increases inequality. In addition, as is further explored in chapter nine, these changes include an altered sense of employer responsibility to employees and changed responses to increasing disparities in income and wealth.

IV. SOCIAL CONTRACT IN ACTION

Occasionally, the idea of the social contract as it affects societal relations is explicitly used in a political context. In such cases, the argument is that a significant affirmation or alteration of existing relationships is about to occur. In relatively recent history, there has been a quasi-successful campaign to undo existing social responsibility for poverty, replacing it with a different version of the relationship between the state and the individual—one that does not involve "entitlement."[44] Republican members of the 104th Congress drew up a document called "The Contract with America," which began a retreat from sixty years of policy guaranteeing a social safety net to poor families with children.[45] Despite its "feel good" rhetoric—it proposed bills with titles such as the Fiscal Responsibility Act, the Personal Responsibility Act, the Family Reinforcement Act, and the Job Creation and Wage Enhancement Act—the "Contract" targeted and reduced or eliminated programs that were originally designed to help low-income and single parents care for their children.

The proposal was to deny to unmarried mothers under the age of twenty-one Aid for Families with Dependent Children (AFDC) benefits, food stamps, and public housing, and to require all mothers to establish the paternity of their child before they were eligible for benefits. Recipients of AFDC were to be required to work thirty-five hours a week, yet the contract made no provisions for caretaking of their dependent children. Recipients who had an additional child while on the program would not receive an increase in benefits, and the funding to nutrition and food programs such as food stamps; the supplemental feeding program for women, infants, and children (WIC); and the school lunch and breakfast programs was to be cut by eleven billion dollars.[46] Many of these proposals found their way into the 1996 Welfare Reform, though in an altered form.

The premise behind a theoretical social contract is that it is an agreement among free and equal individuals to form a state for their mutual benefit. However, the proposed "Contract with America" did not seem to focus on the relationship between the individual and the state as much as on the relationship between the state and the family. The Contract made clear that the family was to provide for the dependency of its members. The Welfare Reform provisions would force young unmarried mothers to reside with their parents or to marry the child's biological father or another man willing to adopt the child, and would require women to establish the paternity of their child before they could receive any funds. In addition, the language of the act specified that the work programs are being implemented "to reduce the amount of time that *families* are on welfare" and that "states must drop *families* from the program after they have received a total of five years of AFDC benefits."[47] On the other hand, the part of the Contract with America that appears to explicitly address and support families—the Family Reinforcement Act—actually contained very few programs at all, and nothing about social programs that would address the health and welfare of children, especially those in low-income families.[48]

By promoting the family as the solution to the problem of poverty, the Republican Contract with America is a proposal to move caretaking and dependency responsibilities back into the private institution of the family. This proposed solution would not increase the likelihood of successfully meeting caretaking needs (how could a single mother work thirty-five hours a week *and* care for her dependent preschool-age children?), but these caretaking needs would be seen as a private problem, not a public one, and not one that the government would have to address.

V. CONCLUSION

I argue that we must look at the reality of the contemporary family and consider the implications of its transformation from the historic model. Additionally, we must look at changes in the workplace and in the state, and explicitly reconsider our existing institutional arrangements.[49] If it seems clear that the contemporary family can no longer be relied upon to fulfill historic expectations in regard to dependency, then some responsibility must be allocated to the market and state.

The concept of background conditions is particularly useful to illustrate why we need to rethink old paradigms, set aside the misleading discourses about personal versus public responsibility, and cast a skeptical eye on current renditions of the social myths of independence and self-sufficiency. Using the idea of changed background conditions, it is possible to argue that it is time to rewrite our social contract, to reconsider the viability and equity of our existing social configurations and assumptions.

Justice requires that we do so. The role assigned to the family has significant implications for the roles within families. These consequences are revealed as a family dissolves with death or divorce, or in cases in which the full complement of roles is not filled. But the consequences are felt not only by an individual family and its members. There are costs to the larger society when things are structured in such a way that many families are doomed to struggle and some to fail in their assigned societal role.

Chapter Nine

The Tentative Workplace

Considering the transformations that have taken place in the workplace strengthens arguments for rethinking the social contract given changes that have made the family a more tenuous institution. Relationships within the workplace are now much more tentative. However, there are important differences in the nature and direction of the changes that have taken place within the two foundational societal spaces of family and workplace. Unlike what we see in the family, transformations in the workplace, for the most part, have not been in the direction of equality. Nor has there been increased participation for workers in the benefits and burdens of the institution.[1] Workplace relationships remain mired in status and hierarchy, and the workplace is an increasingly unstable terrain for the individual worker.

Like the marriage relationship, the employment relationship often is cast in contractual terms, and the contracting parties are seen as having equal control in the bargaining process. As with marriage, the state has the authority to intervene and impose protective or other terms on the contracting parties. Historically, however, the state has been much less likely to recognize that there is a need for protective action in regard to the employment situation. This reluctance seems inappropriate.

Even more than the power imbalance that benefits husbands in the typical marriage, employers hold most of the power in the typical employment relationship. As a result, the terms of that contract are one-sided, and they subordinate the employee to the dictates of a market that is a take-it-or-leave-it system, analogous to contracts of adhesion that consumers face. Nor has the worker been successful in stating a claim to the wealth accumulated by the employer. By contrast, the property (capital) historically held in the hands of husbands is now susceptible to claims that the wife has made a contribution toward its accumulation that is equal in value to the monetary contribution of the husband.

Laws governing the employment relationship have not even begun to unsettle the historic premise that profit goes to the capitalist, while the worker is left with whatever bargain she or he can strike with regard to wages. The laws governing labor relations certainly favor employers. Unlike their European counterparts (and absent a strong union contract or civil service protections), American workers at all levels are employed "at will." The employment-at-will doctrine gives an employer the freedom to dismiss an employee without having to state a reason for the action. This power was modified in the mid-twentieth century by legislation that imposed some restraints on employers, barring employers from firing someone based on factors such as her or his race, gender, or religion.

This lopsided employment arrangement is argued to be contractual in nature, thus carrying with it the implication of equal bargaining power because there is a reciprocal right that accrues to the employee. The employee is also free to leave at will, and the employer cannot stop her or him. But such freedom for the individual employee is largely illusory, an abstract proposition taken out of the context of power relations and economic necessity that inform most employment relationships.

Employers can usually hire someone else easily. For the employee, however, a new job may be hard to find, particularly if the employee is older, less skilled, or trained for a specific set of tasks for which there is not a robust employment market. Increasingly, employers require truly specialized employees or those with knowledge that might prove beneficial to a competitor to sign noncompetition contracts as a condition of employment. These contracts further reduce the possibility of securing new work, should the at-will employee decide to leave.

From the employers' perspective legally, the employment-at-will doctrine has generally meant there was never much security for workers. Yet assumptions about employer responsibility to employees (at least managerial and white-collar employees) and the expectation that employment would secure some basic social goods are widely perceived as having shifted in the past few decades.[2]

A vision of progressive change in the workplace centered on the *individual* worker is hard to articulate because there is no consensus about an idealized form of relationship to exemplify equality between employee and employer. Such a vision was supplied in the context of marriage by the idea of an equal partnership between husband and wife, a metaphor that was transferable in part because the relationship is between two presumptively equal individuals. However, in the workplace we deal with an individual, on the one hand, and quite often a large entity or organization, on the other. Even with small businesses, there is no accepted concept of parity and partnership between employer and employee—the relationship is structured as inherently unequal.

Given this, it is difficult to advance a concept of fair bargaining that does not entail workers' banding together. But in part because they lack proper legal supports, unions have suffered declining membership. One way to establish a more equal social arrangement would be to articulate a theory for more parity in the workplace, in both union and nonunion contexts.

The low level of unionization in the United States leaves most workers without basic equity protections. This would seem to indicate that more regulation is needed to force employers to provide workers with basic protections. Even if the ultimate objective cannot be "equality" in the partnership sense of that term, we could work toward a more just and fair set of conditions governing the individual worker. At a minimum, these conditions should include more job security, better wages, a safe and comfortable working environment, and social benefits such as insurance, thus more "sharing" for the employee in the fruits that her or his labor produces.

In addition, and most significantly for purposes of this book, the basic terms of employment must also take into account changes in the organization and functioning of the family. The workplace must be made more responsive to the needs of workers as members of families, as people who are also responsible for dependency work and who need accommodation as a result. Unfortunately, the direction of the changes now under way in the workplace will make things harder, not easier, for those who are responsible for dependency within the family.

II. THE TENUOUS WORKPLACE

In February 1996, top managers of AT&T described their process for deciding which 40,000 of the company's 300,000 workers were to be cut, as well as the philosophy behind their plan to reevaluate almost every job and worker in the company. "The idea is that everybody has been asked to step out into a parking lot," explained a spokeswoman, offering an analogy for the process described in the *New York Times* as "militaristic in its attempt at precision." [3] The *Times* article cited a 150-page manual for structuring future meetings to be moderated by neutral observers or "facilitators." Managers were to decide who stays and who goes, buffered by job counselors, psychological counselors, and an army of management consultants for the unlucky employee.

What is interesting is that, rather than presenting its actions in traditional terms, such as "layoffs" or "cost cutting," AT&T called them "a forced management program" aimed at reducing an "imbalance of forces or skills." Those workers who were not invited back in from the parking lot were not perceived of as fired; they were simply "unassigned." James Meadows, one of AT&T's vice presidents for human resources, was quoted as saying: "People need to look at themselves as self-employed, as vendors who come to this company to sell their skills. . . . In AT&T we have to promote the whole concept of the work force being contingent, though most of the contingent workers are inside our walls [he should have said "not loitering in the parking lot" to keep the metaphor consistent]. . . . 'Jobs' are being replaced by 'projects' and 'fields of work' [giving rise to a society that is increasingly] jobless, but not workless."

This system replaced company policy that had virtually guaranteed loyal workers a lifetime job. As the *Times* put it, "[h]istorically, AT&T has rivaled the Army as an employer that welcomed minorities and people with only high-school educations, offering training and retraining and the opportunity to rise through the ranks over a lifetime career." Other companies with historically similar policies, such as IBM and Corning, have undergone similar revisioning.

The suggestion that employees should think of themselves as vendors who sell their skills for specific projects obscures what is really going on. Under this system, companies such as AT&T are freed from expectations that they will provide social benefits to workers. The rhetoric of contract and self-employment implies that there is a mutually bargained for agreement between two equals, creating the façade of autonomy. But this change in the employment relationship has been imposed on employees, many of whom suffer under its revised terms. Self-employed vendors must now privately fund all the benefits that companies such as AT&T historically provided, such as health insurance and retirement savings programs.

People who are self-employed, including independent contractors, consultants, and freelancers, may try to compensate for these increased expenses by charging significantly higher rates per hour than are paid to employees. According to the *Wall Street Journal*, people who are self-employed must charge at least 20 percent to 40 percent more per hour than employees who do the same work because, in addition to salaries, they must account for business expenses and for possible future periods without work.

Even assuming that AT&T pays the additional hourly charge for the contingent worker's time, it is still cheaper for the company to organize its work relationships this way. "This is because hiring firms don't have to pay half of [the self-employed person's] Social Security taxes, pay unemployment compensation taxes, provide workers' compensation coverage or employee benefits like health insurance and sick leave."[4]

Employees lose other benefits from their more tentative connection to the workplace. Legal scholar and labor historian Katherine Stone describes corporate workforce organization *prior* to the shift reflected in the AT&T tale as an "internal labor markets" system:[5]

> In internal labor markets, jobs were arranged into hierarchical
> ladders; each job provided the training for the job on the next
> rung up. . . . Employers wanted employees to stay a long time, so
> they gave them implicit promises of long-term employment and
> of orderly and predictable patterns of promotion. . . . Our labor
> and employment laws have been constructed on the basis of a
> view of the employment relationship that saw the employment re-
> lationship as a long-term relationship between a firm and an em-
> ployee in which the employer gave the worker an implicit promise
> of lifetime job security and opportunities for promotion along
> clearly-defined job ladders.[6]

Although she doesn't use the term social contract, Stone explores the notion of a "psychological contract" in her work.[7] She
applies the ideas developed in organizational behavior theory to
discuss the beliefs that an individual forms about reciprocal exchange agreements. She distinguishes this notion of reciprocity
from the unilateral experience of expectation, hope, or aspiration. Stone casts the psychological contract as "a subjective concept, expressing an individual's belief in the existence of a
bilateral relationship such that when expectations are not met,
the employee feels 'wronged,' deceived and betrayed with pervasive implications for the relationship."[8]

Stone goes on to describe how employers have dismantled
this structure in recent years, creating new, more uncertain land-
scapes for the employee. She uses the term "precarious employment," rather than contingent employment, for this evolving
dismantling of the implicit contract between employer and employee because it encompasses all who do not have a long-term
attachment to a firm: those hired as temporary workers, those
hired as provisional or short-term workers, *and* those who have
steady, full-time jobs, but no longer have an implicit or explicit
promise of job security.[9]

Employment relationships are shifting backwards, and while the ultimate direction of change is not as clear as in the case of families, some trends seem apparent. For example, a worker's expectation for employment security, earned through long and loyal service, is now clearly illusory. Corporations favor downsizing in the interests of stockholders and view labor as just another expense of production to be manipulated and contained.[10] Employers and capitalists articulate their social responsibility in terms that leave workers behind. Allegiance is to stockholders, not employees. Various statistical summaries report that temporary employment status is rapidly becoming the norm for many new entries into the workforce, as well as being one of the few options for those terminated from more traditional work situations.[11]

One way that employees react to such changes in the understanding of their relationship to the workplace is by working more, thus taking time away from other endeavors (like family). Today the average American two-parent family needs to work full-time in order to make ends meet.[12] As pointed out in chapter three, Americans surpass workers in every other industrialized nation in time spent on the job.[13] Increasingly, single parents are working year-round (fifty weeks per year), at forty or more hours a week.[14] The typical workweek has increased, not only for America's middle class, but also for the working poor.

In a 1997 Families and Work Institute study that compared 1997 and 1977, respondents indicated their workload had grown. In fact, 51 percent indicated they sometimes or often brought work home. This was compared with 35 percent who reported they did so in 1977. One out of four workers were reported to put in 51 or more hours of work a week. The median workweek had stretched to a bit more than 47 hours. Not surprisingly, a greater number of workers than in 1977 felt their jobs were more demanding and that work interfered with their free time and family life. At the same time, the report found insecurity was on the rise, with 29 percent saying they were fearful of losing their jobs compared with only 15 percent in 1977.[15]

In addition to job insecurity, it is significant to note that over the past thirty years, the minimum wage has not been adjusted to keep up with inflation. As a result, a person working for minimum wage full-time will earn under $11,000 a year, which is almost 40 percent below the national poverty level.[16] In order to provide for the basic needs of a family, these minimum-wage workers are forced to work long hours, sometimes at several jobs. Indeed, increased working hours take time away from children, who must be taken care of by others or stay at home alone because their parents cannot afford child care.[17]

From a historic perspective, real wages for workers have declined, and the idea of a family wage has been replaced by the reality of a dual-earner couple. In response to this situation and the well-documented inability of a family to take care of its basic needs even if it receives full-time minimum-wage pay, living wage campaigns have emerged in several states. A living wage is defined as "the wage required to raise a family of four above the official poverty line."[18] These campaigns urge local legislatures to mandate that public employers, and those who contract with the city or state, provide a living wage for their workers. They argue that such efforts are essential to reduce poverty and dependence on social programs. The campaigns have been successful in thirty-two cities, and there are seventy more campaigns active in the United States.[19]

III. WORK AND SOCIAL GOODS

One of the problems for temporary workers is the lack of social welfare benefits associated with more enduring ties to employers, such as pension plans and health or other forms of insurance. Even those with formally more traditional relationships find their benefits dwindling as increasing numbers of employers scale back on benefits.[20] Attempts to limit existing packages are now part of many collective bargaining negotiations.

In the American scheme of things, the workplace has traditionally been the avenue through which significant social goods were provided. Benefits such as health insurance, sick leave, and retirement savings plans were assumed to be part of the employer-employee implicit contract. Employers received tax incentives to provide some benefits and were directly compelled to offer others, such as Social Security and workmen's compensation protection. This focus on the workplace and the family as mediators stands in contrast to the delivery of social goods in many European systems. In Sweden, for example, basic social goods, such as insurance, are transferred directly from the state to the citizen, independently of either workforce participation or family status.

Because we tie social goods to the workplace and family in America, changes in "entitlement" status affect a large number of individuals, well beyond the number of employees in any organization. A company may cease to provide health insurance, claiming that it is now too expensive a "perk." If an employee is the head of a household, this change may affect not only that individual, but also her or his spouse (perhaps domestic partner) and dependent children, who may have been covered by the plan as well. Private health insurance is available, of course, but it is prohibitively expensive for many families, particularly for those with moderate incomes, since they can't afford a private plan and don't qualify for public programs.

A study published in *Health Affairs*[21] indicates that an increasing number of Americans are being offered health insurance through their jobs. Even so, more and more workers, especially those earning lower wages, are declining to take the benefit. In the decade from 1987 to 1996, the percentage of all workers *offered* insurance grew to 75.4 percent, from 72.4 percent. However, the percentage of workers *holding* insurance slipped to 60.4 percent, from 63.9 percent.[22]

Economists at the Agency for Health Care Policy and Research in the Department of Health and Human Services attributed workers' reluctance to buy employer-based insurance in part to their difficulty in paying their share of the premium. The researchers noted that health insurance premiums "leaped 90 percent from 1987 to 1993," while wages for all workers rose only 28 percent and stagnated for the lowest-paid workers.[23]

Twenty years ago, workers merely signed up for insurance. Employers who offered it typically paid the full cost. Today, a worker contributes on average $1,596 a year for subsidized family coverage by a health maintenance organization or $396 to insure only her- or himself. For someone making $7 an hour, the worker's contribution to the family policy would be 11 percent of the worker's total wages.

In today's employment environment, unless there is some governing labor contract forged with unions, employers do not consider themselves to be responsible for meeting their own workers' social welfare needs. Of course, they may do so, but it is at their option. In recent years, employers have actively resisted the imposition of broader social mandates as well. One such example is the Family Medical Leave Act (FMLA), a very limited form of benefit to workers who have responsibility for the dependency of others. The FMLA mandates only that employers allow their workers to take unpaid leave for caretaking of children and some other, limited situations.

IV. UNIONS, EQUITY, AND MARKET DISTRIBUTION
OF SOCIAL GOODS

While a discussion of labor unions is beyond the scope of this book, they do require a brief mention, if only to note that there may be some recent glimmer of hope provided by increased politicalization of some of these entities. Unions have historically provided a way for workers to act collectively to enhance their benefits vis-à-vis the employer. Unions make actual contracts, demonstrating that the employee/employer relationship can be one of "real," as well as physiological or social, contract. Outside of traditional collective bargaining agreements and some minimal governmental regulations, the historic workplace contract remains mostly an unwritten one, embodied largely in practices that have evolved over time. Employers resist unions, and partly as a result, union membership has declined over the past few decades. In 2001, 13.5 percent of wage and salary workers were union members, which is 20.1 percent less than the 1983 rate.[24]

The decline in union activity may have enabled employers to redefine their responsibilities quietly and rather painlessly. When collective bargaining was in ascendancy, unions functioned to secure some social rights for some workers, moderating the harshness of unfettered capitalism through collective bargaining and contract. These rights not only benefited union members, but also served as models for other workers and employers, even if the specific contract terms did not directly regulate those relationships.

Unions have always been under attack by business and corporate interests, but the attacks have increased in intensity and been better received by politicians in recent decades. Membership declined during the Reagan years, after the air traffic controllers' strike and the passage of legislation designed to weaken unions in the name of individual workers' rights.[25]

In recent years, unions have struggled to reshape themselves, not only by reaching out to new groups of potential members, but also by using political means. Forces like the Working Families Party indicate that union concern continues to be broader than specific member contractual entitlements. Unions are fueling, with their political support, initiatives that benefit society (or workers) in general. A more universalized and class-based approach to the provision of fundamental social goods has emerged.[26]

Corresponding with this increased union activity are the calls by some scholars and activists for new ways of thinking about unionization and collective action. Arguing that the changes in the workplace have revealed the importance of unions in protecting individual workers, and that old forms are ill equipped to deal with the new realities of the workplace, Professor Stone suggests: "As careers become boundaryless and work becomes detached from a single employer, unions need to become boundaryless as well. They need to develop strategies, skills, and strengths that go beyond single contracts with single employers. They need to move beyond the worksite-based collective bargaining and expand . . . upward into the political domain and outward into the community."[27] In particular, she notes the development of "citizens unions," which are not workplace or skill-based entities, but ones anchored in geographic locations. These groups pressure employers in their region to provide appropriate benefits for all workers in that area. While this type of organizing is in its infancy, perhaps the growing strength of the living wage campaigns across various localities demonstrates that this mode of organization could prove productive.

In a related effort, Professors Richard Freeman and Joel Rogers made a proposal in *The Nation* recently to have "open-source" unionization.[28] This was a proposition designed to make unions more receptive to opening up membership to workers who are currently excluded. Freeman and Rogers argue that certain self-imposed limits on the meaning of membership must be discarded, such as the current model in which workers become union members only when the unions gain majority support at a particular workplace. Majority status is very hard to attain because the laws favor employers in resisting unionization.

Open-source unionism would allow workers to become members of the union even without majority status, conferring on them some of the significant benefits of that status, including the protection of some labor laws. Such a plan would benefit unions through increased membership and political influence. Freeman and Rogers describe the possibilities in utopian terms, as dovetailing with the interests of those concerned generally with social justice:

> [Open-source unions] would engage a range of workers in different states of organization rather than discrete majorities of workers in collective-bargaining agreements. There would be traditional employer-specific unions, but there would likely be more cross-employer professional sorts of union formations and more geographically defined ones. Within any of these boundaries, the goal of [the unions] would not be collective bargaining per se but broader worker influence over the terms and conditions of work and working life. Because [these] unions would typically have less clout inside firms or with particular employers, they would probably be more concerned than traditional unionism with the political and policy environment surrounding their employers and employment settings. They would be more open to alliance with nonlabor forces—community forces of various kinds, constituencies organized around interests not yet expressed through work or even class (here think environmental, feminist,

diversity or work/family concerns) that might support them in this work. As a result, labor as a whole would likely have a more pronounced "social" face with [open-source unions] than it has today.[29]

Organizations such as unions that have traditionally fought for higher wages and better working conditions are needed. It is unfortunate that they are no longer as powerful as they were several decades ago.[30]

V. WEALTH AND ENTITLEMENT

Prior to the early 1970s, the United States was becoming progressively more egalitarian.[31] Since that time, however, the reverse has been true—by 1982, income inequality had reverted to its 1947 level, and it has increased further ever since then.[32] In 1968, the household at the ninety-fifth percentile had six times the income of the household at the twentieth percentile, while in 1994, the difference jumped to 8.2 times the income.[33] Between 1977 and 1999, the lowest twentieth percentile of American households dropped 12 percent in average income, and by 1999 the top twentieth percentile was earning half of all the income in the United States.[34]

A. Income Inequality and Family

According to the 2000 census data, although the average family income rose 9.5 percent between 1989 and 1999, about 9.2 percent (or 6.6 million American families) qualified as poor in 1999.[35] In nine states, with New York at the top of the list, the richest 20 percent of households now earn at least eleven times the income of the poorest 20 percent.[36]

There are many reasons that contribute to this increase in inequality. Of particular interest are those associated with business practices and those resulting from state and national governmental policies. In regard to market institutions, factors contributing to inequality that are commonly mentioned include globalization of trade, the decline of trade unions, the drop in well-paying manufacturing jobs, and the growing earnings advantage of better-educated workers.[37]

In addition to increased income inequality, we have seen a general wages decrease since 1973. In his book *The State of Americans*,[38] Urie Brofenbrenner reports that between 1973 and 1994, weekly wages decreased 18.8 percent, and hourly wages decreased 13.5 percent.[39] Family income has been falling slowly since the 1970s; between 1973 and 1992, a family's inflation-adjusted median income decreased by 1.5 percent overall.[40]

Education and change in the nature of jobs can partially explain the high income disparity.[41] In 1979, the average college graduate earned 38 percent more than the average high school graduate.[42] In 1999, the average college graduate earned 71 percent more than the average high school graduate, a significant increase.[43] Even in industries in which there is growth, such as high tech, there are very few or no opportunities for the low-skilled factory worker who is increasingly sliding toward poverty.[44] Yet a college education is not guaranteed to all who could benefit in America because education, even in state schools, comes with high tuitions. Education is a privately supplied good in our scheme of things and is therefore less accessible than in other postindustrial countries.

Of particular concern, of course, are the children; in recent years, about one in five American children (12 to 14 million) have lived in families with income below the poverty line.[45] The United States is the only Western industrialized nation that does not have some form of universal cash benefit for families raising children.[46] In addition, child poverty rates are higher in the

United States than in sixteen other industrialized countries.[47] Poverty has both short- and long-term consequences for children. Evidence supports the conclusion that family income can substantially influence child and adolescent well-being, specifically physical health, cognitive ability, school achievement, emotional and behavioral outcomes, and teenage out-of-wedlock childbearing.[48]

Even in families well above the poverty line, falling economic fortunes create a scramble to stay ahead. "Middle-income" families have experienced stagnant wages for about a decade, their incomes even losing ground due to inflation.[49] Furthermore, these middle-income families are working harder today than they were in 1979.[50] According to the Census Bureau, only 28 percent of the nation's middle-income families have one breadwinner, and this is usually because there is only one parent in the family.[51] Today's complicated lifestyle and society make essentials out of yesterday's luxuries (a car, a television, etc.), demanding income that may have been unnecessary in previous decades.[52] The standards of richer members of society also influence the consumer culture of the lower classes.[53]

Certainly wage and job instability produces stress, encourages longer hours, and pushes more family members into the workplace. In this regard, it is interesting that although families are entering poverty at increasing rates, more married women with young children are entering the labor force.[54] In 1970, 30 percent of married women with young children were in the labor force.[55] In 1987, the rate was 57 percent, and that number has continued to increase.[56]

B. *The Truly Wealthy*

Underscoring concern for the plight of the individual worker is the perception that the rules of the game have changed in America. Wealth distribution has become more skewed because of changes in capitalist structures and attitudes.[57] When one considers the disparity between the prospects and fortunes of the very wealthy and the rest of us in American society, it seems there are no longer any moderating influences to temper a runaway sense of individualism and entitlement.

At the same time that wage workers and others who have previously considered themselves comfortably and securely middle class find that their opportunities to amass a fortune are declining due to job insecurity and wage stagnation, corporate officers and entrepreneurs are making huge fortunes.[58] As one report described: "In 1999, for the first time in the years [the Center on Budget and Policy Priorities] has examined, the top fifth of the population is expected to receive slightly more after-tax income than the rest of the population combined." Even more telling, the same year "the richest one percent of the population [was] projected to receive as much after-tax income as the bottom 38 percent combined."[59] Even companies that are losing money and making their employees make pay or hours sacrifices are seeing an increase in the salaries awarded their chief executive officers.[60] In "Higher Education: The Ultimate Winner-Take-All Market," Robert Frank reports that "[a]s recently as 1980, an average CEO of a large American company earned 42 times the earnings of the average worker; twenty years later, in 2000, the same CEOs earned 419 times an average worker's pay."[61]

By comparing our situation with those of other countries, we see how inappropriate it is. The differentiation between worker and manager pay is greater in the United States than in any other industrialized democracy. In part this may be because European countries have stronger labor union movements and more welfare benefits that have moderated the growth of inequality.[62] There also seems to be a real difference in the ways that nations consider societal responsibility to children.[63] Barbara Ehrenreich, author of *Nickel and Dimed: On (Not) Getting By in*

America, argues that "[m]ost civilized nations compensate for the inadequacy of wages by providing relatively generous public services such as health insurance, free or subsidized child care, subsidized housing and effective public transportation."[64]

Increasing income disparity between the well-being of the richest and the poorest in America, as well as a corresponding decline in the fortunes of the middle class, occurs side-by-side with arguments by governmental policymakers and business leaders for increasing the influence of the market as the ordering mechanism for the distribution of wealth and social goods. Our new vision is of a minimalist government, even considering things such as old-age security. This vision is to be accomplished through the privatization of functions previously performed by government and the devolution of necessary government tasks to the smallest units of government.[65]

VI. RIGHT TO WORK/EQUALITY OF OPPORTUNITY

A. Corporate Responsibility

Wage stagnation and the degree of income inequality that America now experiences violate the spirit of any social contract designed to govern the expectations and relationships in a society that values equality and democracy. This type of inequality demands governmental intervention and some remedial measures directed toward leveling the playing field.

According to Anne Phillips, professor of gender theory at the London School of Economics and Political Science, true equality is achieved not through an equal share of income and wealth, but through opportunities provided. She claims in regard to persons bound in situations in which they cannot help themselves that the state does not have a responsibility to give to them what they lack, but "[t]he state has a responsibility to ensure that opportunities for self-advancement are made equally available to every citizen, an obvious responsibility in the fields of education and training, with perhaps some additional responsibilities to assist lone parents back into the labour market, or to make the feckless take out insurance policies to protect them from future disaster."[66] It is the role of the government to step in and regulate the market to make sure it is functioning fairly to the best interest of society.

To that end, I argue in chapter ten for a "responsive state" and for a "right to work." This concept has many dimensions, including the idea that the state and the market have an obligation to structure things so as to accommodate workers who also have family responsibilities. There are other, far-reaching responsibilities the state should shoulder in regard to the workplace.

It is also important, however, that we as individuals change the way we think about our own relationship with work and with our coworkers and fellow citizens. Within the workplace, we are isolated from others, encouraged to believe that provisions to one group means sacrifice by another.[67] From the perspective of the arguments I have been making in this book, it may be that those without care responsibilities fear that they will be required to bear the burdens in the workplace if there is some accommodation for workers who have responsibilities for caretaking.

But it seems to me that this is the wrong focus. We should instead be questioning a set of employment relationships in which it can be considered just or fair for employers confronted with a demand that they accommodate one group of workers to merely shift the burdens and costs associated with that accommodation to another group of workers. In the case of accommodation for caretakers, employers should not be permitted to evade their responsibility for some of the costs of dependency, even if it means some reduction in profits or diminished returns on capital.

Further, in regard to structuring the workplace differently, we must accept that even if we are unencumbered today, we do not know what the future holds. We may become caretakers ourselves. In this regard, even if we view having children as a choice, all of us had parents (no choice about that) and many of these parents may become dependent on us as they age.[68] Further, since we ourselves might become ill or disabled in the future, we have an interest in securing conditions under which our prospective caretakers can both work and fulfill their responsibility to us.

For those more inclined toward a short-term perspective, there is an additional argument that can be made for regulation of the workplace so as to facilitate caretaking. Caretaking is not something we only do for others. It is also socially productive labor when it provides for our own nonmaterial needs. Beyond our responsibilities as caretakers, citizens, and workers, we have responsibilities to ourselves—to regenerate our energies and resources; to participate in the artistic, nonmaterial, spiritual, or other inner-directed aspects of life upon which we are all dependent for our individual well-being. Society and its institutions must facilitate this type of caretaking also, structuring work so that the rest of life is not forfeited. The scripts of our lives must revolve around more than just work and must not leave the more emotional and spirit-regenerative aspects lying on the cutting room floor.

B. Beyond Caretaking

To take the need for regulating the workplace even further, it is also possible to expand ideas about the social contract and the existence of social debt developed in this book well beyond caretaking labor (for others or for self). We could consider the situation of the worker in general, the conditions of work, and the structure of compensation.[69] The idea of an egalitarian social contract can be the metaphor to bring nonmarket values, such as norms of distributive justice and worker security, to bear on our society as we confront the implications of change.

These norms are part of the scheme of expectations in other industrialized democracies and can be implemented in ours through a regulatory scheme of laws structuring the responsibilities of our workplaces. Particularly in the market context, we need to be reminded that corporations, as abstract legal entities, and those who run, direct, and profit from them cannot function without the labor of others. Secretaries and truck drivers are as essential to commerce as are highly paid CEOs and stockholders.

The arguments made about exploitation in regard to caretaking are applicable to the situation of all those whose labor is undervalued but essential in providing for the needs, growth, and maintenance of society and its institutions. My arguments based on the need for recognition of caretaking can evolve into a general critique of our version of the ideology of free-market capitalism and a claim for universal provision of basic social goods. One's positive contributions to society can thus be valued in a public and egalitarian fashion based on nonmarket values. After all, we are all in this together, and this realization should guide the direction of our discourse about dependency and societal responsibility, as well as actual public policy.

Chapter Ten

The Tenable State

I. STRUCTURING STATE AND SOCIETY

This chapter more fully explores the implications of the concept of collective responsibility for dependency that was introduced in chapter two—the chapter on inevitable and derivative dependency. In that chapter I asserted that dependency is universal and inevitable—the experience of everyone in society and, for that reason, of collective concern, requiring collective response. However, the essential and society-preserving work inevitable dependency demands has been channeled by society in such a way as to make only *some* of its members bear the burdens of this work. As a result, I argue that there is a societal debt owed to caretakers. This debt is a collective one, owed by the whole of society and its members. The existence of this debt must be recognized, and payment accomplished, through policies and laws that provide both some economic compensation and structural accommodation to caretakers.

The state must act for the collective in this regard. In fact, the state is the only societal entity that *can* act for all. It is the only organization in which membership is mandatory and universal (we are all subject to the authority of the state). It is also uniquely and expressly constituted to define the collective rights and responsibilities of its members. Therefore, fulfilling the obligation to caretakers requires a state that assumes an independent and active regulatory role.

This obligation to caretakers can be perceived as one component of a more general state obligation to promote and ensure the conditions of equality, wherein all individuals have an opportunity to achieve security and exercise agency. The state has a responsibility to mediate the structural inequality built into our "free" market system. In regard to caretakers, the inequality is found in the first instance among societal institutions—the family assumes a disproportionate share of responsibility for caretaking and dependency. In the second instance, there results an inequality among family members as responsibility within the family is delegated to some individuals, depriving them of options and opportunities available to less fettered family members.

II. IDEOLOGY AND POLITICS

While it may seem obvious that the national government and its institutions are the only mechanisms with the capability to uniformly regulate the excesses of society, particularly the market, this realization does not alone generate the political will necessary for such regulation. Partly this is because of the corruption visible in the existing system. Our current political climate means that programs and policies that disturb vested interests are stifled at inception or ridiculed if some politician is brave enough to raise them. This situation is not too surprising given the centrality of money to individual and party political success.

Those now in charge of the state seem determined to further limit governmental oversight. Taxation and regulation are often viewed as burdens to be eliminated, not as tools with which to accomplish social and economic justice. Focusing only on recent political history is discouraging for those seeking progressive social-policy changes.

A. The Fabrication of a "Contract with America"

Chapter eight briefly discussed the 1994 conservative Republican Congress's "Contract with America" as an example of a politically motivated maneuver using the rhetoric and imagery of social contractarian theory. The document labeled a "contract" was not the product of negotiations but the result of unilateral and partisan efforts to change the perceived direction of the country. Its terms were little discussed during the election that put its proponents into power. However, that election was later asserted to be a mandate—the basis of the Contract's legitimacy.

The heart and soul of the Contract with America were the ideals of privatization and the mantra of individual responsibility. These ideals were reflected in policies that retreated from the more collective ideal of the 1970s and 1980s, manifested in legislative programs such as the "War on Poverty" and the various provisions enacted at the behest of civil- and political-rights movements. Successful politicians of that earlier era urged measures designed to ensure greater equality, and trusted the accomplishment of this objective to the federal government's oversight.

The revisionists behind the Contract with America specifically went after the poor. The tenets of this so-called "contract" included a "Personal Responsibility Act," which sought to "discourage illegitimacy and teen pregnancy by prohibiting welfare to minor mothers and denying increased [Aid to Families with

Dependent Children payments] for [those who had] additional children while on welfare, cut spending for welfare programs, and enact a tough two-years-and-out provision with work requirements to promote individual responsibility." [1] Such provisions directly aimed to roll back the progressive reforms regarding welfare and child care support of the 1970s and 1980s.

Other provisions also focused on responsibility. The "Fiscal Responsibility Act" sought to rein in governmental spending. The "Family Reinforcement Act" proposed child-support enforcement. The rationale was to "reinforce the central role of families in American society," but the objective was to get individual parents, rather than the state, to pay for their children. Rather than *reinforcing* the families with the economic assistance many so desperately needed, the strategy of the Contract was to pillage and burn the six-decade-old federal entitlement system that provided assistance to needy families with children.

The model of minimal governmental assistance to the poor expounded in the Contract with America positions the national government as a backdrop to other societal institutions, specifically the marital family. The government is also seen as a facilitator of the market and a protector of its private arrangements. Adherents to this philosophy argue that even on a local level, governmental services, such as education, or functions, such as prisons, are more appropriately assigned to the private sphere.

Even though many of its specific provisions, aside from welfare reform, were not enacted into law, the rhetorical and conceptual strategy of the Contract has been very successfully integrated into political rhetoric and formal policy. Shifts in expectations for and attitudes toward the federal government have been accomplished. Cries for minimal government heralded the Contract's inception and its adherents' political approach to issues of national concern. These cries now overwhelm and seemingly have foreclosed the kind of vigorous debate that should attend any significant social transformation.

What is disturbing about the politics associated with the Contract with America is the orchestrated political rhetoric that distorts and oversimplifies social problems and solutions, drawing lines between people and groups by casting only some as worthy. It may be more accurate to read the Contract with America as the surreptitious repealing of earlier understandings of governmental and social responsibility, not a newly negotiated set of social-contract provisions. The Republican Contract is clearly premised on ideology rather than being a response to empirical realities. It does not reflect any vigorous public discourse about future direction and aspiration.

There is also an important question for politicians to ponder: in a political system in which only a minority of eligible citizens vote, some of them un- or misinformed, should election results be used to legitimate major shifts in policy direction without thorough and focused further debate in a nonpoliticized context?[2] Government has not provided the structures or fostered the ethical and political culture to promote a balanced exchange of information, debate, and deliberation, giving all segments of society inclusion. As a result, our politics do not reflect the diversity of our pluralistic society.

B. Economics Are Us: The "Democratization" of Supply and Demand

Complementing the Contract with America (and perhaps laying an essential foundation for it) was the ascendancy of economic principles as the preferred method of assessing social policy. President Ronald Reagan introduced a philosophy of supply-side economics, which posits that the well-being of the capitalist class will ultimately provide for the rest of society. Termed "trickle-down" economics, this idea was shown by many economists to be an unwise illusion.[3] Similar policies of supply-side economics have been recently resurrected with a vengeance by President George W. Bush's administration in the form of massive tax cuts for the wealthiest Americans. Bush seems to have forgotten his father's label for such attempted manipulations when he was competing with Ronald Reagan for the Republican nomination: "voodoo economics."[4]

The focus on the wealthy as the road to prosperity for all became entrenched in popular culture during the 1990s. In that decade a focus on market well-being supplanted more inclusive and nuanced public assessments about the state of our nation. This economic-sphere focus is best captured in one of the ways in which the pulse of the nation is currently measured. Today the Dow Jones average is reported daily (sometimes hourly), even on public radio, as though this specific measure accurately reflects our country's general health and wealth. In this way, an economic indicator is substituted for other forms of evaluation of national standing, such as the equitableness of wealth distribution or the well-being of our most vulnerable citizens. How would we assess our nation's well-being if what was reported on a daily basis instead were the increases or declines in the number of children or elderly having health insurance coverage, or the fluctuations in the number of Americans living in poverty, perhaps going to bed hungry at night?

During the boom of the 1990s we seemed blinded in a reverie of self-satisfaction, even as the position of our children and historically disadvantaged subgroups deteriorated, both in terms of where they were a few decades earlier and relative to the position of comparable groups in other industrialized democracies. Tellingly, the obsession with market indicators has not been displaced now that the economy is less robust.

Today it seems as though the function and role of the state have been merged with those of the market. A goal of governmental policy is still to address market confidence, as though the market and not the government could be the primary guarantor of general citizen well-being. Progressive politicians seem to buy into this fallacy as much as their conservative counterparts do. There is some effort to defend public programs such as education, but the basic tenets of a privatized and individualized philosophy seem to be driving policy on all political sides. Missing from mainstream political and public discourse is any strong support for the state to act as a vigorous mediator of market excesses and active guarantor of a more equitable allocation of wealth.

III. POSING THE PHILOSOPHY FOR AN ACTIVE STATE

A. Relating State and Market

While it would seem obvious to most citizens of other Western countries that the state would be implicated in any discussion of possible solutions to the problem of inequality in society, many progressive Americans are almost as suspicious of governmental action as their conservative counterparts. Perhaps this is why the political will to expand the states' regulatory responsibilities has lagged over the past decades, even as recognition of persistent inequality has grown and notions about justice have evolved.

The state is held in much more suspicion in the United States than in other Western democracies, and arguments about transforming its role to be more active are bound to be subjected to scrutiny and skepticism. Contemporary legal and policy discussions (which are part of the process whereby a state can be altered) are overwhelmingly concerned with limiting and restricting the state, particularly with regard to the economic areas of policy-making. Those who reject the idea that the government has a basic and explicit role in monitoring and mediating change vigorously resist a more regulatory response to market developments. With regard to the market, increasingly the state is either cast in the role of cheerleader or urged to facilitate, not regulate, economic arenas.[5]

In the United States such arguments have culminated in a philosophy espoused widely from center to right of the political spectrum—by business leaders, politicians, and policymakers who urge an increase in the sphere of influence and power of the market, and a weakening of the power of the federal government. Their shared vision is of a minimalist national sphere, ideally accomplished through the privatization of functions previously performed by the government. When government is necessary, the ideal route is through the devolution of responsibility to the smallest, most local units.

This desired withdrawal of the national level of regulation and responsibility is urged even though the history of the United States shows that local rule on some issues cannot be effective and sometimes results in discrimination and concession to local passion and prejudice. It is urged even though it is clear that it has always been a struggle to get businesses to accept progressive labor practices. It is urged even though the market has shirked responsibility for the provision of social goods, such as health insurance, family and medical leave, day care, and a minimum family wage unless "encouraged" to do so by the state.

To abandon progressive aspirations for the state given this history of failure of the market to make progressive adjustments without coercion is to abandon all hope for progressive change. The national government is the only organization with the potential to impose such measures. At a minimum, the state must strive to eliminate major disparities that result from unequal social relations. This book has been concerned with remedying one obvious point of economic exploitation—that of those in our society who make the essential yet unrecognized contribution of caretaking. A strong and vital state is necessary to even begin to undertake, let alone accomplish, that task.

Instead of fighting for the shrinking and weakening of a national government, progressives should be focusing on articulating appropriate objectives for the state to pursue. Defining the norms and aspirations that should replace the impoverished concepts provided by economics would be the place to start. There must be a change in the discourse of politics, with a new paradigm to guide state policy replacing that of the free market, in which there is no collective responsibility but only an exaggerated sense of individual autonomy.

B. Concepts and Meaning—
The Connection Between Autonomy and Equality

A notion of collective responsibility for dependency has to begin with the creation of an alternative paradigm of state regulation and responsibility. This is necessary in order to counter the non-regulatory philosophy of the current manifestation of American free-market capitalism.

This paradigm would present an alternative to that which now drives our politics, because it would explicitly build upon the premise that there is a fundamental connection between autonomy—an individual's ability to make choices in her or his life—and equality, which demands that the state exercise some responsibility to ensure that each individual has the necessary basic resources to allow choices to be made and to be meaningful. In this paradigm the state is not a default (therefore stigmatized) port of last resort, but an active partner with the individual in realizing her or his capabilities and capacities to the fullest extent. In this vision, the equal opportunity guaranteed by the state would also be an individualized one, in that it would bear some relationship to a person's situation and reflect her or his circumstances.

As discussed in chapter one, both autonomy and equality are accepted as core values and essential components in our American foundational myths. Both remain potent verbal mainstays in contemporary political discourse. Yet certain interpretations of the meanings of these two ideals can place them in tension—even in conflict—with one another. If the state obligation with regard to equality is processed and shaped by an ideological system in which autonomy is primary and also understood as the right to be free of governmental intrusion and regulation, then it can mean little more than state neutrality. In this scheme, absent discrimination or some other distortions of the market, any regulatory action by the state trying to confer more than neutral process in order to help some individuals is susceptible to being interpreted as an intrusion on the autonomy of others. This is so regardless of how desperate or (therefore) unequal the circumstances of those the state sought to assist or how privileged and (therefore) unequal the position of those who seek to shield themselves in autonomy's mantle.

As discussed in the first section of this book, autonomy is often presented as a state of being that is attainable by all. It is also perceived as an individually (and autonomously) developed characteristic that ultimately reflects the worth (or lack thereof) of the person. In this simplistic version of autonomy, the realities of inevitable and derivative dependency are absent. In fact, the world that this vision of autonomy imagines is a world that can only be populated by adults, and then only by those adults possessing sufficient capabilities and competencies to make it possible that their only demand of government (aside from the provision of security and courts of law) be for rules that guarantee their right to be left alone to realize the gains and glory their individual talents may bring. The majority of arguments made in this book are presented to show that such a vision is a chimera, and that this version of autonomy is both undesirable and unattainable on an individual level and, therefore, destructive from a policy perspective. We all experience dependency, and we are all subsidized during our lives (although unequally and inequitably so).

C. Giving Substance to Equality

In a paradigm that privileges an uncomplicated notion of autonomy, equality is inevitably also presented in a narrow and simplistic manner. A simplistic autonomy discourse increasingly dominates American politics. State affirmative attempts to guarantee equality in more than a formal, procedural sense are considered suspect; some regard this as "special treatment," or the very opposite of state neutrality that the autonomy-driven version of equality is deemed to demand. But the circumstances of privileged members of society are not deemed "special" in the same way. It is only explicit governmental attempts to assist those who are disadvantaged that are to be prohibited. The laws and structures that perpetuate wealth and privilege are not considered special treatment, even thought they benefit only those with "special" status and economic standing.

In this regard, it is important to note that the term "equality" may be defined in several different ways. "Formal equality" is the circumstance in which universal laws are applied equally to everyone. Formal equality does not, however, guarantee that everyone is treated equally. In fact, given existing inequalities, formal equality ensures that there will be unequal results or implications. It is procedural, not remedial, in nature.

Of course, formal equality may prevent laws from drawing distinctions on the basis of personal characteristics, such as the United States Supreme Court's decision in *Brown v. Board of Education*,[6] in which it ruled that segregated education was an equal-rights violation. However, a formal equality approach ignores the fact that neutrality is seldom sufficient when there are gross underlying disparities in position. Nor does it address those many situations in which laws that are neutral on their face have an unequal impact. As the French quipped during their revolution, the rich and the poor are equally punished if found sleeping under bridges; the point being that a prohibition on such conduct in reality only impacted the poor. It is those groups that have traditionally suffered deprivation and discrimination that are too often only further disadvantaged by the application of the rules of formal equality.

Affirmative action programs or other remedial measures that would draw distinctions between groups, even though designed to help create a more level playing field, are attacked under the rhetoric of formal equality.[7] Yet it seems obvious that some level of substantive or material well-being is a precondition for both equal opportunity and the realization of a degree of individual autonomy or choice. One cannot exercise freedom to pursue options without a certain degree of social equity and capital. In fact, some restructuring of the economic status quo would be essential in order to achieve a situation in which most people could effectively strive for meaningful equality.

There is a competing way of thinking about equality. The concept of "substantive equality" entails the "elimination of major disparities in people's material resources, well-being, opportunities, and political and social power. It also ideally seeks to minimize economic, social, and cultural oppression and exploitation."[8] In order to achieve the goals of substantive equality, it is necessary to address systemic inequality, assessing laws and regulations in the context of historical discrimination, keeping in mind the goal of reducing oppression.[9]

Joel Bakan attempts to describe the conditions to which a more substantively equal society would aspire:

> [E]quality entails elimination of major disparities in people's material resources, well-being, opportunities, and political and social

power, and an absence of economic, social, and cultural oppression and exploitation. Perfect social equality may be impossible, but the aspiration to rid society of oppressive and exploitative disparities, based on unequal social relations—such as those of class, gender, and race—is realistic and worth fighting for.[10]

Bakan may be correct that it is impossible to achieve a perfectly classless, genderless, and nonracist society—a true society of equals—and yet we will surely never achieve even diminishment of the social constraints of inequality if we cannot envision such a society and move toward it.

The situation where the state ignores everyone's needs equally should no longer be tolerated. Some robust version of substantive equality is essential in a society that imposes on individuals an expectation that they can attain a degree of self-sufficiency as adults. In order to eventually develop competency to the fullest extent possible, an individual during her or his formative stages of life must have access to basic material and social resources. The assurance of some fundamental level of economic security guaranteed to all caretaking units in which such individuals are nurtured would be foundational in this regard. The state must subsidize caretaking just as it does other socially productive labor. It is the articulation of this aspiration for substantive equality that is the first step in building a politics to demand it.

IV. THE POLITICS OF SUBSTANTIVE EQUALITY

There are several important questions to ask both our politicians and ourselves as we seek to refine and further define an otherwise abstract commitment to substantive equality with which to replace our current formal version. As with many concepts of historic magnitude, some of the most significant questions to pose about equality have to do with how we should respond to evolutions in understanding and changes in aspiration for the term: is a mere commitment to formal equality sufficient for a humane and modern state?[11] How should the state respond to the fact that increasingly our society is one in which a privileged few command more resources than the struggling many, and individuals are born into and continue to experience disparities in well-being that are built upon existing inequitable distributions of society's resources?

In the United States today, some live in real poverty and deprivation while a few have more wealth than they could spend in ten lifetimes. Of course there also is the vast majority, who view themselves as "middle class." These Americans have homes, automobiles, and even small stock portfolios. Most of them, nonetheless, live in a state of insecurity. Given the way things are organized in our system of privatized and individualized responsibility, they are only a few paychecks, a catastrophic illness, or a divorce away from economic disintegration and despair.

The insecurity and unfairness generated in the current political and economic organization of this society suggest that we should fashion a sense of equality that is more concerned with ultimate outcome or results. In such a society a more substantive notion of equality would warrant that the rewards that it and its resources produce are more equitably distributed among its members. This would be a society with some basic guarantees of social goods—a society that would not tolerate any *person* left behind,[12] without adequate resources to allow them and their children to succeed to the fullest extent possible.

T. H. Marshall argued that there are three separate categories of citizenship rights in any democracy—civil, political, and social—and that these rights develop in historically successive stages. According to Marshall, civil rights include "the rights necessary for individual freedom—liberty of the person, freedom of speech, thought and faith, the right to own property and to conclude valid contracts, and the right to justice"; political rights include "the right to participate in the exercise of political power, as a member of a body invested with political authority or as an elector of the members of such a body"; and social rights "range from the right to a modicum of economic welfare and security to the right to share to the full in the social heritage and to live the life of a civilized being according to the standards prevailing in the society." [13] Each one has developed out of conflicts arising from a society's attempts to realize the earlier attempt. Marshall did not claim that his theory represented a final and definitive description—because of the ongoing conflicts involved in implementing them, he believed that citizenship rights, and the ways in which they could be realized, would continue to evolve and develop. Marshall coined the term "social citizenship" to describe the status conferred by such an approach to state responsibility. [14]

Marshall's vision can form the foundation for an argument that the state must provide the "rights of autonomous citizenship" in order for Americans to actually effectively exercise our civil and political rights. Without the autonomy that basic social goods provide, the rights of citizenship are merely formal, not substantive.

While it is possible to appreciate Marshall's notions of citizenship, the current politics in the United States are such that substantive equality arguments are likely to be banished to the realm of utopian visions. Absent some vigorous democratic movement for change based on outrage stemming from the badly skewed and unequal distribution of material, political, and social goods, those who control the American state are likely to do no more than continue it in its current role as reactive facilitator of the market and its institutions.

V. HISTORICAL ROOTS FOR A MORE SUBSTANTIVE EQUALITY

One task for scholars and others interested in resurrecting the foundation for a more equitable America is the excavation and dissemination of progressive history. This is necessary in order to counter the asserted inevitability of today's narrow and restricted political will.

Constructing such histories is beyond the scope of this book, but a few examples are warranted. One rich source is the aspirations set forth in Franklin D. Roosevelt's Second Inaugural Address, delivered January 20, 1937, and touching on the objectives of the New Deal. Several should resonate with those disturbed by the direction of today's political climate. On economic forces, FDR stated:

> [W]e recognized a deeper need—the need to find through government the instrument of our united purpose to solve for the individual the ever-rising problems of complex civilization. . . . To do this we knew we must find practical controls over blind economic forces and blindly selfish men.

In a utopian vein, he continued:

> We have always known that heedless self-interest was bad morals; we know now that it is bad economics. Out of the collapse of prosperity whose builders boasted their practicality has come the conviction that in the long run economic morality pays. We are beginning to wipe out the line that divides the practical from the ideal; and in so doing we are fashioning an instrument of unimagined power for the establishment of a morally better world.
>
> This new understanding undermines the old admiration of worldly success as such. We are beginning to abandon our toler-

ance of the abuse of power by those who betray for profit the elementary decencies of life.

And recognizing that progress often carries amnesia along with it:

> To hold to progress today, however, is more difficult. Dulled conscience, irresponsibility, and ruthless self-interest already reappear. Such symptoms of prosperity may become portents of disaster! Prosperity already tests the persistence of our progressive purpose.

Further, it was clear that the government had a vital role to play:

> I see a United States which can demonstrate that, under democratic methods of government, national wealth can be translated into a spreading volume of human comforts hitherto unknown, and the lowest standard of living can be raised far above the level of mere subsistence.

The appropriate means to measure progress were also clear:

> The test of our progress is not whether we add more to the abundance of those who have much; it is whether we provide enough for those who have too little.

Progressive history is not only to be found in Democratic administrations, nor do we have to retreat to the 1930s to discover it. For example, the 1970s and 1980s marked an increase in workers' benefits. This increase was generated under the guidance of a Republican president. Professor Martha T. McCluskey describes the development of the Occupational Safety and Health

Act of 1970, which highlighted "serious questions about the fairness and adequacy of present workmen's compensation laws in light of economic, medical, and technological changes."[15] A bipartisan national commission, appointed by President Richard Nixon, had been unanimous in finding that contemporary state protection was both "inadequate and inequitable." According to McCluskey, as a result of this examination, over the next decade, the majority of states enacted legislation that liberalized benefits to workers.[16]

Professor Sonya Michel traces the movement to bring social welfare benefits to poor families that began in the 1960s. She notes that the discourse employed then "open[ed] the way for a major shift in public policy toward low-income women."[17] Over the course of the 1970s and 1980s, this discourse about society's responsibility to mothers entered the discussion regarding the progressive expansion of child-care benefits. This discourse is a background for the arguments made in this book, which also expands on T. H. Marshall's notion of citizenship by arguing that child-care allowances and other forms of compensation and accommodation are necessary social goods that must be provided to caretakers.

VI. INTERNATIONAL NORMS

The practices and aspirations of other societies might also provide additional inspiration for the beleaguered American progressive. The problems presented by dependency and poverty are not unique to American society. Other states have gone through the process of allocating responsibility for dependency among its institutions and determining what role it will play in regard to supplying social goods and guaranteeing nonexploitative practices.

Norms have been developed in the international context that suggest a definition of the role and responsibilities of the state with regard to citizens that is far more expansive than the one ensconced in American constitutional principles of equality. For example, international human rights documents describe the obligations the state has to guarantee certain rights. They are far-reaching and diverse in subject matter and include the Universal Declaration of Human Rights (which was the first international statement to use the term "human rights");[18] the International Covenant on Economic, Social and Cultural Rights (which includes as basic rights such things as sufficient wages to support a minimum standard of living, equal pay for equal work, equal opportunity for advancement, and paid or otherwise compensated maternity leave);[19] the American Convention on Human Rights (which sets forth a commitment to adopt measures with a view to achieve economic, social, educational, scientific, and cultural standards);[20] the African Charter on Human and Peoples' Rights (linking civil and political rights to economic, social, and cultural rights);[21] and the European Convention for the Protection of Human Rights and Fundamental Freedoms (recognizing the obligation to respect human rights);[22] among others.[23]

While it is true that these documents have not been ratified by every country (most notably the United States) and their principles are not uniformly followed in those states that have adopted them, they do set out aspirational terms. They stand witness to what are generally considered desirable, normative standards that have been widely accepted in many societies.

The United States has not even gone as far as to agree to the desirability of many of the provisions, and even some of those documents that have been signed remain unratified (and unimplemented) by the Senate.[24] American reluctance to accept international norms is based partly on the fact that some of the documents embody an alternative to the formal vision of equal opportunity entrenched in the jurisprudence of the United States. For example, the International Covenant on Economic, Social and Cultural Rights recognizes "the right to work, which includes the right of everyone to the opportunity to gain his living by work which he freely chooses or accepts."[25] The Covenant goes on to set out as governmental responsibility the obligation to ensure "fair wages and equal remuneration for work of equal value" (thus stating the principle of "comparable worth" in addition to the equal-pay-for-equal-work formal equality notion behind United States law). It also places on the state an obligation to ensure for citizens "a decent living for themselves and their families."[26]

Further, rather than confirming the role of the state as a supporter of the market and its institutions, these documents overwhelmingly suggest that governments are responsible for countering and correcting for the natural imbalances and inequalities that result from the actions of market institutions. They focus on rights that would further the development of progressive social equality, and emphasize remedial actions in regard to traditionally disadvantaged societal groups.

While the documents all place a heavy emphasis on equality and equal rights, and discourage discrimination, they generally promote a vision of equality that goes beyond formally treating every member of a society in the same way. They recognize that some members of society may justifiably need different treatment and different societal resources in order to gain an equal opportunity within society.[27]

Many of the international documents include provisions specifying that members of traditionally disadvantaged groups—women, racial and ethnic minorities, people with disabilities, the elderly, and children of unmarried parents—should not suffer discrimination. Affirmative action–type programs are recognized as sometimes necessary to achieve such an inclusive vision.

Further, international human rights documents also recognize the issue of dependency with provisions for the needs of those who are elderly,[28] ill,[29] or handicapped,[30] members of "the highest risk groups . . . [or] those whose poverty makes them the most vulnerable."[31] In this context, some provisions acknowledge the special burdens that are placed on the family—the societal institution traditionally responsible for dependency—and specifically mandate that the state play an active role in supporting the family. The International Covenant on Economic, Social and Cultural Rights states that "[t]he widest possible protection and assistance should be accorded to the family . . . [particularly] while it is responsible for the care and education of dependent children."[32]

States use these norms in crafting their own laws. The Constitution for the Republic of South Africa, for example, includes in its Bill of Rights the guarantee that "everyone has the right to have access to . . . social security, including, if they are unable to support themselves and their dependents, appropriate assistance."[33] The same constitution mandates that "the state must take reasonable legislative and other measures, within its available resources, to achieve the progressive realization of [the right to have access to adequate housing]."[34]

In addition, courts all over the world are using these concepts and norms and communicating with one another with regard to human rights. These documents provide the bases for discussion and for demands. They are the substance of a growing consensus, the principles in a discourse that is shockingly muted in the United States.

Interestingly, as the international norms are filtered through local laws and made viable within jurisdictions, court cases from other states are increasingly relied upon in countries that adhere to international human rights standards.[35] This process of globalization of decisional standards in which various nations' experiences can inform and inspire other nations with regard to human rights, occurring with frequency in countries such as Australia, South Africa, and Canada, is *not* common in the United States. We remain isolationist in our jurisprudence.

Just a few years ago Justice Ruth Bader Ginsburg, commenting on other countries with regard to this development, noted the lack of integration of international norms in America, "the same readiness to look beyond one's own shores has not marked the decisions of the [United States Supreme Court]."[36] At that time, before *Lawrence v. Texas*,[37] Ginsburg found only five mentions of the Universal Declaration of Human Rights in Supreme Court cases. Out of these few acknowledgments to our sister countries' courts, only two were to be found in the opinions of the Supreme Court's majority. Ginsburg also documented that the most recent of the citations appeared thirty-two years earlier in a dissenting opinion written by Justice Thurgood Marshall.

The concepts underlying these universal documents—inherent human dignity, equality, freedom, and justice—are well worth exploring and advocating. They go beyond the purely economic justifications of the market that have been used to promote much of contemporary American social policy.

VII. FORGING A MORE JUST SOCIAL CONTRACT

A. Subsidies and Support

Distilling the arguments that have been made in the preceding pages in order to reimagine the respective responsibility of family, market, and state in regard to dependency would yield a few basic premises. First, the state provision or assurance of basic social goods to all individuals is essential in a humane modern society. Second, as argued in chapter two, inevitable dependency is of general concern and may, therefore, be conceived of as a generalized or collective responsibility. Third, undertaking caretaking exacts a unique cost from an individual caretaker, who becomes derivatively dependent on society and its institutions for additional material and structural resources necessary to do care work well.

With these premises in mind, an argument flows that a just state would provide two different types of subsidies to individuals—lifelong provision of fundamental social goods, which are necessary for individual survival and flourishing, and specific additional subsidies that support the caretaker and caretaking. Basic social goods are economic or material in nature and include essentials such as housing, health care, a minimum income guarantee, and other necessities that complement and facilitate the expression of an individual's civil and political rights in a democracy. This responsibility for some minimal form of substantive equality marks a right of humanity no less important and worthy of governmental protection than are already-guaranteed formal civil and political rights and equalities. The initial governmental task, therefore, would be to ensure a more just allocation of the goods society and its institutions are producing.

The second type of subsidy, which is specifically directed at supporting caretaking, requires the state to ensure both material and structural accommodation. In this regard, the state would provide some subsidies directly, such as child-care allowances, but also oversee and facilitate the restructuring of the workplace so that market institutions accommodate caretaking and, in this way, assume some fair share of the burdens of dependency.

The mechanisms that might be available for funding these subsidies include the current tax and subsidy systems that so effectively channel rewards to corporate and business interests. The state could assess (and ultimately tax) the market institutions based on the imputed benefits they receive from uncompensated caretaking labor.[38] Other societies, such as those of Canada and the European Union countries, routinely provide support and subsidies to the family in numerous ways, such as child tax benefits, universal health care, and governmentally subsidized higher education.[39] These collectively provided supports would be welcome in our privatized system, where currently health insurance and a college savings fund represent a significant portion of the budget of even a middle-class family—a system in which single mothers, dually burdened with caretaking and economic responsibility, may find even basic health care prohibitively expensive.

The restructuring must not be blind to the transnational nature of caretaking work. As suggested in chapter two, the devaluing of dependency work left it classified (or ignored) "outside" of the market. Much of this labor is still ungoverned by market institutions.

The National Bureau of Labor Statistics marks 416,540 individuals as employed as "child care" workers, yet this figure obviously excludes nannies, au pairs, and other dependent laborers who are employed illegally.[40] Significantly, if the middle class is compensated for derivative dependency, the work may simply fall to immigrants (legal and illegal) who in turn will be exploited for their caretaking labor. This is especially true when one considers the massive global-wealth divide. After all, structural accommodations that exclude the great number of noncitizens would merely force one class's exploitation onto another. Grace Chang, in *Disposable Domestics,* documents the trend of middle- and upper-class women hiring poor immigrant women as "affordable" care. She asserts that "the advances of many middle-class white women in the workforce have been largely predicated on the exploitation of poor, immigrant women."[41]

While the precise number of illegal child-care workers may be next to impossible to ascertain, the recognition of their importance must include an acknowledgment that the market has ignored this essential work, and may continue to ignore it, if it is not recognized throughout economic classes. Without an eye ultimately toward global reformation, subsidies for caretaking labor may serve only a temporary solution. These problems provide a roadmap for future explorations in accommodation and reform surrounding dependency work.

The additional state responsibility in regard to caretakers involves supervision of a restructured market sphere, a subsidy that is every bit as important and essential to caretakers as are economic adjustments. The state must ensure that market institutions respond appropriately to the dependency burdens borne by the workers. Workplaces must be restructured so that responsibility for dependency is distributed more justly between family and market, thus alleviating the conflict between care work and workplace responsibilities that often results in neither being done well. This restructuring must include options in accommodation, such as flexible workweeks, job sharing without penalty, and paid family leave. Along with the economic reforms noted above, including a guarantee of a living wage, these adjustments to the workplace would create a more equitable arrangement for distributing the burdens of dependency between the market and the family.[42]

B. Generalizing the Concept of Care

Some conservative commentators will doubtless respond to these (relatively) modest economic proposals by trumpeting notions such as individual choice and attendant consequences, or waxing eloquent on the sanctity of personal responsibility. I suspect a problem for more progressive readers, however, will be the accommodation or restructuring of the workplace component of my arguments. In contemplating the implications of a restructured workplace, those without caretaking responsibility may fear that they would be ultimately forced to bear the costs of accommodation and change.[43] Workers without children may resist my suggestion because they would be the ones who had to work longer hours to fill in for absent colleagues. They might wonder how much their salary might be reduced to pay for benefits they will never use, such as family leave or day care on site. I have two responses to such concerns. One is pragmatic, the other more philosophical in nature.

In the first instance, we all must realize that even if we are unencumbered by dependents today, we do not know what the future holds for us with regard to the relevancy of dependency for the options we have in our lives. We may become caretakers even if we plan not to. We might avoid having children, but all of us have parents, and many of these parents become disabled as they age and become dependent on their adult children.[44] In addition, we ourselves might become disabled—become the dependent rather than the caretaker in the caretaking relationship. In that instance we would certainly want our caretakers to have the resources they would need to undertake our care.

In this regard, considering our own individual need for care, we should take an expansive view and include the need for self-care. Caretaking is not socially productive only when it is improving the situation of others. Human beings must also care for our own nonmaterial or spiritual needs.

Respect for a need for self-care is particularly important in our increasingly workaholic society. Americans work longer hours and more weeks of the year than do our European counterparts. We have little time left to regenerate our energies and resources, to participate in the artistic, nonmaterial, spiritual, or other inner-directed aspects of life upon which we all depend for our individual well-being. A commitment to caretaking should include this concern, along with the demand that society and its institutions be organized so that the emotional and nonmaterial aspects of life are not ignored.

From a philosophical perspective, it is important to point out that focusing on the caretaker's position ultimately illuminates something general about the organization of society: what is valued and respected. Generalizing from the initial perspective of exploitation of caretaking labor, it becomes possible to argue that such exploitation is also the norm in other forms of work. Expanding the idea of a collective or societal debt based on society-preserving labor beyond caretaking labor, one can argue for accommodation of others who are overlooked and undervalued. There are many workers whose labor provides for the needs, growth, and maintenance of society and its institutions, but whose contributions are undercompensated. They are also owed some material and structural adjustments in our current version of free-market capitalism.[45]

Particularly in the market context, we need to be reminded that corporations and those who run, direct, and profit from them cannot function without the labor of others. The contributions of secretaries and truck drivers are as essential to commerce as are those of highly paid CEOs and stockholders. Thus, the arguments that began with recognition of caretaking can evolve into a claim for universal provision of basic social goods grounded in basic humanity and the recognition of societal contributions that are nonmonetary and currently undercompensated. These contributions should be valued in a public, positive, and egalitarian fashion.

The idea of societal debt, coupled with the social-contract

metaphor, can provide a way to reintroduce and reinforce noneconomic values, such as norms of distributive justice or provision of worker security, into contemporary American political ideology. These concepts are realized in a consistent political and material way in other industrialized democracies. For those who question the wisdom of starting from caretaking and then expanding to the "larger" word of wage workers, I can only respond that it is necessary to secure the foundation before we rehabilitate all that is built upon it.

This argument can be carried to relationships that exist beyond the borders of the United States. A consideration of the international implications of rethinking the state's responsibility with regard to dependency and subsidy is beyond the scope of this book. Future work, however, may fruitfully explore the many ways in which our economic and material success is grounded on the provision of subsidies from other nations: goods and services that are appropriated through a system in which Western domination is built on centuries of colonization and exploitation that to some extent parallels the appropriation of women's labor in the family.

Just as the family performs essential but invisible work, and some necessary tasks are undervalued in the market, various countries and their citizens' labor directly contribute to the well-being of American multinational corporations, and hence also to the American state. Often this contribution to market and state is accomplished at the expense of individual American workers, as production is shifted abroad to take advantage of labor systems that pay mere fractions of what homegrown workers would demand.

The United States has a responsibility to monitor these relationships and the corporations that create and exploit them. It also has a responsibility to acknowledge and heed in fashioning policy our dependence on the rest of the world.

Just as there are no autonomous, independent, and self-sufficient individuals, no nation can stand alone. Yet, we now face a situation in which the rhetoric and actions of our political leaders evidence a willful disregard of the international community and other alliances of nations.

Postscript

What Place for Family Privacy?

In this book, I have been rethinking the arrangement among family, market, and state by undermining the idea of autonomy and articulating a theory of collective responsibility for dependency. In the process, I reconfigured certain core concepts in American policy discourse in order to make an argument for the redistribution of responsibility for dependency across these coercive institutions. I used the term "coercive" to distinguish these highly regulated, legally defined institutions from more voluntary social structures such as philanthropy, religion, or charity.

My argument has been that dependency, which is seen, at least partially, in many other systems as a collective responsibility, in ours is privatized through the institution of the family. Our state, through its capitalist nature, is perceived as having a role in the delivery of social goods only in the case of family default. In such instances, the state might provide highly stigmatized assistance (welfare) for those (deviant) families unable to provide for their members' needs.[1] Market institutions have little, if any, direct responsibility for the family, even for the families of their own workers.

A more appropriate and equitable scheme would redistribute the burdens for inevitable dependency, causing the market and the state to assume some of the up-front share of the economic and social costs (the subsidy) inherent in the reproduction of society. One conceptual problem with the idea of collective responsibility for dependency is the corresponding argument that assumption of such responsibility must be accompanied by collective *control* over the circumstances leading to that dependency. If society has obligations to subsidize and support caretakers, then society should have a correlative right to control intimate decisions that produce or effect dependency decisions concerning reproduction, family formation, and family function.

Some concept of privacy is necessary for resisting assertions about the appropriateness of collective control. In fact, weaving a reconfigured concept of family privacy into the arguments for collective responsibility strengthens both concepts. Collective responsibility accompanied by a well-developed notion of privacy for the caretaking unit can provide autonomy for that unit. Collective resources provide the ability, while the norm of nonintervention provides the freedom, for families to freely undertake the societal tasks they have been assigned.

In regard to our current social scheme, we use a notion of privacy to give the family coherence. We perceive a line of privacy drawn around certain intimate units that distinguishes them as "family." The privacy line defines the relationship of individuals within the family entity and mediates their relationship to the state.[2] This line of privacy currently shields few entities. Although it has historically been drawn around the traditional marital family, it should instead be drawn around caretaking or dependency units.

In fact, rethinking our ideas about dependency and self-sufficiency mandates a corresponding reconsideration of other assumptions about the family as an institution and a reconceptualization of the family's relationship with the state. As part of this process, the question is whether we can modernize the concept of family privacy, making it a complement to our restructured vision of the family. This will involve looking at both intrafamily ties and the position the family occupies in relation to the state.

The task of reconfiguring privacy has two related components: a shift in our understanding as to what privacy attaches—family *function* and not family *form*—and the development of family privacy as an entity-based entitlement to self-government or autonomy. Thus conceived, privacy would not be a right to separation, secrecy, or seclusion, but rather the right to autonomy or self-determination for the family, even as it is firmly located within a supportive and reciprocal state.[3]

I distinguish family or entity privacy from constitutional or individual privacy. Family privacy is a common-law concept that is not individualized, but founded on the nature of the protected relationship. Family privacy attaches to the entity of the family, not to the individuals who compose it. Historically, this has meant that, in certain situations, the doctrine operates to shield the family unit from state interference, even when the request for intervention comes from one of the family members.

Recognizing the typical critiques of family privacy, in this postscript I argue that we must think beyond the historic manifestations of the concept. My reconstruction of family privacy is more ideological than doctrinal. It is also a necessary part of re-visioning the family along functional lines.

I. PRIVACIES

Most commentators focus on privacy as a matter of federal constitutional doctrine. This strand of privacy jurisprudence is individualistic in nature and has been the basis for some important decisions protecting reproductive choice. This individual or constitutional notion of privacy is certainly necessary to deter certain impulses toward collective control in sexual and reproductive areas.[4] In fact, there has been quite a bit of debate in recent years about the effectiveness, as well as the wisdom, of using privacy to secure individual rights. I remain an agnostic on questions such as whether equality or privacy is the most potent concept with which to preserve individual reproductive rights. Nor do I offer an opinion as to whether some form of sexual privacy is essential for the development of individual personhood.

My interest in the legal or doctrinal idea of privacy is focused on its use in consideration of the institution of the family—privacy in its common-law sense. The notion of the private family predates, and is analytically separate from, the constitutional idea of individual privacy, although this new arena of privacy seems rooted in older notions about family relations. For example, *Griswold v. Connecticut is* often cited as the bedrock case for the development of our constitutional concept of individual privacy in regard to reproductive decisions.[5] But the *Griswold* opinion, articulating the concept of privacy, clearly looks beyond the individual, referencing an entity or marital concept of privacy.

The question *Griswold* explicitly presents is whether there is a constitutional right for *married* couples to use contraception.[6] Justice Douglas's majority opinion may characterize the right to this type of privacy as located in the now-well-known penumbras, but its presence transcends those shadows. The privacy interests at issue were deemed "older than the Bill of Rights—older than our political parties, older than our school system."[7]

There is little ambiguity about what is being protected: "[m]arriage is a coming together for better or worse, hopefully enduring, and intimate to the degree of being sacred."[8] Justice Goldberg's concurring opinion reiterated the point that it is marriage that deserves protection, stating that the statute at issue deals "with a particularly important and sensitive area of privacy—that of the marital relation and the marital home."[9]

From the family law perspective, *Eisenstadt v. Baira*[10] is the radical departure, because it takes the idea of entity or marital privacy and expands constitutional protection beyond the common-law limitations of the family relationship. In *Eisenstadt,* the court stated:

> It is true that in Griswold the right of privacy in question inhered in the marital relationship. Yet the marital couple is not an independent entity with a mind and heart of its own, but an association of two individuals each with a separate intellectual and emotional makeup. If the right of privacy means anything, it is the right of the individual, married or single, to be free from unwarranted governmental intrusion into matters so fundamentally affecting a person as the decision whether to bear or beget a child.[11]

This articulation of the principles enumerated in *Griswold* establishes the individual as the relevant subject of privacy inquiry. In effect, a constitutional cloak of privacy was thrown over certain individual decisions involving sex and reproduction.[12]

If we were to return to the doctrine of family or marital privacy, we would see that it is distinguishable from the new individual variety in several significant ways. The obvious difference is in the designation of the relevant unit for protection, entity verses individual. Also important, however, is the historic fact that family privacy operated as a generalized protection. What was shielded from state intervention and control was not only specific, weighty, intimate decisions, such as the decision to beget or bear a child, but also mundane, day-to-day family interactions.

Although the Supreme Court has brought some aspects of family privacy into constitutional law, the cases that are most relevant in discerning the characteristics of family privacy are state, not federal, decisions.[13] The task of the state family privacy cases is not to pronounce grand principles or to figure out how to mesh family privacy with other constitutional limitations. Instead, these cases address expectations and aspirations for families, articulating in the process what might be characterized as an ethic or ideology of family privacy. This ideology, which is noninterventionist, is rooted in an idealization of the family, and it references the perceived pragmatics of family relationships as well as the acknowledged limitations of legal (particularly judicial) systems as substitutes for family decision making. The ideology expresses the norm of nonintervention in ongoing families—a principle of state restraint because of the needs of the functioning family.[14]

The facts of *McGuire v. McGuire*,[15] a Nebraska state court spousal support case, illustrate the contours of the common-law doctrine of family privacy. Mrs. McGuire had asked the court to intervene and require her husband to provide suitable maintenance and support for her. She did not want a divorce or legal separation, but instead she sought the enforcement of the terms of the *state-defined* marriage contract, which required husbands to support their wives. Her complaints about her husband's lack of adequate support were rather compelling. For example, although her husband was a fairly wealthy man, she had not received money to buy clothing for several years. Further, she lived in a house with no indoor bathroom, kitchen sink, or functioning central heating. The Nebraska Supreme Court, while indicating that the husband's behavior was inappropriate, nonetheless held that his marital obligations could not be enforced if Mrs. McGuire chose to remain in her family relationship:

> The living standards of a family are a matter of concern to the household, and not for the courts to determine, even though the husband's attitude toward his wife, according to his wealth and circumstances, leaves little to be said in his behalf. As long as the home is maintained and the parties are living as husband and wife it may be said that the husband is legally supporting his wife and the purpose of the marriage relation is being carried out. Public policy requires such a holding.[16]

Mrs. McGuire's petition for a level of support consistent with the family's wealth and income would be granted only if she left the relationship. As long as the marriage lasted, the courts would not intervene, even when asked to by one of the spouses and even if all that was requested was the enforcement of state-imposed family obligations.

Of course, children present a more problematic situation. We are less certain that children can protect themselves within the family, much less *from* the family. The nature of the parent-child relationship has occupied state courts' attention. Parental conduct, be it disciplinary or decision making, is generally protected unless it constitutes abuse or neglect of the child. Courts consistently reiterate the common-law presumption that parents act in the best interests of their children. The law's concept of the family rests on the presumption that parents possess what children lack in maturity, experience, and capacity for judgment.[17]

The parent-child connection has also received some attention by the United States Supreme Court.[18] Consistent with the approach undertaken in *Griswold* to find sources for a married couple's constitutional right to privacy in their bedroom, the Supreme Court opinions about parent-child relationships excavate parental rights not from explicit textual provisions, but from the history and functioning of the family itself.[19]

II. LIMITATIONS OF PRIVACY

Both individual and entity versions of privacy have limitations.[20] For example, family privacy is limited in two important senses. First, there is the historic doctrinal limitation that family privacy apply primarily to family units that conform to ideological conventions about appropriate form and function—meaning, intact nuclear families. Second, in recent decades the idea of family privacy has been severely criticized by feminists: children's rights proponents; and others concerned with the potential for physical, emotional, or psychological abuse of some family members by others. Family privacy has been charged with obscuring and fostering inequality and exploitation.[21]

Somewhat of a dilemma is presented for those of us who view privacy as essential and necessary to the very concept of family. While we recognize its significance, we must concede that privacy can conceal, even foster, situations dangerous to the individuals who comprise the family unit. The focus on the necessity of privacy for family formation and functioning arises from concern with abuses associated with state intervention and regulation of intimacy. If there is no privacy attached to the family and its functioning, we must be concerned with state intervention and regulation of intimate relationships.

By contrast, if we are attuned to potential abuses within the family, we are reminded that often they are hidden beneath the cloak of privacy and that power imbalances provide incentives for stronger family members to prey upon or exploit weaker ones.[22] When we consult the empirical data, it seems both concerns are warranted. Therefore, the obvious goal should be to reconcile both concerns and to balance family privacy with protection for family members. Too often, however, advocates discard one (particularly family privacy) for the sake of the other.

III. REVISIONING PRIVACY

In attempting to reconcile the need of the family for privacy with the obligation of the state to protect its citizens, we should first resolve the question of family population. How are we going to define the family that will be entitled to privacy protection? Existing law defines the family through legal affiliations. Only certain ties are significant for the establishment of the status of family. Some ties are purely legally contrived, such as those in the construct of marriage, while others are considered to be reflective of more "natural" links, such as the parent-child bond.[23]

The legally conceived family presumptively is, or has been, a reproductive unit. As argued in chapter four, the primary tie that gives the family its current privileged form is the heterosexual affiliation of husband and wife.[24] Theirs is a connection considered basic to family and to state, and therefore historically legally mandated to be permanent, exclusive, and stable.[25] This traditional family was hierarchically organized with well-defined gendered divisions of labor. It is this family that is reflected in much of the feminist criticism of recent years, as indicated in chapter five. The introduction to part three discussed the work of Professor MacKinnon, which critiques family privacy as allowing the oppression of women by men. It also highlighted the work of Professor Allen, which urges feminists to develop a concept of privacy that could protect women's autonomy within families, in some regard freeing them from the demands of children and spouse.

A more central criticism of privacy, from the perspective of this postscript, is presented by those who focus on the rights of children. Family privacy in this regard protects parental authority and autonomy.[26] In this area, the tendency of privacy critics who see abuses has been to individualize the family, by separating children out for special concern and state protection. Some child advocates focus on physical and psychological abuse of children within families. These seem to me to be easy issues (problems of definition aside). Privacy should never be used to condone or obscure abuse.

What are of concern, however, are the more sweeping claims of the child advocates—those who focus on the very basic question of how children are described and treated in law. The discomfort of child advocates in this regard seems to be related to the traditional hierarchical or unequal nature of the parent-child relationship. The charge often leveled is that the law treats children as though they are the property of their parents, an inflammatory characterization that does more to obscure than to illuminate the issues.

There are a number of suggestions for recasting the relationship between parent and child, for example, substituting concepts such as stewardship or trusteeship for the more traditional notion of parental authority, and thus leveling out the relationship.[27] These ideals, amorphously appealing on a rhetorical level, seem harmless enough as aspirations. The problems arise when they are implemented into laws that can be used at the relatively unfettered discretion of various state actors to undermine, even usurp, parental decision-making authority.

From the perspective of my project, notions of child advocacy can raise some interesting issues. How might a general and broadly construed norm of child advocacy relate to the concepts of collective responsibility without collective control? Perhaps advocacy may be of benefit to the project. For example, noted child advocate Professor Barbara Woodhouse has urged the idea of stewardship. She uses the child advocates' claim that children must be treated as "people in their own right" to argue for laws and policies that focus on children's welfare.[28]

Although she does believe that children's welfare might necessitate some monitoring of parental authority, Woodhouse reaches for more than mere control over parents. With the objective of children's welfare as the organizing tool, she advocates for a more extensive sense of children's rights—"needs-based rights." These rights are not associated with children's rights to autonomy or independence, but are the basis for a positive claim for basic nurture and protection.[29] These rights create responsibility, not only for individual parents, but also for the larger community, and require political responses.

To some extent, Woodhouse's concern with basic-needs rights reflects my own call for collective responsibility for dependency. However, the identity of the rights holder and the source of the right are different in important ways. My claim is a communal one—entity focused and based on a claim of entitlement or right originating as a result of the societal work performed by caretakers.[30] Woodhouse's model is not a compensatory one, but is based on the status of the child as a future citizen. She positions the child as the claim holder and, in doing so, conceptually breaks up the family into individual and therefore potentially competing interests. This paves the way for claims of collective supervision and monitoring of parental stewardship.

IV. AUTONOMY FOR FAMILY FUNCTIONING

Rethinking the family and its relationship to the state requires a corresponding rethinking of other primary institutions and foundational concepts.[31] As part of this process, I suggest that we can and should rethink privacy in such a way as to confer autonomy on caretaking or dependency units. The beneficiary of this privacy is the unit, defined through its functioning, not its form. In fact, the caretaking unit could adopt a multitude of possible forms. The unifying idea that creates a new family is the existence of a caretaker-dependent relationship.

My version of the new entity privacy, designed to complement the new family, could be called "autonomy." Autonomy in this sense would protect entity decision making, giving the unit the space and authority to self-govern, and including the right of self-definition. Autonomy does not presuppose that the family would be separate from society. The family would be anchored firmly within society, and subsidized and supported by market and state, but would retain authority within its parameters.[32] Privacy, just like subsidy, should attach to units performing societally necessary and essential functions, such as caretaking.[33]

This version of a reconceived family, entitled to privacy or autonomy, is responsive to some of the critics of old forms of family privacy. For example, if the family is defined functionally, focused on the caretaker-dependent relationship, the traditionally problematic interactions of sexual affiliates (formerly designated "spouses") are not protected by notions of family privacy. MacKinnon's charge that men will exploit women in an intimate context may still be a problem, but it will no longer be a privacy problem. The fact that privacy is refocused removes from the special or family context the entire range of relationships between sexual affiliates, opening them up to public scrutiny.[34]

This opening up of some relationships to scrutiny does not mean that my reconfigured family model is going to escape feminist criticism, however. The criticism is most likely to be that a notion of collective responsibility (and therefore social subsidy) and privacy protection for the caretaking-dependent relationship will permanently enthrall women as dependency laborers. As I argued earlier, I think such arguments are based in part on assumptions about women's false consciousness.

In any case, my objective is not social engineering. I do not consider it my place to persuade women not to undertake care-taking; rather, I seek to ensure that if they do undertake it, they will not be systemically disadvantaged and rendered economi-cally dependent on men or on highly stigmatized state assistance as a result. I do believe in the possibility of women's agency—the ability to choose among options—including the option to undertake a caretaking role. This position, I believe, is compati-ble with the aspiration of gender equality. Although we all oper-ate within societal and cultural constraints, we can determine direction and decide to take one path rather than another. Women should have the ability (subsidy and privacy) to under-take a caretaking role.

The problems suggested by child advocates will be more on point for challenging privacy for the new family I envision. This is true because the exemplar of the caretaker-dependent rela-tionship is the parent-child relationship. Significantly, these are relationships of inherent inequality, reflecting the fact that one role is that of child or dependent, while the other is that of par-ent or caretaker. To point out an inequality in a relationship is not to make an assertion as to how we should value children.

Children (or any other inevitably dependent person) are as important and valuable as caretakers, but they are typically not equals in the sense that society does not presume that they are equivalent to adults in capability or in their ability to make judg-ments. Therefore it is more appropriate to view the parent-child relationship not as one of equality (as with sexual affiliates), but as one of responsibility. It is not about individuals, but about a relationship. And the relationship, defined by responsibility, re-quires privacy or autonomy for the caretaking entity.

It is this distinction between equality and responsibility—

between valuing the individuals and assessing the relationship—that many child advocates fail to make. In fact, some child advocates' attempts seem like efforts to equalize the relationship between parent and child by adding the supposedly leveling force of the advocate (as stand-in for the state). My argument about autonomy for the caretaking unit is an assertion that some relationships should be considered outside of the equality paradigm that so dominates liberal legal scholarship.[35] The reasoning of some child advocates presents the danger that, under the rubric of protecting the child, we facilitate state intervention and control, and potentially undermine the autonomy of caretaking units.

The fact that we can think that some intimate relationships are inherently unequal does not mean that they will inevitably be exploitative and oppressive or that the less powerful participant will have no voice within the relationship.[36] I explicitly mention this because it seems that many child advocates assume that exploitation necessarily follows once the inequality of the child is posited.[37] In the same way, the lack of a legal voice is equated with the lack of an actual voice.

Of course, the determination of typical and atypical modes of operation in caretaker-dependent units presents an empirical question. My assumption is that a careful study would show that the relationship between typical caretakers and dependents is dynamic (it is in motion), fluid (easily changing shape), and interactive (the participants act upon each other). The reciprocal interactive nature of the relationship ensures that it will not be fixed. The reciprocity also means that in regard to family decision making, the dependent will seldom, if ever, be absent.

Caretakers typically consider dependents' needs. Often dependents are an explicit part of the process of decision making, and at times they are even in control of it. Just as the relationship is fluid within daily interaction, it is dynamic over time. While the authority of a parent over a child will decline as the years pass, an adult child's authority over (and responsibility for) an elderly or ill parent may increase. This is not to assert that there will never be wrong decisions made by caretakers, or even that there will never be outright abuse. No system of child advocacy, no matter how interventionist and regulatory, can deliver only optimal, nonabusive caretaking.

It is important in this regard to realize that the debates about child advocacy are, to a large extent, only arguments about legal relationships and how legal authority is distributed. As a practical matter, they are arguments about the relationship between state and family more than attempts to define and regulate intrafamily interactions. By contrast, if we focus, as I urge, on entity autonomy and responsibility, we are at least attempting to understand and respond to how family units function. Reflecting on the discussion about marriage in chapter four, it is important to recall that legal relationships capture only some things about "real" families, often distorting a family's reality in the process. This distortion results, in part, from the adversarial nature of legal relationships.

One danger of imposing an equality aspiration on relationships of responsibility is pertinent for the ideas of subsidy and collective responsibility discussed earlier.[38] If we look at the child as the recipient of the subsidy and not the unit (in which the caretaker is the "head"), several issues arise. Foremost is the very real possibility that if the child is seen as the object of social policy and justification for subsidy, some form of quality control will be considered appropriate. Standardization and normative judgments in a diverse and pluralistic society can be problematic and contentious.

By contrast, if subsidy is perceived as going to the caretaker-dependent entity or unit, it is more likely that autonomy over decision making will follow. Units may make mistakes, but if it is not abuse or neglect (we can argue about where to draw those lines later), then the unit as recipient of the subsidy should decide how it is to be used. This way of looking at what is the appropriate focus for policy also gives value to caretaking labor. The dependent may be the beneficiary, but the labor of the caretaker is what has societal value.

V. CONCLUSION

To protect caretaking relationships, we must extend the right to privacy beyond individuals. A concept of individual privacy, particularly in regard to the formation of intimate connections, can complement family privacy, but some protection that transcends the interests of individual members of the entity is essential. When a caretaking-dependent unit has formed, family privacy would serve to shield and protect the functioning relationships within it. The protection would dissolve only if the entity grossly fails in the performance of its responsibilities or because the underlying relationship has itself dissolved.[39]

Entity privacy would denote a line of nonintervention drawn around ongoing functioning relationships.[40] This version of privacy can provide a barrier between an entity performing family functions, such as the caretaker-dependent unit, and the potentially overreaching state seeking to impose collective standards or controls. Properly conceived, privacy as a principle of self-government allows the caretaker-dependent unit to flourish, supported and subsidized by the larger society without the imposition of conformity.

Notes

Introduction

1. This attack is epitomized by the Personal Responsibility and Work Opportunity Reconciliation Act of 1996, which limited aid to families in poverty in order to "end the dependence of needy parents." Pub. L. No. 104-93, §401(a)(2), 110 Stat. 2105 (1996). *See also* Elinor Burkett, *The Baby Boon* (Free Press, 2000) (arguing that childless workers are stigmatized and exploited, in order to accommodate parents in the workplace). For a discussion of Burkett's book, *see* Andrew Hacker, "The Case Against Kids," *The New York Review of Books*, November 30, 2000, at 12.

2. Not all children are viewed as presumptively private. As documented in Martha Albertson Fineman, *The Neutered Mother, the Sexual Family, and Other Twentieth Century Tragedies* (Routledge, 1995) [herein after *The Neutered Mother*], children are a matter of public concern when they are located in public (as contrasted with private) families—families that are poor, thus not self-sufficient, or defective in form, such as headed by a single mother. These families are subjected to regulation and control because of the public interest in the children within them who are deemed endangered by their family's nonconformity to societal norms in regard to marriage and financial stability.

3. *See* Personal Responsibility and Work Opportunity Reconciliation Act of 1996, *supra* note 1, §408(a)(5) (seeking to "solve" teenage parenting concerns by requiring denial of public assistance to teenage parents unless they live with their parents—in other words, sending them back to their families).

Chapter One: Exploring Foundational Myths

1. Looking at inheritance practice from a comparative perspective can be useful. In the United Kingdom, the inheritance is taxed to the recipient and the estate is, therefore, "tax-free." This would remove the kind of objections based on the idea that inheritance tax is a "death tax" that accompanied the recent reforms in the United States. Also of interest is the fact that the United States is virtually alone in not requiring a testator to leave a certain percentage to his or her children. We allow parents to disinherit their children, a practice considered "unnatural" (or at least bad social policy) in other industrialized democracies where there is a strong sense of intergenerational obligation and responsibility and less attention to individual autonomy and testamentary freedom.

2. Jeanne Brooks-Gunn and Greg J. Duncan, "The Effects of Poverty on Children," *The Future of Children: Children and Poverty,* Summer/ Fall 1997, at 55 (reporting that in recent years about one in five American children [12 to 14 million] have lived in families with incomes below the poverty line). The 2000 census reports that the number of people under the age of eighteen living in poverty is 16.3 percent. United States Census 2000, *at* www.census.gov (visited June 1, 2003). Whichever figure is used, the number is appalling in such a wealthy country, particularly one that aspires to democratic and egalitarian principles. *2002 Annual Demographic Supplement to the Current Population Survey.*

3. The 2000 census reports that the number of people age sixty-five and older living in poverty is 10.1 percent. United States Census 2000, *supra* note 2. *See also* Beth Haller, "Disability Rights—and Wrongs," *at* www.horizonmag.com/poverty/disability-rights.asp (last visited June 3, 2003); "The Disability Equation: Does Disability = Poverty?" (Madeline S. Bergstrom, ed.) *at* www.horizonmag.com/poverty/disabilitytnt.asp (last visited June 1, 2003).

4. The 2000 census estimates the number of Americans without health insurance is 41.2 million. United States Census 2000, *supra* note 2.

5. William W. Cobb, *The American Foundation Myth in Vietnam* passim (University Press of America, Inc., 1984); Gilbert Morris Cuthbertson, *Political Myth and Epic* 173 (Michigan State University Press, 1975); Tom Garvin, *Mythical Thinking in Political Life: Reflections on Nationalism and Social Science* 12, 22–23 (Academia Press, 2001).

6. *The New Webster's Encyclopedic Dictionary of the English Language* (Random House, 1997).

7. Cobb, *supra* note 5, at 2, 12, 157; Garvin, *supra* note 5, at 16.

8. Cobb, *supra* note 5, at 3.

9. This theory is associated with John Locke.

10. In fact, at the time of the establishment of the American Constitution, many Americans were indifferent or strongly opposed to the document and the ideas it embodied. Rhode Island only ratified the Constitution after being threatened with blockades and invasions.

11. Henry Tudor, *Political Myth* 14, 17 (Praeger Publishers, 1972).

12. *Id.* at 16–17.

13. *Id.* at 15.

14. *Id.* at 97.

15. Cobb, *supra* note 5, at 188.

16. Mircea Eliade, *Myth and Reality* 2, 5–6 (Harper & Row, 1975) (1963).

17. Tudor, *supra* note 11, at 23–24.

18. Tudor, *supra* note 11, at 16–17, 91. One of the most famous political myths in the ancient world was the myth of the foundation of Rome. This was a story, based on the legend of Aeneas, that the Romans were actually the descendents of the Trojans. Since the Trojans had been enemies of the Greeks, this political myth was used to justify the Roman wars against and triumph over Greece, since the Romans could believe they were avenging ancient wrongs. As time passed, and the myth was handed down through generations, it evolved to meet the changing political needs of Roman society. The story of Trojan descent could be interpreted in numerous ways, and could be used for many purposes, even if they were contradictory. By the time of the Punic Wars, the Romans had assimilated a significant amount of Greek culture, and considered Rome to be a center of Hellenic civilization. As a result, they used the story of their Trojan origins to invoke the Homeric past, and declare themselves an integral part of the Greek world. Thus, the Roman foundation myth could be used to support anti-Greek, and later pro-Greek, politics, depending on the evolving needs of Roman society.

Foundation myths are complex and multidimensional. The Roman claim to Trojan decent was a major component of the Roman foundational story, but there were other facets to the myth as well. One part of the myth was that it was Rome's geographic location that had allowed it to rise to preeminence in the ancient world. Like the American Founding Fathers, who established their nation on a large piece of rich and fertile land, protected from hostile enemies by the surrounding oceans, the founders and mythical ancestors of the Romans had wisely chosen to situate the city on the banks of a navigable river, essential for commerce and travel, yet far enough inland to be safe from foreign attack.

19. Cobb, *supra* note 5, at 18; Cuthbertson, *supra* note 5, at 174; Colin Grant, *Myths We Live By* ix (University of Ottawa Press, 1998).

20. Cuthbertson, *supra* note 5, at 16.

21. Tudor, *supra* note 11, at 72.

22. Ennius, Ann. 467.

23. Cuthbertson, *supra* note 5, at 197.

24. Tudor, *supra* note 11, at 91.

25. Cobb, *supra* note 5, at 188.

26. Cuthbertson, *supra* note 5, at 8.

27. Tudor, *supra* note 11, at 15–16.

28. We see this in American constitutional law with the doctrine of strict construction of the constitutional intent of the framers. Justice Scalia and others would have us use only the original intent (as if that could be determined) as a guide, not the individual perceptions of contemporary judges of what should be considered fair or just.

29. Susan Sterett, *Service and Charity: Social Welfare in the States* (forthcoming, introduction, on file with the author).

30. Amy Dru Stanley, *From Bondage to Contract* 9 (Cambridge University Press, 1998).

31. *Id.* at 9, 105, passim.

32. Cobb, *supra* note 5, at 11, 18–19, passim.

33. Tudor, *supra* note 11, at 121.

34. *Id.* at 126–7.

35. *Id.* at 91.

36. *Id.* at 9.

37. Jack Zipes has conducted extensive research on myths and fairy tales and concludes that they play a significant role in educating, socializing, and civilizing both children and adults. Jack Zipes, *Fairy Tale as Myth: Myth as Fairy Tale* 8, 17, passim (University Press of Kentucky, 1994); Jack Zipes, *Happily Ever After: Fairy Tales, Children, and the Culture Industry* (Routledge, 1997). *See also* Cuthbertson, *supra* note 5, at 197.

38. Values are also viewed as exceptional or unique characteristics of a society—used to favorably distinguish us from others. Thus, we see values associated with certain political stances expressed as "American" (or "un-American"). Values language can also be used to obliterate different or competing values such as when a certain form of family is asserted to express "American family values."

39. Cobb, *supra* note 5, at 17; Cuthbertson, *supra* note 5, at 2, 14.

40. Cuthbertson, *supra* note 5, at 5; Garvin, *supra* note 5, at 15.

41. Cobb, *supra* note 5, at 33; Garvin, *supra* note 5, at 26.

42. Zipes, *Fairy Tale as Myth, supra* note 37, at 4, 5.

43. More than ten million copies of *The Seven Habits of Highly Effective People* have been sold since its publication in 1989. The Franklin-Covey organization markets books, cassette tapes, electronic and paper planners, classes, seminars, other training opportunities, and "accessories" *at* www.franklincovey.com (visited June 1, 2003).

44. Stephen R. Covey, *The Seven Habits of Highly Effective People* (Simon & Schuster, 1989).

45. *Id.* at 50.

Chapter Two: Dependency and Social Debt: Cracking the Foundational Myths

1. Other recent political decisions also reflect a trend toward the adoption of policies that rely on the individual and remove responsibility from government, thereby increasing the possibility of income inequities. Instead of relying on Social Security supplemented by employer-funded pension plans, people are being encouraged to arrange for their retirement through 401(k) savings plans and private investments free from governmental oversight and protection.

2. Louis Uchitelle, "A Shift to Self-Reliance: Proposals to Revamp Social Security Reflect the Larger National Trend," *New York Times,* January 13, 1997, A15.

3. Even women on welfare themselves perpetuate a feeling of shame and stigmatize their condition. George W. Bush used the statement of a woman who had worked her way off welfare to illustrate the point: "the success of it is my children see me go to work every day. And that makes them go to school every day, because they see mama isn't staying at home." President Bush applauded this particular mother by stating, "The ability

for somebody to realize kind of an independent life, less dependent upon government not only affects that person but also affects a lot of other people, starting with the children—starting with the children." George W. Bush, "Remarks to the North Carolina Chamber of Commerce," February 27, 2002, *available at* LEXIS, Federal News Service.

4. *See* Peter Edelman, "Prepared Testimony of Peter Edelman, Professor of Law, Georgetown University Law Center, Before the Senate Health, Education, Labor and Pensions Committee," February 14, 2002, *available at* LEXIS, Federal News Service.

5. Juliet Schor argues that because domestic work has been excluded from the realm of labor, that work is taken for granted, and competitive alternatives are artificially inflated. Schor quotes economist Nancy Folbre suggesting that in colonial times, women's household activities were not devalued this way: "By 1900, however, [women] had been formally relegated to the census category of 'dependents' that included infants, young children, the sick, and elderly." In *The Overworked American* 84–5 (Basic Books, 1992).

6. *See* Martha Albertson Fineman, "Limits of Privacy—The Public Family," in *The Neutered Mother* 177.

7. *See* Linda J. Waite and Maggie Gallagher, *The Case for Marriage: Why Married People are Happier, Healthier, and Better off Financially* 107 (Doubleday, 2000).

8. *See* Vicki Schultz, "Life's Work," 100 *Columbia Law Review* 1881, n. 62 (2000).

9. *See* Thomas Gabe et al., "Child Care Subsidies: Federal Grants and Tax Benefits for Working Families," in *The Child Care Disaster in America: Disdain or Disgrace?* 25, 58 (Nova Science, 2001).

10. *Ibid.*

11. *See supra* note 3 (referring to ideals of hard work and self-sufficiency).

12. *Ibid.*

13. *See* Nick Gillespie, "The Kids Are Alright: The White House Invents a Child Care Crisis," *Reason*, December 1997, *available at* http://reason.com/9801/ed.nick.shtml (last visited June 1, 2003); Dearborn, "Press Release: Libertarians Give Mixed Reviews to Day Care Reform Proposals," Libertarian Party of Michigan, *at* www.mi.lp.org/press/112299.htm (last visited June 1, 2003).

14. *See* Gillespie, *supra* note 13. It seems as though Gillespie-type argu-

ments are not challenging the mythological role of the family, but still envisioning the individual ideal since it depends on the individual choice of parents to result in a satisfactory solution.

15. *See* Edelman, *supra* note 4.

16. *See* Kimberly Porrazzo, *The Nanny Kit* 12 (Penguin Books, updated ed., 1999). ("Nannies' salaries vary greatly from region to region. In the northeast, nannies are often paid $400-$500 or more per week. In California, however, the average nanny's weekly salary is closer to $300-$350 per week. Within Southern California, wages are higher in Los Angeles County than in Orange County or San Diego County, probably because Orange and San Diego counties are close to the Mexican border and a large number of illegal immigrants are seeking domestic work and will accept a lower salary.")

17. *See* Katherine M. Frank, "Theorizing Yes: An Essay on Feminism, Law, and Desire," 101 *Columbia Law Review* 181, 183-7 (2001).

18. *See id.*, at 185.

19. *See* Suzanne Lamorey et al., *Latchkey Kids: Unlocking Doors for Children and Their Families* 19 (Sage Publications, 2nd. ed., 1999) (arguing that the major myth that expects mothers to stay at home and be the primary caretaker of children arises from society's negative attitude toward maternal employment, divorce, day care, single parenting, and latchkey children).

20. Porrazzo, *supra* note 16. (Approximately 60 to 70 percent of those who videotape their nannies end up firing them. One parent found a nanny to be taking wonderful care of the child, but witnessed the nanny saying, "I take much better care of you than your mother.")

21. Deborah Belle, *The After-School Lives of Children: Alone and with Others While Parents Work* 7 (Lawrence Erlbaum Associates, 1999). ("The U.S. public school day is substantially shorter than the full-time work day and shorter than the school day in many other nations of the world. The school year is also interrupted by frequent holidays, early release days, and closings for inclement weather, and then concluded with a lengthy summer vacation, all of which vastly exceeds the vacation allotments of most employed parents. Nor are extended day or after-school programs available in many communities or to many children who need them.")

22. *See* Frank, *supra* note 17, at 190-91.

23. *See* Suzanne W. Helburn and Barbara R. Bergmann, *America's Child Care Problem* 98 (St. Martin's Press, 2002). *See also* Belle, *supra* note 21, at 12.

24. *See* Helburn and Bergmann, *supra* note 23. (When a family at or near the poverty level is looking for child care, it will obviously look for the cheapest available, which is most likely to be unlicensed care; furthermore, if there are any questions as to the quality, many families in this situation would resolve them in favor of cheapness.)

25. *See* Helburn and Bergmann, *supra* note 23. (Two parents working at minimum wage, for fifty-two forty-hour weeks, with two preschool children earn $27,962 in disposable income—after taxes. With the official U.S. poverty-line living expenses set at $17,493, the family only has $10,496 to spend on child care estimated to cost between $9,980 and $11,870.)

26. *See* Helburn and Bergmann, *supra* note 23. (One parent, with two preschool children, working at minimum wage for fifty-two forty-hour weeks, with government benefits earns $15,736 in disposable income. With official U.S. poverty-line living expenses set at $13,898, the mother has only $1,838 to spend on care estimated to cost between $9,980 and $11,870.)

27. *See* Waite, *supra* note 7, at 99.

28. *See* Edelman, *supra* note 4.

29. *See* Belle, *supra* note 21, at 7.

30. *See* Waite, *supra* note 7, at 99.

31. *See* Victor R. Fuchs, *Women's Quest for Economic Equality* 60–64 (Harvard University Press, 1998) (discussing the hidden costs of children for women in the workplace); Shultz, *supra* note 8, at 1881, 1894 (arguing that women do not choose lower-paying, lower-status jobs because of their heavier family obligations, but rather that the segregation of women into these jobs forces women into household labor).

32. *See* Julie Novkov, "A Deconstruction of Motherhood and a Reconstruction of Parenthood," 19 *New York University Review Law and Social Change* 155, 165–66 (1991) (discussing the role of working mothers).

33. *See* Belle, *supra* note 21, at 75–8.

34. *See* Martha Albertson Fineman, "Cracking the Foundational Myths: Independence, Autonomy, and Self-Sufficiency," 8 *American University Journal of Gender, Social Policy and the Law* 18 (2000).

35. *Ibid.* at 13, 21, n. 15.

36. *Ibid.* at 19.

37. *See generally* Christine N. Cimini, "Welfare Entitlements in the Era of Devolution," *Georgetown Journal on Poverty Law and Policy* (Winter 2002).

38. *See* Kenneth A. Cook, "The Cash Croppers," at www.ewg.org/pub/home/reports/croppers/chapter_1.html (visited June 1, 2003).

39. *See* Daniel S. Goldberg, "Tax Subsidies: One-Time vs. Periodic, an Economic Analysis of the Tax Policy Alternatives," 49 *Tax Law Review* 305, 306–307 (1994) (discussing the elements of tax subsidies). See also Martha McCluskey, "Subsidized Lives and the Ideology of Efficiency," 8 *American University Journal of Gender, Social Policy and the Law* (2000).

40. Torrey, as quoted in Robert B. Reich and John D. Donahue, *New Deals: The Chrysler Revival and the American System* (Times Books, 1985), 50. A brief excursus back to 1996 provides an illuminating example of how rhetoric surrounding subsidies is more muddied than one might expect. President Clinton, along with then–Secretary of Labor Reich and a Republican-led Congress, promised to curtail corporate welfare. (*See e.g.* Stephen Moore and Dean Stansel, "How Corporate Welfare Won: Clinton and Congress Retreat from Cutting Business Subsidies," Cato Policy Analysis No. 254 [1996].) Reich championed the cause, proclaiming, "If we're asking middle-class people to work smarter and welfare mothers to play by the rules, it seems important to ask corporate America to get off welfare and play by the rules as well." (As quoted in Brian Kelly, "The Pork That Just Won't Slice; Everything Gets Cut—But Not Corporate Welfare," *Washington Post*, December 10, 1995.).

The strange consensus included Ralph Nader as well as the Cato Institute, yet the government ultimately failed to make good on its promise. In shocking frankness, Republican Representative Scott Klug of Wisconsin admitted, "We have not shown the same kind of fervor in cutting corporate welfare as we have in the social area." (Quoted in Kelly, "The Pork That Just Won't Slice," at C4.)

41. *See* Douglas MacKinnon, "The Welfare Washington Doesn't Know," *New York Times*, May 21, 2002, at A21 (discussing how most congressmen cannot comprehend the amount of shame and pain that comes with being in poverty, or the frustration of trying to help yourself out of it).

42. *See* "Making Hay," *New Republic*, May 20, 2002, at 9 (pointing out that President Bush is not keeping with his market-driven approach to agriculture).

43. *See* Dick Lugar, "The Farm Bill Charade," *New York Times*, January 21, 2002, at A15. (The majority of payments in most states go to the top tenth of farmers. Farms in just six states will take almost half of the federal payments. According to the *Times*, "Ineffective agricultural policy has, over the years, led to a ritual of overproduction in many crops and

most certainly in the heavily supported crops of corn, wheat, cotton, rice and soybeans and the protected specialty products like milk, sugar and peanuts.") *See also* Elizabeth Becker, "Farmers Market Program Wins Support but Loses Subsidy," *New York Times,* March 17, 2002, at 32.

44. *See* "Statement by the President," Office of the Press Secretary, May 2, 2002, at www.whitehouse.gov/news/releases/2002/05/ 20020502.html (visited June 2003).

45. Laura D' Andrea Tyson, "The Farm Bill Is a $200 Billion Disaster," *Business Week,* June 3, 2003, at 26.

46. *See* Bush, *supra* note 3 (referring to ideals of hard work and self-sufficiency).

47. *See* Center for Law and Social Policy, *at* www.clasp.org/ pubs/ TANF/finalregs.html (last visited June 1, 2003). The proposed bill would also require welfare recipients to work forty hours a week, up from the current requirement of thirty hours per week; Personal Responsibility, Work, and Family Promotion Act of 2002, H.R. 4737, 107th Cong. (2002); Sarah Lueck, "House Passes Bill Lengthening Workdays of Welfare Recipients," *Wall Street Journal,* May 17, 2002 (quoting Health and Human Services Secretary Tommy Thompson, who was a key player in the overhaul of the state welfare system when he was governor of Wisconsin).

48. This family cap is being challenged in court. *See* Leslie Brody, "Welfare Reform in Spotlight as Milestone Nears," *New Jersey News,* March 24, 2002 (20 percent of the families no longer on welfare in New Jersey are living in poverty).

Existing Societal Arrangements

1. *See* Nancy F. Cott, "Giving Character to Our Whole Civil Polity: Marriage and the Public Order in the Late Nineteenth Century," in *U.S. History as Women's History* 107 (L.K. Kerber, A. Kessler-Harris, and K.K. Sklar, eds., 1995) (giving a historian's perspective on the family as an institution). Professor Cott states that "one might go so far as to say the institution of marriage and the modern state have been mutually constitutive . . . one of the principal means that the state can use to prove its existence . . . is its authority over marriage." *Id.* at 109.

2. I use this term to indicate a reciprocity or mutualism, although the term "containment" might also be appropriate. Containing family within

its traditional form and function is certainly the goal of some political actors.

3. Amitai Etzioni, "A Moderate Communitarian Proposal," *Political Theory* 24, no. 2 (May 1996) at 3.

4. *See*, generally, chapter three.

Chapter Three: The Family in the Rhetoric of Civil Society— Privileging Marriage

1. Council on Civil Society, "A Call to Civil Society: Why Democracy Needs Moral Truths" 7 (1998).

2. The National Commission on Civic Renewal has sponsored a series of scholarly working papers and created an Index of National Civic Health. National Commission on Civic Renewal, "A Nation of Spectators: How Civic Disengagement Weakens America and What We Can Do About It" (1998).

3. Council on Civil Society, *supra* note 1; National Commission on Civic Renewal, *supra* note 2.

4. Council on Civil Society, *supra* note 1, at 65, 66; National Commission on Civic Renewal, *supra* note 2, at 29.

5. Council on Civil Society, *supra* note 1, at 4–6: National Commission on Civic Renewal, *supra* note 2, at 23–36, 45.

6. Council on Civil Society, *supra* note 1, at 4–6, 19–26; National Commission on Civic Renewal, *supra* note 2, at 5.

7. David S. Broder, "Should the Government Be in the Business of Promoting Marriage?" *at* www.mncaa.orgMedia/GovPromotMarriage 040102.htm (last visited June 1, 2003).

8. This chapter will use the report of the National Commission on Civic Renewal as the basis for a general criticism of the civil society movement in regard to its positioning and consideration of the family. *See* National Commission on Civic Renewal, *supra* note 2. Most of the major players in the civil society debate were associated with the Commission. *See id.* at 65, 66. I am using "civil" and "civic" as interchangeable terms reflecting the idea that individuals live a secular collective or corporate life.

9. *Id.* at 5.

10. *Ibid.* (quoting Andrew Kohut, Pew Research Center for the People

and the Press, "Deconstructing Distrust: How Americans View Government" (1998).

11. *Id.* at 6.

12. *Id.* at 10.

13. *Id.* at 7 (citing Daniel Yankelovich, "How Changes in the Economy Are Reshaping American Values," *Values and Public Policy* [Henry J. Aaron et al., eds., 1994]). This seems to be particularly ironic given that the implications of current economic arrangements on civic health are not seriously considered in the Commission's Final Report.

14. National Commission on Civic Renewal, *supra* note 2, at 20.

15. Council on Civil Society, *supra* note 1, at 7.

16. National Commission on Civic Renewal, *supra* note 2, at 13.

17. *Id.* at 24.

18. *Id.* at 13.

19. *See Loving v. Virginia.* 87 S.Ct. 1817 (1967) (holding that statues barring interracial marriage violated the equal protection and due process clauses of the Fourteenth Amendment). It is interesting to note, however, that South Carolina and Alabama retained antimiscegenation clauses in their state constitutions until 1998 and 2000, respectively, despite this Supreme Court holding.

20. "No State, territory, or possession of the United States, or Indian tribe, shall be required to give effect to any public act, record, or judicial proceeding of any other State, territory, possession, or tribe respecting a relationship between persons of the same sex that is treated as a marriage under the laws of such other State, territory, possession, or tribe, or a right or claim arising from such relationship." Defense of Marriage Act, 28 USC 1738C (1996).

21. National Commission on Civic Renewal, *supra* note 2, at 41.

22. *Id.*

23. This second objection gives rise to some confusion in considerations of civil society—it is not always clear who is in and who is outside of civil society. At one point, the Commission defines civil society as "meaning free markets and private associations," suggesting that all nongovernmental institutions might be considered civil. *Id.* at 43, n. 16. At another point, however, civil society is seemingly restricted to "the network of voluntary associations and activities." *Id.* at 39.

24. *Id.* at 23.

25. Council on Civil Society, *supra* note 1, at 18.

26. *Id.* at 5. This use of the term "morality" is different than that in the report of the Commission. The Commission's report opted for morality "based not on any particular denominational creed, but on the constitutional faith we share—in the moral principles set forth in the Declaration of Independence, and the public purposes set forth in the Preamble to the Constitution." National Commission on Civic Renewal, *supra* note 2, at 12. The Council's report cites as indications of a weakened morality "behavior that threatens family cohesiveness," although it also noted weakening morality was evidenced by "uncivil" behavior and behavior that "violates the norm of personal responsibility." Council on Civil Society, *supra* note 1, at 5. Examples of moral decline included unwed childbearing, extramarital affairs, and easy sex as a normal part of life. Uncivil behavior included children's disrespecting adults, declining loyalty between employers and employees, and the absence of common courtesy. A pop star's announcing a preference for single motherhood is offered as one example of violating the norm of personal responsibility. *Id.*

27. The Council writes that "the steady break-up of the married couple child-raising unit [is] the leading propeller of our overall social deterioration. . . ." Council on Civil Society, *supra* note 1, at 18.

28. *Id.* at 6.

29. *Id.* at 5.

30. *Id.* at 18; National Commission on Civic Renewal, *supra* note 2, at 24.

31. The Council defines civil society in part as referring "specifically to relationships and institutions that are neither created nor controlled by the state." Council on Civil Society, *supra* note 1, at 6. The Commission indicates "the institutions of civil society are organic, not mechanical, and can at best be nurtured, not engineered." National Commission on Civic Renewal, *supra* note 2, at 12. One would assume that they cannot be legislated, either.

32. Council on Civil Society, *supra* note 1, at 19.

33. In Arkansas, Arizona, and Louisiana, persons may now enter a covenant marriage contract, which encourages them to seek marriage counseling if they are having marital difficulty and limits their ability to divorce to just a few instances, such as adultery, physical or sexual abuse, or the commission of a felony by one spouse.

34. Council on Civil Society, *supra* note 1, at 20.

35. *Id.* at 25.

36. *Id.* at 24–5.

37. Conclusions about popular notions of morality based on opinion surveys may be questioned, particularly if they are the basis for legal reforms with the potential to make people in unhappy, and sometimes violent and emotionally abusive, marriages less able to escape.

38. William A. Galston, "A Liberal-Democratic Case for the Two-Parent Family," 1 *The Responsive Community* 14 (1990–91).

39. *Id.*

40. *Id.* at 15–6.

41. *Id.* at 16.

42. *Id.* Galston also notes this position in his book. *See* William A. Galston, *Liberal Purposes: Goods, Virtues, and Diversity in the Liberal State* 283–87 (Cambridge University Press, 1991).

43. Galston, *supra* note 38, at 15.

44. *Id.*

45. *See* Terry Lugalia, United States Department of Commerce. Series P-23, No. 181, "Households, Families, and Children: A 30-Year Perspective" 14 (1992).

46. *See* Authur J. Norton and Louisa F. Miller, United States Department of Commerce, "Marriage, Divorce, and Remarriage in the 1990's" 1–4 (1992).

47. Theodore Caplow, *American Social Trends* 63 (Harcourt Brace Jovanovich, 1991). Caplow questions whether there is even a crisis of the family. Despite the fact that Americans have been told the family is in crisis, they tend to see their own families as happy and successful.

48. Galston, *supra* note 38, at 15.

49. *Id.*

50. *Id.* at 16–7.

51. *Id.*

52. *Id.* at 16.

53. *Id.* at 16–7. Galston continues, "[c]onversely, family disintegration is a major reason why after a decade-long economic expansion—the poverty rate among children is nearly twice as high as it is among elderly Americans." *Id.* at 17.

54. *Id.* at 17.

55. *Id.*

56. *Id.* at 18 (emphasis in original).

57. *Id.* at 17.

58. *Id.*

59. *Id.* at 19. He is also clear that he does not "advocate a return to the single-breadwinner 'traditional' family of the 1950s." *Id.*

60. *Id.* at 20.

61. *Id.* at 21–2 (emphasis in original).

62. *Id.*

63. *Id.* at 23–4.

64. *Id.* at 16–7.

65. *See* Judith Stacey, *In the Name of the Family* (Beacon Press, 1996).

66. *Id.* at 59.

67. Henry Ricciuti, "Single Parenthood and School Readiness in White, Black, and Hispanic 6- and 7-Year-Olds," 13 *Journal of Family Psychology* 450 (1999). School readiness was found to be about the same in large samples of single- and two-parent families.

68. *Id.*

69. E. Mavis Hetherington and John Kelly, *For Better or For Worse* 7 (W. W. Norton & Company, 2002).

70. *See id.* at 5.

71. *See id.* at 7.

72. Andrew Lister, "A Family Affair: The Causal Basis of Communitarian Family Values," presented at the 1999 Annual Meeting of the American Political Science Association (September 2–5, 1999). Lister considered Judith Stacey's charge about the selection and exaggeration of only some social science information, finding "a good deal of evidence of exaggeration." *Id.* at 11. Lister states, however, that the "best research" does seem to indicate that growing up in a single-parent family is not good for children. Lister then sets forth his analysis of the difficulties with such studies.

73. *Id.* at 12.

74. *Id.*

75. *Id.* at 12–3. (Caveats are from S. McLanahan and G.D. Sandefur, *Growing Up With a Single Parent: What Hurts, What Helps* [Harvard University Press, 1994]).

76. *Id.* at 23.

77. Iris M. Young, "Mothers, Citizenship, and Independence: A Critique of Pure Family Values," 105 *Ethics* 545 (1995).

78. Pepper Schwartz, "Gender and the Liberal Family," 1 *The Responsive Community* 87 (1990–91).

79. Susan Moller Okin, *Justice, Gender, and Family* 139 (Basic Books, 1989).

80. *Id.*

81. Young, *supra* note 77, at 545.

82. Susan B. Apel, "Communitarianism and Feminism: The Case Against the Preference for the Two-Parent Family," *Wisconsin Women's Law Journal* 1, 10–14 (1995) (citing statistics demonstrating the extent of violence in the homes: "Forty-one percent of all women who are murdered are murdered by their husband; violence is the leading cause of injury to women between the ages of fifteen and forty-four, more common than car accidents and cancer deaths combined"; and "in 1989, more women were abused by their husbands than got married").

83. *See* Daniel H. Weinberg. United States Department of Commerce, Pub. No. P60-191, "A Brief Look at Postwar U.S. Income Inequality," *Current Population Reports: Household and Economic Studies* 1 (1996); Rodger Doyle, "Income Inequality in the U.S.," *Scientific American* (June 1999).

84. Urie Brofenbrenner et al., *The State of Americans* 56 (Free Press, 1996).

85. Center for the Future of Children, "Executive Summary," *The Future of Children: Children and Poverty,* Summer/Fall 1997, at 2–3.

86. Lee Rainwater and Timothy M. Smeeding, "Doing Poorly: The Real Income of American Children in a Comparative Perspective" (Luxembourg Income Study Working Paper No. 127, 1995).

87. *Id.* at 10.

88. *Id.* at 21.

89. *Id.*

90. Council on Civil Society, *supra* note 1, at 4. Perhaps this attention to inequality reflects the fact that one of the Council's sponsors is the University of Chicago Divinity School.

91. *Id.*

92. *Id.* at 5.

93. *Id.* at 7.

94. National Commission on Civic Renewal, *supra* note 2, at 24.

95. *See* Brofenbrenner, *supra* note 84, at 56; Weinberg, *supra* note 83, at 1; Doyle, *supra* note 83.

96. Kathryn Larin and Elizabeth McNichol, Center on Budget and Policy Priorities, "Pulling Apart: A State-by-State Analysis of Income Trends," www.cbpp.org/pa-4.htm (visited June 1, 2003).

97. National Commission on Civic Renewal, *supra* note 2, at 24.

98. Brofenbrenner, *supra* note 84, at 66.

99. *Id.*

100. *See* Nina Bernstein, "Poverty Rate Persists Despite Boom: Twice as High as Nation. Analysis of Data Shows," *New York Times*, October 7, 1999, at B1.

101. Jeanne Brooks-Gunn and Greg J. Duncan, "The Effects of Poverty on Children," *The Future of Children: Children and Poverty*, Summer/Fall 1997, at 55.

102. Center for the Future of Children, *supra* note 85, at 3.

103. *Id.*

104. Brooks-Gunn and Duncan, *supra* note 101, at 57. This report collects and assesses the available research in regard to each of these dimensions of the well-being of children in poverty. The authors conclude that income can substantially influence children's well-being, finding that the associations between income and child outcomes are more complex and varied than is suggested in simple tables. "Family income seems to be more strongly related to children's ability and achievement-related outcomes than to emotional outcomes. In addition, the effects are particularly pronounced for children who live below the poverty line for multiple years and for children who live in extreme poverty." *Id.* at 67–8.

105. Caplow, *supra* note 47, at 59.

106. *Id.*

107. *Id.* Even two-parent families are experiencing poverty, so revering the two-parent family as an ideal economic unit is not the answer.

108. Kristin Downey Grimsley and Jacqueline L. Salmon, "For Working Parents, Mixed News at Home: Children Praise Them but Note Stress," *Washington Post*, September 27, 1999, at A1.

109. *Id.*

110. *Id.*

111. *Id.*

112. A recent study by Cornell sociologist Phyllis Moen reports that couples that feel burdened by long work hours, demanding jobs, and conflict between work and personal life report the lowest quality of life among working couples surveyed. *See* "Working Couples Burdened by Time at Work Say Their Lives Are Beset by Stress, Conflict and Overload, Cornell Sociologist Reports," *Cornell University News, at* www.news.cornell.edu/releases/Jan99/AAAS.couples. strategies.html (last visited June 1, 2003).

113. Richard K. Caputo, "Economic Well-Being in a Youth Cohort," *Families in Society: The Journal of Contemporary Human Services,* January 1, 1998, at 83.

114. John Ehrenberg, *Civil Society: The Critical History of an Idea* 246 (New York University Press, 1999), 240.

115. *Id.* at 247.

116. *Id.*

117. *See* Lugalia, *supra* note 45.

Chapter Four: Why Marriage?

1. Predictability is one of the major objectives of family law reform. *See* American Law Institute, *Principles of the Law of Family Dissolution: Analysis and Recommendations* (May 16, 2000), 42.

2. "Developments in the Law: Legal Responses to Domestic Violence" 106 *Harvard Law Review* 1498, 1501–04, 1528–29, 1534–43 (1993); Harry D. Krause et al., *Family Law: Cases, Comments and Questions* 152 (West Group, 4th ed., 1998) (under common law, a husband and wife cannot sue each other in tort).

3. *Trammel v. United States,* 445 U.S. 40 (1980); *see also* Frances E. Olson, "The Family and the Market: A Study of Ideology and Legal Reform," 96 *Harvard Law Review* 1497, 1504–05 (1983).

4. She may be able to use the doctrine of "necessaries" if she is able to persuade a third person, such as a merchant, to provide her with essential goods or services without her husband's consent and knowledge. In those instances, however, the action is the merchant's, not the spouse's. D. Kelly Weisberg and Susan Frelich Appleton, *Modern Family Law: Cases and Materials* 262–5 (Aspen, 2nd ed., 2002).

5. *See McGuire v. McGuire,* 157 Neb. 226 (Sup. Ct. of Neb. 1953), *discussed in* Martha Albertson Fineman, "What Place for Family Privacy?" 67 *George Washington Law Review* 1207, 1209 (1999).

6. *See* Lloyd Cohen, "Rhetoric, the Unnatural Family, and Women's Work," 81 *Virginia Law Review* 2275, 2286 (1995). I think this argument raises an important empirical question—do men crave intimacy, not only sexual, but that of the connection with children? I believe they do, but are hampered in acting on that need in today's society, which assigns them to the workplace as the economic provider.

7. *See also* Randy Thornhill and Craig Palmer, *A Natural History of Rape: Biological Basis of Sexual Coercion* (MIT Press, 2000).

8. *Prince v. Massachusetts,* 321 U.S. 158 (1994). Note that most of the debate about the state's interest in precluding same-sex couples from the institution of marriage focused on the negative effect this would have on children (this was true in both the Hawaii and Vermont cases). The other arguments focused on the possibility that same-sex marriage would weaken "real" marriage as an institution.

9. 127 U.S. 190, 205–6 (1888) ("[M]arriage, as creating the most important relation in life [has] more to do with the morals and civilization of a people than any other institution . . .").

10. 98 U.S. 145, 165 (1878) ("Upon it society may be said to be built, and out of its fruits spring social relations and societal obligations and duties, with which government is necessarily required to deal").

11. Benjamin Franklin: "only a virtuous people are capable of freedom." Samuel Adams: "neither the wisest constitution nor the wisest laws will secure the liberty and happiness of a people whose manners are universally corrupt." John Adams: "our constitution was made only for a moral and religious people. It is wholly inadequate to the government of any other." As quoted in Lynn Wardle, "The Bonds of Matrimony and the Bonds of Constitutional Democracy," draft of comments made at Hofstra University, March 5, 2003 (on file with author), 3.

12. *Id.*

13. *Id.*

14. *Baker v. State,* 744 A.2d 864 (Vt. 1999) (holding that the State of Vermont may not exclude same-sex couples from the benefits and protections that its laws provide to opposite-sex married couples).

15. As the Hawaii Supreme Court noted in *Baehr v. Lewin,* benefits associated with marriage may include (1) a variety of state income tax advan-

tages, including deductions, credits, rates, exemptions, and estimates; (2) public assistance from and exemptions relating to the Department of Human Services; (3) control, division, acquisition, and disposition of community property; (4) rights relating to dower, curtsey, and inheritance; (5) rights to notice, protection, benefits, and inheritance; (6) award of child custody and support payments in divorce proceedings; (7) the right to spousal support; (8) the right to enter into premarital agreements; (9) the right to change of name; (10) the right to file a nonsupport action; (11) post-divorce rights relating to support and property division; (12) the benefit of the spousal privilege and confidential marital communications; (13) the benefit of the exemption of real property from attachment or execution; and (14) the right to bring a wrongful death action. *Baehr v. Lewin* 74 Hawaii 530 (1993).

16.   Some of the critics of civil unions in Vermont, where it is now legal, cite religious belief. *See* Julie Deardorff, "Vermont Is Front Line of Gay Marriage Fight," *Chicago Tribune,* April 3, 2001, at 1. The use of history and tradition is more common. *See also Bowers v. Hardwick* and state court decisions in the 1970s limiting marriages to heterosexuals often assumed marriage was by definition between a man and a woman; Martha Chamallas, *Introduction to Feminist Legal Theory* 265–6 (Aspen Law & Business, 1999), citing *Baker v. Nelson,* 191 N.W.2d 185 (Minn. 1971), *Jones v. Hallahan,* 501 S.W.2d 588 (Ky. 1973), *Singer v. Hara,* 522 P.2d 1187 (Wash. Ct. App. 1974).

17.   *See also Baker v. State,* 170 Vt. 194 (1999); *Baehr v. Lewin,* 74 Haw. 530 (1993).

18.   *Baehr v. Lewin,* 74 Haw. 530 (1993).

19.   James A. Henderson Jr., Richard N. Pearson, and John A. Siliciano, *The Torts Process* (Aspen Publishers, Inc., 5th ed., 1999) (duty to rescue as contrasted with strangers); Krause et al., *Cases, Comments and Questions* 157 (West Group, 4th ed., 1998). *See also State v. Mally,* 139 Mont. 599 (1961); *State v. Smith,* 65 Me. 257 (1876) (spouses have an affirmative obligation to obtain medical assistance for each other); *McGuire v. McGuire,* 157 Neb. 226 (Sup. Ct. of Neb. 1953) (duty to financially support one's spouse).

20.   *See Griswold v. Connecticut,* 381 U.S. 479 (1965); *McGuire v. McGuire,* 157 Neb. 226 (Sup. Ct. of Neb. 1953).

21.   John Demos, "Images of the American Family, Then and Now," in *Changing Images of the Family* 43–60 (Virginia Tufte and Barbara Myerhoff, eds., 1979).

22.   *See* Lynn D. Wardle. "A Critical Analysis of Constitutional Claims

for Same-Sex Marriage," 1996 *BYU Law Review* 1; Curt Pham. "Let's Get Married in Hawaii: A Story of Conflicting Laws, Same-Sex Couples, and Marriage," 30 *Family Law Quarterly* 727 (1996); Linda Nielsen, "Family Rights and the Registered Partnership in Denmark," 4 *The International Journal of Law and the Family* 297 (1990).

23. Tavia Simmons and Martin O'Connell, "Married-Couple and Unmarried-Partner Households: 2000," Census 2000 Special Reports, U.S. Census Bureau (issued February 2003); Jason Fields and Lynne M. Casper, "America's Families and Living Arrangements: March 2001," *Current Population Reports*, 20–537 (2001). Commentators point out that this can be the result of a number of factors, such as couples' living longer after their adult children have "left the nest," many men and women delaying marriage and children until they are older than in previous generations, and the relatively more rapid growth of single-parent families over those of married parents.

24. Families headed by single mothers account for nearly 7 percent of all households. Single-mother families increased from 3 million in 1970 to 10 million in 2000. *See* Jason Fields, "Living Arrangments of Children," *Current Population Reports* (1996).

25. Simmons and O'Connell, *supra* note 23, at 1.

26. *See* Fields, *supra* note 24.

27. *Id.*

28. Simmons and O'Connell, *supra* note 23, at 1.

29. The categories of relatives include husband/wife, natural-born son/daughter, adopted son/daughter, stepson/stepdaughter, brother/sister, father/mother, grandchild, parent-in-law, son-in-law/daughter-in-law, and "other relative—print exact relationship." The categories of nonrelatives include roomer/boarder, housemate/roommate, unmarried partner, foster child, and other nonrelatives.

30. *Id.*

31. This book focuses on heterosexual marital relationships simply because family law and our political sense of family have been organized around that particular intimate configuration. Same-sex couples are organizing around demands for access to marriage, and this is increasingly a topic of scholarship.

32. *See* Simmons and O'Connell, *supra* note 28.

33. *Maynard v. Hill*, 125 US 190 (1887).

34. *Feliciano v. Rosemar Silver Co.*, 514 N.E.2d 1095, 1097 (1987).

35. Personal Responsibility and Work Opportunity Reconciliation Act of 1996, §101, 1996 HR 3734 (1996).

36. Geraldine Sealey, "Marriage Proposal Debate Looms over Bush Plan to Spend $300 Million Promoting Unions," *at* abcnews.go.com/sections/us/dailynews/marriage020305.html (visited June 1, 2003).

37. Krause et al., *supra* note 2, at 47.

38. *Id.*

39. Krause et al., *supra* note 2, at 533 (on annulment); Lawrence M. Friedman, *A History of American Law* 204–08, 498–504 (Simon and Schuster, 2d ed., 1988) (on desertion).

40. Krause et al., *supra* note 2, at 534.

41. Weisberg and Appleton, *supra* note 4, at 533. In any case, such a bill would only have been available to the wealthiest members of society.

42. *Id.* at 533–4.

43. "Cause" could include adultery (in New York this was the only cause that justified divorce in 1787), as well as "impotence, adultery, intolerable severity, three years' willful desertion, and long absence with presumption of death" (Vermont in 1798) and "gross misbehavior and wickedness in either of the parties, repugnant to and in violation of the marriage covenant" (Rhode Island). *Id.* at 534.

44. *See* Krause et al., *supra* note 2, at 534.

45. *Muhammad v. Muhammad*, 622 So.2d 1239 (Miss. 1993). *See also* Weisberg and Appleton, *supra* note 4, at 549. The supposed special nature of the marital family is also significant outside of family law. Many other areas of law incorporate and utilize the concept of the family—tort, criminal, and property laws have historically distinguished family relationships from those of "strangers" and established exceptions or alternatives to the general rules for family members. Such exceptions include the marital rape exemption and various spousal privileges—domestic violence, tort immunity, fornication, adultery, cohabitation, etc. These exceptions and alternatives are based on the belief that a family connection signifies a special relationship, one that justifies a different regulatory regime.

46. *See* Krause et al., *supra* note 2, at 534. *See also* Glenda Riley, *Divorce: An American Tradition* 8–29 (University of Nebraska Press, 1991).

47. *Loving v. Virginia*, 388 U.S. 1 (1967) (the trial judge's opinion stated, "Almighty God created the races white, black, yellow, Malay and red, and

he placed them on separate continents. And but for the interference with his arrangement there would be no cause for such marriages. The fact that he separated the races shows that he did not intend for the races to mix . . ."); *Potter v. Murray City,* 760 F.2d 1065 (10th Cir. 1985), *cert. denied,* 474 U.S. 849 (1988) ("monogamy is inextricably woven into the fabric of our society. It is the bedrock upon which our culture is built").

48. *Bradwell v. Illinois,* 83 US 130 (1873) (saying a woman cannot get admitted to the Illinois bar).

49. Blackstone, Commentaries 442–5.

50. *See generally Graham v. Graham,* 33 F. Supp. 936, 938 (E.D. Mich. 1940) (holding that a contract between spouses to change the roles of husband and wife—the essential incidents of the marriage—is void).

51. Beatrice Gottlieb, *The Family in the Western World: From the Black Death to the Industrial Age* 90–92 (Oxford University Press, 1993).

52. Krause et al., *supra* note 2, at 152.

53. *See generally* June Carbone and Margaret Brinig, "Rethinking Marriage: Feminist Ideology, Economic Change and Divorce Reform," 65 *Tulane Law Review* 953 (1991).

54. Lenore J. Weitzman, *The Divorce Revolution* 74, 164–7 (Free Press, 1985); *Wirth v. Wirth,* 38 A.D.2d 611 (App. Div. 1971).

Chapter Five: The Future of Marriage

1. In recent years, it seems there has been a rise in orthodoxy in Jewish and Christian religions that is very marital family–based and biased. Indeed, religious imagery and sensibilities about the institution are more frequently explicitly finding their ways into policy discussions under the presidency of George W. Bush.

2. "[1] The right of citizens of the United States to vote shall not be denied or abridged by the United States or by any State on account of sex." U.S. Constitutional Amendment XIX.

3. Grace Raymond Hebard, "The First Woman Jury," 7 *The Journal of American History* 1293, 1302–03 (1913); Joanna L. Grossman. "Women's Jury Service: Right of Citizenship or Privilege of Difference?" 46 *Stanford Law Review* 1115, 1131 (1994).

4. *J.E.B. v. T.B.,* 114 S.Ct. 1419 (1994).

5. "Law in Fifty States: Case Digests" 30 *Family Law Quarterly* 811 (1997).

6. *See* D. Kelly Weisberg and Susan Frelich Appleton, *Modern Family Law: Cases and Materials* 284–5. (Aspen, 2nd ed., 2002). *See also Samuel v. University of Pittsburgh,* 375 F. Supp. 1119 (W.D. Pa. 1974), decision to decertify class vacated (invalidating, on equal protection grounds, university residency rules that assigned the husband's domicile to the wife for determination of tuition); Restatement (Second) of Conflict of Laws § 21 (Supp. 1988) ("rules for the acquisition of a domicile of choice are the same for both married and unmarried persons").

7. *Stratton v. Wilson,* 185 S.W. 522, 532 (1916).

8. *Edwardson v. Edwardson,* Supreme Court of Kentucky, 798 S.W.2d 941 (1990). *See also* Uniform Premarital Agreement Act (UPAA), 9C U.L.A. 35 (2001) (premarital agreements are valid unless they are "unconscionable").

9. *Simeone v. Simeone,* 581 A.2d 162 (Pa. 1990).

10. *Edwardson v. Edwardson,* 798 S.W.2d 941 (1990) (quoting *Clark v. Clark,* 192 S.W.2d 968, 970 [1946]).

11. *Button v. Button,* 388 N.W.2d 546 (Wis. 1986).

12. *In Re Marriage of Greenwald,* 454 N.W.2d 34 (Wis. Ct. App. 1990).

13. American Law Institute, "Principles of the Law of Family Dissolution: Analysis and Recommendations" (Tentative Draft No. 4, April 10, 2000) Chapter 7 (Agreements), Topic 2 (Requirements for an Enforceable Agreement), §7.05 (Procedural Requirements), 88.

14. *Id.*

15. It also recognizes, however, that the state might want to reserve the right to oversee and amend these agreements in conformance with public policy to a much greater degree than is permitted with commercial contracts that arise in the public sphere of the market.

16. *Marvin v. Marvin,* 557 P.2d 106 (Cal. 1976).

17. American Law Institute, *supra* note 13, Chapter 6 (Domestic Partners), § 6.05 (Allocation of Domestic-Partnership Property), 55. ("Domestic-partnership property should be divided according to the principles set forth for the division of marital property in § 4.15 and § 4.16.")

18. *Baker v. State,* 744 A.2d 864 (Vt. 1999).

19. American Law Institute, *supra* note 13 § 6.01 (Scope), 1.

20. *Id.* § 6.03 (Determination that Persons are Domestic Partners).

21. www.promisekeepers.org/faqs/core/faqscore24.htm (visited June 1, 2003).

22. www.now.org/issues/right/promise/mythfact.html (visited June 1, 2003).

23. Ephesians 5 (Darby translation).

24. www.baptist2baptist.net.

25. This discussion of the Southern Baptists is based on an article by Chad Brand, Ph.D., "Christ-Centered Marriages: Husbands and Wives Complementing One Another" (September 1998) *at* www.baptist2baptist. net (visited June 1, 2003) (material on this site is described as "information and inspiration on issues of importance to Baptists . . . from supporters of the Southern Baptist Convention").

26. *Id.* at 3.

27. *Id.* at 4 (emphasis in original).

28. www.now.org/issues/right/promise/quotes.html (visited June 1, 2003).

29. Laura Sanchez, "The Implementation of Covenant Marriage in Louisiana." *Virginia Journal of Social Policy and the Law,* 9(1) 194 (Fall 2001).

30. La. Rev. Stat. Ann. § 9:273(A).

31. Sanchez, *supra* note 29, at 221.

32. Jason Fields and Lynne M. Casper, "America's Families and Living Arrangements: March 2001," *Current Population Reports* P20-537 (2001).

33. This is common with prenuptial agreements and doctrinally required (even if not typically practiced) with settlement agreements.

34. I am uncommitted to any particular set of principles for these default rules at this time. The only requirement would be that they apply to all types of transactions between legally competent adults and that specific categories of affiliation not be segregated for different treatment.

35. In the past, certain types of domestic violence were not even considered criminal behavior. Husbands had not only a right, but also a duty to chastise and punish wives and children. Physical chastisement was considered appropriate as long as it did not exceed certain limits. This principle is often suggested as the basis for the "rule of thumb" reform in which a man was admonished not to beat his wife with a rod thicker than his thumb.

36. There are some moves to do this in the context of divorce already. *See Ruprecht v. Ruprecht,* 252 N.J.Super.230, 599 A.2d 604 (Ch. Div. 1991) (allowing for suit for intentional infliction of emotional harm without physical injury in the context of a divorce). *See also Hakkila v. Hakkila,* 112 N.M. 172, 812 P.2d 1320 (App. 1991).

37. Other areas of law that would substitute for (or be supplemented by) the abolition of marriage and divorce rules would include bankruptcy, fiduciary responsibility, equity, and ethics.

38. The exceptions to this general principle should be obvious—rape and child molestation would still be prohibited and punished by law; criminal and civil law would still restrict and limit coercive or exploitive sexual acts.

39. This method of reproduction might be preferred once such restraints were removed. It avoids any questions about "consent" vis-à-vis the sperm donor since he would have alienated his interest in his contribution of reproductive material by his donation to the sperm bank.

40. This is particularly true in modern family law jurisprudence, in which marriage is referred to as a "partnership" and some of the economic consequences may be tailored to individual preferences through prenuptial contracts and/or separation agreements.

41. More specifically, these areas were set aside and governed by special rules regulating marriage.

42. Historically, reasons for annulment had to do with sex and reproduction. Typical grounds included inability to consummate the relationship, lying about pregnancy or about fertility, having a venereal disease, and so on. The ability to function in an appropriate manner sexually is considered by the law to be an "essential" aspect of the marriage relationship. Without that ability, the courts could determine that a real marriage had not taken place—it was void.

43. *People v. Liberta,* 474 N.E.2d 567 (N.Y. 1984), *cert. denied,* 471 U.S. 1020 (1985) (holding that the marital exemption for rape no longer applies).

44. I Hale P.C. 629, as quoted in *Warren v. State,* 336 S.E.2d 221 (1985).

45. These rules include not only the laws of marriage and divorce, but also large areas of criminal and civil law that bolster the institution of marriage and penalize sexual affiliations that do not conform to the marriage model, e.g., laws against prostitution, fornication, adultery, and cohabitation, as well as inheritance and probate laws, property rules, and tax laws

that treat economic exchanges between marital partners differently than those that occur between other members of society.

46. Kant struggled with the idea that rights to persons are akin to rights to things—describing marital or family status as entailing "neither [a right] to a thing nor merely a right against a person but also possession of a person . . ." Kant described the objects to be acquired as three: "a man acquires a wife, a couple acquires children, and a family acquires servants." We are also told that "whatever is acquired in this way is also inalienable and [that] the right of possessors of these objects is the more personal of all rights." One outgrowth of the (obviously patriarchal) assertion that what is acquired in marriage is a woman (wife) by a possessor (husband or man) was the common-law rule that marriage was a defense to rape. Fortunately, the system of obligations and entitlements thus built has been undermined. This undermining would seem to beg a reexamination of other basic principles and assumptions.

47. The prospect of opening up all these areas to reconsideration presents exciting possibilities for reexamination of whole areas of substantive law in which assumptions about interactions between independent, equal, and autonomous individuals govern terms and consequences. This project, however, is beyond the scope of this book, which has as its task the reevaluation of the relationship among societal institutions in regard to dependency.

48. Robert Mnookin and Lewis Kornhauser, "Bargaining in the Shadow of the Law: The Case of Divorce," 88 *Yale Law Journal* 950 (1979), 951, 954–7.

49. *Levy v. Louisiana*, Supreme Court of the United States, 1968, 88 S.Ct. 1509, 20 L.Ed.2d 436 (denial of damages to "illegitimate" children as a result of the wrongful death of their mother is a violation of the Equal Protection clause of the Fourteenth Amendment).

50. *Gomez v. Perez*, 409 U.S. 535, 93 S.Ct. 872, 35 L.Ed.2d 56 (1973) (nonmarital child has a right to paternal support); *Weber v. Aetna Casualty & Surety Co.*, 406 U.S. 164, 92 S.Ct. 1400, 31 L.Ed.2d 768 (1972) (state law that denied worker's compensation benefits to nonmarital dependent children is a violation of the Equal Protection and Due Process clauses of the Fourteenth Amendment); *Levy v. Louisiana*, 391 U.S. 68 (1968).

51. *Clark v. Jeter*, 486 U.S. 456 (1988).

Equality and Family

1. Harry D. Krause et al., *Family Law: Cases, Comments and Questions* 113 (4th ed., West Group, 1998).

2. *Ferguson v. Ferguson*, 639 So.2d 921 (Miss. 1994) (en banc).

3. D. Kelly Weisberg and Susan Frelich Appleton, *Modern Family Law: Cases and Materials* 663 (Aspen Law and Business, 2nd ed., 2002).

4. This is manifest in the historic designation of the "separate spheres" in common law. The family and other institutions of care and altruism occupied the private (female) sphere, while the market and state were in the public (male) domain. See *Bradwell v. Illinois*, 83 U.S. (16 Wall.) 130, 132 (1873) (Bradley, J., concurring) (commenting "[t]hat God designed the sexes to occupy different spheres of action, and that it belonged to men to make, apply, and execute the laws").

5. A traditional family is typically imagined: a husband and wife—formally married and living together—with their biological children. The husband performs as the head of the household, providing economic support and discipline for the dependent wife and children, who correspondingly owe him duties of obedience and respect.

6. Marriage has shaped women's dependency responsibilities. Their caretaking responsibilities often prevent them from being able to take advantage of opportunities in the workplace. Traditionally, the uncompensated tasks of caretaking are placed with women while men pursue careers that provide economically for the family but also enhance their individual career or work prospects.

7. Women's Rights Convention, "Declaration of Sentiments," 1848.

8. Frances E. Olsen, "The Myth of State Intervention in the Family," 18 *University of Michigan Journal of Law Reform* 835 (1985).

9. *See, e.g.,* Uniform Marriage and Divorce Act (UMDA) §§ 205, 207 (amended 1971 and 1973), 9A U.L.A. 181, 183 (1998) (limiting the ability of minors to marry and prohibiting marriages between close relations—siblings or parent and child, respectively).

10. *See, e.g.,* Uniform Marital Property Act § 4, 9A U.L.A. 116 (1998) (classifying property of spouses).

11. Catherine A. MacKinnon, "*Roe v. Wade:* A Study in Male Ideology," in *Abortion: Moral and Legal Perspective* 45 (Jay L. Garfield and Patricia Hennessey, eds., 1984).

12. *Id.* at 53.

13. *See generally* Catherine A. MacKinnon, *Toward a Feminist Theory of the State* (Harvard University Press, 1989).

14. *See generally* Martha Fineman and Roxanne Mykitiuak, *The Public Nature of Private Violence* (Routledge, 1994). Increasingly, such critiques have been accepted, and intervention in certain domestic situations has become more common. There has been a change in the way society reacts to spousal violence, for example. Marital exemptions to rape statutes have been successfully attacked and repealed in many states. Police are trained to respond to domestic calls and to take them seriously or risk legal responses. Sexual intimacy is no longer considered to carry with it a corresponding right to rape or batter. This change in societal perception about male family prerogative is largely the result of the feminist movement and its egalitarian premises. I do not mean to imply that there is now freedom from abuse in intimate situations; rather I want to indicate that the ideological underpinnings for such violence have been successfully challenged.

15. *Id.* at 193.

16. *See* Anita Allen, "Privacy at Home: The Twofold Problem," in *Revisioning the Political: Feminist Reconstructions of Traditional Concepts in Western Political Theory* 193 (Nancy J. Hirschmann et al., eds., Westview Press, 1996).

17. *Id.* at 194.

18. *Id.* at 209, n. 1.

19. *Id.* at 201.

20. *Id.* at 198.

21. *Id.* at 205. Allen's position seems to be that reproduction and caretaking functions subvert women's positive liberty interests in solitude, self-satisfaction, and fulfillment.

Chapter Six: Feminism and the Family: Implementing Equality, Achieving Autonomy

1. Theoretical and conceptual differences make sweeping generalizations difficult. By contrast, those outside of feminism tend to collapse the divisions and divides and cast all the sisters the same. I make this observation because, for the most part, nonfeminist legal scholars remain ignorant of the differences among feminists and feminisms. This is not the same as

stating that feminism is ignored. One can find at least some token gesture to a feminist perspective in liberal scholarship in virtually all academic areas. But knowledge of feminism remains rudimentary. A few well-worn ideas attributed to a few well-recognized names may be a marginal part of the discourse, but beyond this, most legal scholars seem unfamiliar with the rich and varied work that has been produced by feminists over the past several decades.

2. Recent feminist literature in a variety of disciplines has focused on this process. *See* Judith Butler, *Gender Trouble* xiv–xv (Routledge, 1999).

3. There is no recognition that there may be more than two sexes, let alone many variations and combinations of gender attributes.

4. *Brown v. Board of Education*, 347 U.S. 483 (1954).

5. Ruth Bader Ginsburg, "Sex Equality and the Constitution," 52 *Tulane Law Review* 451 (1978).

6. The feminist legal theorist's story is similar to that of nonlegal feminists. Barrie Thorne asserts that in the so-called first wave of feminism, patriarchal laws, such as those that gave husbands control over wives' bodies and property, occasioned outrage and generated calls for reform. In the second wave (which occurred in the mid-twentieth century), feminists explicitly analyzed the family as a site of oppression and inequality. The family under such consideration was identified as both an idealized household arrangement and an ideology. Barrie Thorne, "Feminism and the Family," in *Rethinking the Family* 7 (1992).

7. 83 U.S. 130 (1873) (plaintiff denied admission to the bar solely because of her sex).

8. Of course we no longer think about marriage or women in the common-law terms—we have undergone a gender-equality revolution. Women are now found in the profession of law, as well as in the nursery. The model for femaleness is no longer as rigidly defined as it was in the nineteenth century. Women can now occupy traditional male spaces, such as the military and the boxing ring, without forfeiting their claim to womanliness. Nonetheless, many feminists would argue that marriage, as the site of what has been considered to be the most intimate connection between women and men, continues to play an important ideological and institutional role. Our beliefs about marriage shape our understandings of masculinity and femininity today, as they did in the past. In turn, our beliefs about masculinity and femininity shape the expectations and aspirations we have for ourselves and others—expectations and aspirations that

remain gendered. In this regard, marriage, tied to the foundational institution of the family, remains central to the way we understand and assess other societal institutions, and is in need of feminist analysis and critique.

9. *See* Elizabeth M. Schneider, "The Violence of Privacy," 23 *Connecticut Law Review* 973, 985–9 (1991).

10. *See Roe v. Wade,* 410 U.S. 113 (1973).

11. Katherine T. Bartlett, "Feminism and Family Law," 33 *Family Law Quarterly* 475, 475 (1999).

12. *Id.* at 500 (noting also that "the least divisive issues in family law, such as domestic violence, have been those that have been resolved by reference to familiar principles outside of family law. By the same token, the most visible conflicts outside family law, such as the debate among feminists over maternity leave, have related to gender roles").

13. *Id.*

14. *See id.* at 475. Bartlett addresses the tensions within feminism in regard to the areas she does discuss. In doing so, she of necessity also touches on marriage and the child-support system (which is the privatized solution for economic dependency and, therefore, tied to any discussion of welfare). Perhaps this demonstrates how difficult it is to address any one area of central concern in family law without bumping into others, because they are related conceptually and politically as well as in practice.

15. *Id.*

16. This is not to suggest that there is no sex discrimination remaining in the workplace. Rather, the nature or character of discrimination has changed. It is not the fact of being a woman that typically places one in the margins of the workplace, but the culturally and socially imposed consequences of sex (gender) that are incompatible with the culture of the workforce.

17. *See* Arlie Russell Hochschild, *The Time Bind: When Work Becomes Home and Home Becomes Work* 117–21 (Metropolitan Books, 1997) (men who asked for parental leave were seen as not dedicated to their career); *see also* Gene Koretz, "Hazardous to Your Career: The Risks of Taking Unpaid Leaves," *Business Week,* January 17, 2000, at 26.

18. Marilyn J. Essex and Marjorie H. Klein, "The Wisconsin Parental Leave Study: The Role of Fathers" in *Parental Leave and Child Care: Setting a Research and Policy Agenda* (Janet Shibley Hyde and Marilyn J. Essex, eds., Temple University Press, 1991).

19. These concepts helped to make it clear that historically the law has treated women unequally and unjustly in the contexts of divorce, reproduction, and family violence, contexts in which women were victimized to begin with. These contexts are also areas in which we are clear(er) about our aspirations for society and its institutions in regard to women's quest for equality. Victor R. Fuchs, *Women's Quest for Economic Equality* (Harvard University Press, 1988), 72 (noting that despite equality, children are still predominately the concern of women).

20. These concepts of unequal worth and unequal ability are very difficult to discuss in noncondescending or -patronizing ways. *See* Barbara Bennett Woodhouse, "The Dark Side of Family Privacy," 67 *George Washington Law Review* 1247, 1250, n. 21 (1999) (advocating use of the "stewardship" model and the "notion of children's 'need-based rights' ").

21. *Foundations of the Economic Approach to Law* 410 (Avery Wiener Katz, ed., 1998).

22. *Id.* at 410–11.

23. *Id.* at 411.

24. *Id.*

25. *Id.* Katz states that, due to the complexity inherent in the family, some may see economic modeling as inappropriate. In this regard, he recognizes there are "competing disciplines," specifically psychology and biology. Feminism is not mentioned as a competing discipline.

26. This does not mean that economists have not used their model to predict and explain family behavior or to argue for policy (*see, e.g.,* Gary Becker). *Id.* at 410–39.

27. *See* Martha A. Fineman, "Masking Dependency: The Political Role of Family Rhetoric," 81 *Virginia Law Review* 2181, 2208–9 (1995).

28. Women of all marital statuses without children earn on average $467 a week, compared to $552 earned by similarly situated men. When women, again of all marital statuses, have children under eighteen, their weekly earnings fall to $440. Surprisingly, though, when men have children under the age of eighteen, their earnings increase to $663 per week. The addition of children to a family increases the wage gap to 84 cents per dollar from 66 cents per dollar. Thus, although policies of equality have worked to decrease income gaps in the workplace, families have not yet adopted models of equality. Women still bear the cost of having children. Labor force statistics from the Current Population Survey, "Highlight of

Women's Earnings in 1998," *available at* www.bls.gov/cps/cpswom98.htm (visited June 1, 2003).

29. Martha Minow, "Introduction: Finding Our Paradoxes, Affirming Our Beyond," 24 *Harvard Civil Rights-Civil Liberties Law Review* 1, 2–4 (1989).

30. *Id.*

31. Wendy W. Williams, "The Equality Crisis: Some Reflections of Culture, Courts, and Feminism," 7 *Women's Rights Law Reporter* 175, 196, 200 (1982).

Chapter Seven: Mothering in a Gender-Neutral World

1. *See* Martha Albertson Fineman, *The Illusion of Equality: The Rhetoric and Reality of Divorce Reform* (University of Chicago Press, 1991) for a description of this phenomenon, especially chapter four, "Embracing Equality: A Case Study," 53–75.

2. " . . . until the division of household labor and child care is more nearly equalized, the revolution in the family will remain unfinished." Bart Landry, *Black Working Wives: Pioneers of the American Family Revolution* 190 (University of California Press, 2000); *see also* Scott Coltrane, *Family Man: Fatherhood, Housework, and Gender Equity* 197 (Oxford University Press, 1996).

3. The language of the recent TANF bill requires that the states assess the employability of each work-eligible individual receiving assistance and establish a self-sufficiency plan to assist the family in achieving its "maximum degree of self-sufficiency." Personal Responsibility, Work, and Family Promotion Act of 2002, H.R. 4737, 107th Cong. § 109b (2002).

4. *See* Scott Coltrane, "Gender, Culture, and Fatherhood," in *Family Man* 177–98 (1996) for a discussion of this argument.

5. *See* Linda J. Waite and Maggie Gallagher, *The Case for Marriage: Why Married People Are Happier, Healthier and Better Off Financially* 102–103 (Broadway Books, 2000) on the explanation that marriage allows men to specialize in making money, and that this is perhaps due to their greater willingness to put their careers first.

6. This was a favorite suggestion of Newt Gingrich.

7. Personal Responsibility, Work, and Family Promotion Act, *supra* note 3, §103b.

8. *See* Sally Sheldon, *Terminating Men's Child Support Obligations? Abortion,*

Unwilling Fathers and Child Support 17 (unpublished manuscript, on file with author).

9. *See* Deborah Belle, *The After-School Lives of Children: Alone and With Others While Parents Work* 77 (Lawrence Erlbaum Associates, 1999).

10. *See* Ross D. Parke and Armin A. Brott, *Throwaway Dads: The Myths and Barriers that Keep Men from Being the Fathers They Want to Be* 59 (Houghton Mifflin, 1999).

11. One group of fathers' rights activists goes so far as saying that the feminist movement is a reemergence of the Women's Ku Klux Klan of the early 1900s, and that, as a result of it and of deeply rooted sexism, fathers are being driven from their homes and families. *See* Dads NOW, "Sexism in America," *at* www.dadsnow.org (visited June 1, 2003) (the Dads NOW motto reads: "We must now grant fathers the same rights to be in the family as we have granted to women in the workplace").

12. At the turn of the century, family law reform was also related to women's push for equality. Ironically, in attacking the rule of father custody, feminists of that era privileged motherhood by casting caretaking as gendered work that is deserving of recognition in custody determinations. Seeking to enshrine gender neutrality and equality primarily focused on women's participation in the public sphere, contemporary feminists attacked their foremothers' efforts to displace fathers' rights and foster maternal preferences for young children.

13. *See* Joseph Goldstein, Albert J. Solnit, Sonja Goldstein, and Anna Freud, *The Best Interests of the Child: The Least Detrimental Alternative* 186–89 (The Free Press, 1996).

14. *See* Waite and Gallagher, *supra* note 5, at 97.

15. It should be obvious that even in situations in which both parents work, typically one assumes primary responsibility for securing, organizing, and supervising alternative care and is the one who steps in if glitches or crises disrupt such arrangements.

16. *Linda R. v. Richard E.*, 162 A.D.2d 48, 561 N.Y.S.2d 29 (1990).

17. *See* Joseph Goldstein et al., "Why Should the Child's Interests be Paramount?" in *Best Interests* 81–82 (2000).

18. *See* Coltrane, *supra* note 2, at 106.

19. *See* Parke and Brott, *supra* note 10, at 119–20, 169–78 (going as far as blaming feminism for America's fatherlessness).

20. *See id.*

21. *See* Coltrane, *supra* note 2, at 227–8.

22. *See id.* at 102.

23. *See id.* at 103.

24. *See* Richard Collier, "Waiting Till Father Gets Home: The Reconstructing of Fatherhood in Family Law," *Social and Legal Studies* 4(1), 8 (1995) ("He [father] is marked by all the trappings of a benign and safe/domesticated masculinity—a masculinity pervaded by the dualism of a public/private divide which legitimated his absence from childcare whilst simultaneously maintaining the structural supports whence he derived his economic power").

25. The traditional male preoccupation with the workplace has also been characterized as "breadwinner masculinity." Men are seen as economic providers and women are seen as caretakers. The law sanctions the philosophy of male physical absence from the family in order to make money. *See* Collier, *supra* note 24, at 8.

26. *See* Parke and Brott, "Lazy Dads and Deadbeat Dads," in *Throwaway Dads, supra* note 10, at 65–9.

27. *See id.*

28. Ira Daniel Turkat, Ph.D., "Divorce Related Malicious Mother Syndrome" 10(3) *Journal of Family Violence* 253–64 (1995); W. J. Holly, Ph.D., "Questions and Answers on California's New Child Support Guidelines: Questions Not Frequently Asked on Guidelines (from the website of the Fathers' Rights and Equality Exchange), *at* http://dadsrights.org/fmo/ca_support.html (last visited June 1, 2003).

29. *See, e.g.,* Children's Justice, "Sample Resolution for United States Legislatures to Adopt," *at* http://childrens-justice.org/legislature.htm (last visited June 1, 2003).

30. See discussion of fatherhood and economic opportunity in Fineman, *The Neutered Mother,* 204–205.

31. This is reflected in legislative initiatives such as North Carolina's "Helping Dads" program, which focuses on incarcerated and low-income fathers. The mission statement of the program equates economic provision with positive fathering, stating that "[b]eing a good dad starts with being a good provider." *See* "Press Release: North Carolina: Helping Dads Initiative," *at* www.dhhs.state.nc.us/docs/ fathers.htm (last visited June 1, 2003).

32. *See* Landry, *supra* note 2, at 57–60, 71–2.

33. Personal Responsibility, Work, and Family Promotion Act of 2002, *supra* note 3, §103c, §109b.

34. Iris Marion Young, "Mothers, Citizenship and Independence: A Critique of Pure Family Values," 105(3) *Ethics* 535 (1995) (critiquing Galston's *Liberal Purposes*).

35. *Id.* at 537–8.

36. *Id.* at 536 (citing Galston 280).

37. *Id.* at 542 (citing Galston 285).

38. *Id.* at 545.

39. *See* Jane Jenson and Mariette Sineau, *Who Cares? Women's Work, Childcare, and Welfare State Redesign* 6–8 (University of Toronto Press, 2001).

40. *See id.* at 148–59.

41. *See* chapter two of this book.

42. Even the most liberal government initiatives that recognize the social significance of male/female roles simply recognize the roles—they do not offer a framework for change, but only make broad statements. The Colorado Initiative for Responsible Fatherhood, for example, states that in order "[t]o support fatherhood Colorado must: [r]ecognize the need and moral right of children to know and meaningfully interact with both their parents as they grow up, [h]old fathers morally, emotionally and financially responsible for the welfare of their children, [r]ecognize that a father's involvement in his child's life is multi-faceted, [p]rovide role models of responsible fathering/male behavior, [and a]ccept fathers' roles in the home just as women are accepted in the work place." *At* www.peak. org/~jedwards/COLORADO.HTM (last visited June 1, 2003).

43. *See* chapter eight of this book.

44. *See* Sheldon, *supra* note 8, at 21. Sheldon further asserts that if advocates of men's rights are serious about problems facing individual unwilling fathers, then they should also advocate that children be considered the responsibility not just of their parents, but also of society as a whole.

45. *See id.*

46. *See* Martha Albertson Fineman, "Child Support Is Not the Answer: The Nature of Dependencies and Welfare Reform," in *Child Support: The Next Frontier* 217 (J. Thomas Oldhan and Marygold S. Melli, eds., University of Michigan Press, 2000); *see also* Promise Keepers, paid advertisement, *The Ithaca Journal,* June 3, 2002, at 9A. (The advertisement depicts a

picture of a girl playing soccer, asking her mom who is the "crazy guy" in the stands cheering for her. Her mother replies that this is her father. The advertisement pledges, "Promise Keepers wants to help you be the man your family needs you to be.")

47. *See* Fineman, *supra* note 46, at 221.

48. Institute for Women's Policy Research, "Research-in-Brief" (March 1999).

49. *See* the Honorable Evelyn Lynn, "Prepared Testimony of the Honorable Evelyn Lynn," Florida House of Representatives on Behalf of the National Conference of State Legislatures Before the Senate Committee on Finance Subcommittee on Social Security and Family Policy (July 25, 2000) (LEXIS, Federal News Service) *see also* Fineman, *supra* note 46, at 217 (poor and unemployed men have trouble providing for themselves, much less a family).

50. Institute for Women's Policy Research, *supra* note 48, at 6.

Part Four: The Autonomous Individual and the Autonomous Family Within the Social Contract

1. It is interesting to note that the "private" sphere of the family is subject to heavy public regulation, mostly because it retains aspects of "status" and is not governed by contract. In contrast, bodies of designated "private" law, such as contract, govern the "public" arena of the marketplace. These contrary characterizations have ideological nuances.

2. *See generally* Sir Henry Summer Maine, Ancient Law 174 (6th prtg. 1920) (1864). ("[T]he movement of the progressive societies has hitherto been a movement *from Status to Contract*"; emphasis added.)

3. Christina Boswell, "Social Contract Theory, Global Justice and Motivation," paper for the Political Studies Association–UK 50th Annual Conference, 2000, 2, *at* www.psa.ac.uk/cps/2000/Boswell%20Christina. pdf (last visited June 1, 2003).

4. Stanford Encyclopedia of Philosophy, "Contemporary Approaches to the Social Contract," 1, *at* http://plato.stanford. edu/ entries/ contractarianism-contemporary (last visited June 1, 2003).

5. Boswell, *supra* note 3, at 3.

6. *Id.*

7. *Id.*

8. David de Carvalho, "The Social Contract Renegotiated: Protecting Public Values in the Age of Contracting," 2, *at* www.sprc.unsw.edu. au/nspc2001/NSPC%202001Papers/deCarvalho.pdf (last visited June 1, 2003).

9. Restatement (Second) of Contracts § 17 (1979) (Requirement of a Bargain—the formation of a contract requires mutual assent).

10. *See generally* Robert Nozick, *Anarchy, State, and Utopia* (Basic Books, 1974).

11. An influential exposition of this perspective is found in George Gilder, *Wealth and Poverty* 63 (Basic Books, 1981). Also illustrative are the debates concerning the revision of the welfare system. *See* Personal Responsibility and Work Opportunity Reconciliation Act of 1996, Pub. L. No. 104-103, § 101, 110 Stat. 2105, 2110–12 (1996).

12. *See generally* John Rawls, *A Theory of Justice* (Belknap Press, 1971).

13. John Locke, "An Essay Concerning the True Original, Extent, and End of Civil Government" (Chapter 11, No. 140) (George Bonham, 1798).

14. *See* Susan Moller Okin, *Justice, Gender and the Family* (Basic Books, 1989).

15. Eva Feder Kittay, *Love's Labor: Essays on Women, Equality, and Dependency* 76 (Routledge, 1998).

16. Martha L.A. Fineman, "Dependencies," in *Women and Welfare: Theory and Practice in the United States and Europe* (Nancy J. Hirschmann and Ulrike Liebert, eds., 2001); Martha L. A. Fineman, "Contract and Care" (Symposium on the Structures of Care Work) 76 *Chicago Kent Law Review* 1403–40 (2001); Martha L.A. Fineman, 'Why Marriage?' *Virginia Journal of Social Policy and the Law* 239–71 (2001); Martha L.A. Fineman, "Cracking the Foundational Myths: Independence, Autonomy, and Self-Sufficiency" (Symposium: Gender, Work and Family Project Inaugural Feminist Legal Theory Lecture) 8 *American University Journal of Gender, Social Policy and the Law* 13–29 (2000); Martha L.A. Fineman, "The Family in Civil Society" (Civil Society Symposium) 75 *Chicago Kent Law Review* 531–54 (2000); Martha L.A. Fineman, "What Place for Family Privacy?" 67 *George Washington Law Review* 1207–24 (1999); Martha L.A. Fineman, "The Inevitability of Dependency and the Politics of Subsidy" (Symposium on Welfare Reform) 9 *Stanford Law and Policy Review* 89–99 (1998); Martha L.A. Fineman, "The Nature of Dependencies and Welfare Reform" (Symposium on Ethics, Public Policy, and the Future of the Family) 36 *Santa Clara Law*

Review 287–311 (1996); Martha L.A. Fineman, "Masking Dependency: The Political Role of Family Rhetoric" (Symposium on New Directions in Family Law) 81 *Virginia Law Review* 2181–2215 (1995).

17. John Rawls, *Justice as Fairness: A Restatement* 10–11 (Erin Kelly, ed., Harvard University Press, 2001).

18. *Id.* at 11.

19. *Id.* at 163.

20. *Id.* at 164.

21. *Id.*

Chapter Eight: Recasting the Social Contract

1. Christopher W. Morris, ed., *The Social Contract Theorists: Critical Essays on Hobbes, Locke and Rousseau* (Rowman & Littlefield, 1999), ix; *see, e.g.* Edgar Faure, *Pour un Nouveau Contrat Social* (1973); Ralf Dahrendorf, *Conflict and Contract: Industrial Relations and the Political Community in Times of Crisis* (Liverpool University Press, 1975); James M. Buchanan, *Freedom in Constitutional Contract: Perspectives of a Political Economist* (A & M University Press, 1977); Kai Nielsen and Roger A. Shiner, *New Essays on Contract Theory* (Canadian Association for Publishing in Philosophy, 1977); Geraint Parry, Jack Lively, and Pierre Birnbaum, *Democracy, Consensus and Social Contract* (Sage Publications, 1978); Ilyas Ahmad, *The Social Contract and the Islamic State* (Shahzad Publisher, 1979); Ian R. Macneil, *The New Social Contract: An Inquiry into Modern Contractual Relations* (Yale University Press, 1980); Ron Replogle, *Recovering the Social Contract* (Rowman & Littlefield, 1989); Robert C. Solomon, *A Passion for Justice: Emotions and the Origins of the Social Contract* (Rowman & Littlefield, 1995); Brian Skyrms, *Evolution of the Social Contract* (Cambridge University Press, 1996); Charles W. Mills, *The Racial Contract* (Cornell University Press, 1997); Frances Fox Piven and Richard A. Cloward, *The Breaking of the American Social Compact* (The New Press, 1997).

2. Christopher Morris explains John Locke's definition of the social contract in this way: "A complete political society, Locke suggests, is created in two logically separable stages (which may or may not be separated by an interesting temporal gap). The society itself is created by a contract among all those who wish to be part of it. The society's government is formed by society's granting a separate trust, which conveys to government the political power that was previously invested in the society by its

members. Political power is given first 'into the hands of the society, and therein to the governors whom the society has set over itself, with this express or tacit trust: that it shall be employed for their good and the preservation of their property' " (II, 171; *see also* II, 243). While the creation of the "Legislative" (the "soul" of the commonwealth) is "the first and fundamental act of society" (II, 212), the body politic is created "by barely agreeing to unite into one political society" (II, 99). Consent to membership in the body politic must be unanimous ("by the consent of every individual" [II, 96]), for "only a person's *own* consent can remove that individual from the state of nature. But this consent *entails*, Locke believes, consent to rule by the majority of the members in all subsequent matters (including, of course, the creation of government)" (internal footnotes removed). A. John Simmons, "Political Consent," in *The Social Contract Theorists, supra* note 1, at 127.

3. I find in the course of my teaching that law students are very attached to the idea of contract. Many would use it to resolve all sorts of difficult social policy and economic resource issues. The idea of consent is particularly potent (she or he "asked for it"). *See generally* Restatement (Second) of Contracts §§1, 3 (1979) (contract, agreement, and bargain defined).

4. Relationships within the family are considered to exist beyond and outside contract, their legality and consequences governed by status or policy principles, but to a large degree the product of state-imposed obligations.

5. W. David Slawson, "Standard Form Contracts and Democratic Control of Law Making Power" 84 *Harvard Law Review* 529, 530, 532 (1971).

6. Karl N. Llewellyn, "Book Review: O. Prausnitz, The Standardization of Commercial Contracts in English and Continental Law," 52 *Harvard Law Review* 700, 702–3 (1939); *see also Steiner v. Mobil Oil Corp.*, 569 P.2d 751 758 (1977) ("[A]dhesion contract analysis teaches us not to enforce contracts until we look behind the façade of the formalistic standardized agreement in order to determine whether any inequality of bargaining power between the parties renders contractual terms unconscionable").

7. *See, e.g., NLRB v. Burns International Security Services, Inc.*, 406 U.S. 272 (1972) (The Supreme Court emphasized the importance of freedom of contract in its decision that it was improper to hold a successor employer to the substantive terms of a collective bargaining agreement that it had neither expressly nor implicitly assumed).

8. Simmons, *supra* note 2, at 122.

9. James Boyle, "Legal Realism and the Social Contract: Fuller's Public Jurisprudence of Form, Private Jurisprudence of Substance," 78 *Cornell Law Review* 371 (1993).

10. Simmons, *supra* note 2, at 131.

11. *Id.* at 128–9.

12. Roland Benabou, "Unequal Societies: Income Distribution and the Social Contract," 90 *American Economic Review* 96 (2000).

13. *Id.* at 97. He proposes a "simple theory of inequality and the social contract," which is based on two mechanisms: redistribution receives "less political support in an unequal society than in a more homogenous one . . . [and a] lower rate of redistribution, in turn, increases inequality of future income due to wealth constraints on investment in human or physical capital." *Id.* at 119. He concludes that these mechanisms have produced "two stable steady-states, the archetypes for which could be the United States and Western Europe: one with high inequality yet low redistribution, the other with the reverse configuration." *Id.* He concludes his article by stating: "the original question of why the social contract differs across countries, and whether these choices are sustainable in the long run, remains an important topic for further research." *Id.* It seems that this issue is the one being played out in current European politics. *See, e.g.,* Robert Schuman Centre for Advanced Studies, "Recasting the European Welfare State: Options, Constraints, Actors" (1998–99 European Forum), *at* www.fue.it/RSCAS/Research/EuropeanForum/EF_1998–1999.shtml (last visited June 1, 2003); Peter Flora, "Welfare State Analysis" (Research Programme 1996–1999–Research Department I), *at* www.mzes.uni-mannheim.de/res_prog_e/fb_ab106. html (last visited June 1, 2003).

14. For a succinct description of libertarian policy and theory, including free-market conservatism, *see* Libertarian.Org, "An Introduction to Libertarianism," *at* www.libertarian.org (last visited June 1, 2003).

15. The economic redistribution in our welfare policy (however limited) and in the legal rules readjusting traditional patriarchal power within families were products of a liberal political view. For a brief discussion of the historical development of distrust in the market and the rise of "new" liberalism, *see* "Liberalism in Liberalism as a Political Theory, Property and Market," Stanford Encyclopedia of Philosophy, *at* http://plato.stanford.edu/entries/liberalism (last visited June 1, 2003).

16. Restatement (Second) of Contracts § 19 (Conduct as Manifestation of Assent).

17. Linda McClain, "Care as a Public Value: Linking Responsibility, Resources, and Republicanism," 76 *Chicago Kent Law Review* 1673, 1675–6 (2001).

18. *See e.g.,* the relevantly named Personal Responsibility and Work Opportunity Reconciliation Act, Pub. L. No. 104–103, § 101, 110 Stat. 2105, 2110–12 (1996). *See also* Linda McClain, in *Homo Economicus,* Fineman and Dougherty (eds.) forthcoming (2004).

19. For further discussion of unpacking choice, see Martha Albertson Fineman, *The Neutered Mother* 148–50, 165–6.

20. Restatement (Second) of Contracts § 208 (Unconscionable Contract or Term;) § 152 (When Mistake of Both Parties Makes a Contract Voidable); § 261 (Discharge by Supervening Impracticability).

21. Matthew Swanson. *The Social Contract Tradition and the Question of Political Legitimacy* 11 (Edwin Mellen Press, 2001).

22. *See* Fineman, *supra* note 19, at 177 ("The Limits of Privacy—The Public Family").

23. *See* chapter one.

24. *See, e.g.,* Owen Fiss, "The Autonomy of Law" 3–4, *at* www. yale.edu/lawweb/lawfac/fiss/efiss.pdf (last visited June 1, 2003) ("any well-functioning market needs law . . . [t]he market also needs an institution that can interpret and implement relevant rules of law: a judiciary").

25. *See* the Uniform Commercial Code (U.C.C.) § 2–302 (2000) (discussing court treatment of an unconscionable contract or clause).

26. The U.C.C., recognizes background conditions in several different forms. U.C.C. § 1–205 (2000) (Course of Dealing and Usage of Trade: "A course of dealing is a sequence of previous conduct between the parties to a particular transaction which is fairly to be regarded as establishing a common basis of understanding for interpreting their expressions and other conduct. . . . A usage of trade is any practice or method of dealing having such regularity of observance in a place, vocation or trade as to justify an expectation that it will be observed with respect to the transaction in question").

27. The U.C.C. contemplates changes in background conditions and assigns liability. U.C.C. § 2–615 (2000) (providing for excuse by failure of presupposed conditions). *See* Stephen G. York, "Re: The Impracticability

Doctrine of the U.C.C.," 29 *Duquesne Law Review* 221 (1991) (arguing for a broad interpretation of § 2–615, with greater consideration of background conditions especially due to the relational nature of the relevant contracts). Jeremy Waldron argues that in order for agreements and transactions between individuals, or between an individual and the state, to be operational, there needs to be a context of "rights" upon which the agreements are based—in other words, a fallback position. Jeremy Waldron, "When Justice Replaces Affection: The Need for Rights," in *Liberal Rights: Collected Papers, 1981–1991,* 370–91 (Cambridge University Press, 1993). Waldron's "rights" represent the background conditions upon which individuals can reasonably rely in the event that goodwill and affection fail in interpersonal relation. *Id.*

28. *Id.* at 385–6.

29. *Id.* at 387.

30. *Id.* at 370–91.

31. *Id.* at 376.

32. *Id.* at 379.

33. Restatement (Second) of Contracts §205 (1979) (Duty of Good Faith and Fair Dealing).

34. Restatement (Second) of Contracts §261 (1979) (Discharge by Supervening Impracticability) and §265 (Discharge by Supervening Frustration).

35. Other questions might include: What is the scope of the obligation of law and policy (and, hence, the state) to accommodate significant societal change? Can societal change achieve such a transformation in context that injustice can be said to result without accommodation and incorporation of the new background conditions into a new version of the social contract?

36. Arising within this inquiry are questions concerning the bargaining opportunities that have been excluded from the generalized realm of "private" contract by being relegated to the special (and "publicly" regulated) category of marriage. Of course, a related question that arises from this articulation of this issue is whether such exclusion undermines the use of contract theory as the way to generate universal concepts to discuss abstract interactions of bargain and exchange in society.

37. *See* chapter four.

38. *See* Vicki Schultz, "Life's Work," 100 *Columbia Law Review* 1919 (2000)

(noting that the changes in the workplace are creating a situation in which all workers are experiencing the problems and dilemmas that have traditionally faced women).

39. *Id.* at 1921–8 (documenting the threatening changes in the workplace).

40. *But see id.* at 1925 (noting the growing number of contingent and temporary workers working without benefits).

41. *But see id.* at 1928 (arguing for a right to work).

42. Many of the ways in which the state has participated in changing the historic premises of the social contract are discussed in chapter four. They include increased legal recognition of and response to domestic abuse and neglect; removal of common-law interspousal tort immunity, which precluded one spouse from recovering from the other for negligently inflicted injuries; no-fault divorce statutes; changes in the workplace that acknowledge women's ability to bargain and conduct business; the courts' changing approach to the validity of prenuptial agreements; increased legal recognition of nonmarital relationships between sexual affiliates; the legal entitlement of nonmarital children to benefits historically reserved for their marital counterparts; and a growing acceptance of a contractual view of marriage, based on the parties' equal status. *See* chapter four.

43. See the discussion of changes in family law in chapter four.

44. *See* the "Republican Contract with America," *at* www.house. gov/house/Contract/CONTRACT.html (last visited June 1, 2003). The section called the Personal Responsibility Act, on "Capping the Growth of Welfare Spending," says that "[t]he entitlement status of these programs [Aid for Families with Dependent Children, Social Security Insurance, and public housing programs] is ended"; *see also, e.g.,* Personal Responsibility and Work Opportunity Reconciliation Act of 1996, Pub. L. No. 104–103, § 101, 110 Stat. 2105, 2110–12 (1996).

45. "Republican Contract with America," *supra* note 44.

46. "Republican Contract with America," *supra* note 44 "Personal Responsibility Act (Welfare Reform)," *at* www.house.gov/house/ Contract/ persrespd.txt (visited June 1, 2003).

47. *Ibid.* (emphasis added).

48. "The Family Reinforcement Act," *at* www.house.gov/Contract/ familiesd.txt (last visited June 1, 2003); *see also* "The Contract with America," *at* www.spectacle.org/295/contract.html (last visited June 1, 2003).

49. *See* Eva Kittay, *Love's Labor: Essays on Women, Equality, and Dependency* 76 (Routledge, 1999); *see also* Victor R. Fuchs, *Women's Quest for Economic Equality* 60–4, 133–4 (Harvard University Press, 1988).

Chapter Nine: The Tentative Workplace

1. *But see* Unlawful Employment Practices, 42 U.S.C. § 2000e-2 (a)(1) (1994) (prohibiting employment discrimination on the basis of race, color, religion, sex, or national origin).

2. *See* Katherine V.W. Stone, *The New Psychological Contract and the Boundaryless Workplace* (reviewing the history of employment trends through the twentieth century).

3. Edmund L. Andrews, "Don't Go Away Mad, Just Go Away," *New York Times,* February 13, 1996, D1.

4. Stephen Fishman, *Working for Yourself: Law and Taxes for Independent Contractors, Freelancers and Consultants,* chapter 1 (3rd ed., Nolo, 2000).

5. Katherine V.W. Stone, "Knowledge at Work," 34 *Connecticut Law Review* 721, 725 (2002).

6. *Id.*

7. Katherine Stone, "The New Psychological Contract: Implications of the Changing Workplace for Labor and Employment Law," 48 *UCLA Law Review* 519 (2001).

8. *Id.* at 550.

9. *Id.* at 542.

10. *See* Vickie Schultz, "Life's Work," 100 *Columbia Law Review,* at 1881, 1924–25 (discussing the decline in job security and an increase in contingent work).

11. *Id.*

12. *See* Deborah Belle, *The After-School Lives of Children: Alone and With Others While Parents Work* 7 (Lawrence Erlbaum Associates, 1999). For further elaboration on the effects of employment on time parents spend with their children, *please see* chapter two of this book.

13. *See* Kristin Downey, Grimsley and Jacqueline L. Salmon, "For Working Parents, Mixed News at Home: Children Praise Them but Note Stress," *Washington Post,* September 27, 1999, A1.

14. *See* Deanna M. Lyter et al., "New Welfare Proposals Would Require Mothers Receiving Assistance to Work More than the Average American

Mom: Child Care Inadequate," Institute of Women's Policy Research (2002).

15. Ellen Galinaky, President of the Families and Work Institute reporting to the Association of Work/Life Professionals, reported in *Miami Herald*, February 7, 1998, §C, at 1C.

16. Sarah Anderson et al., "A Decade of Executive Excess: The 1990s," *at* http://www.ufenet.org/press/archive/1999/Executive_Excess/decade_of_executive_excess.html (visited June 1, 2003).

17. *See* Belle, *supra* note 12, at 7.

18. *See id.*

19. *See id.*

20. *Id.* at 1924.

21. *See* Peter T. Kilborn, "Poor Workers Turning Down Employers' Health Benefits," *New York Times*, November 10, 1997, at A24 (reporting on a government study authored by Barbara Steinberg Schone and Phillip F. Cooper, economists at the Agency for Health Care Policy and Research in the Department of Health and Human Services, that was published in the journal *Health Affairs*).

22. *See id.*

23. *See id.*

24. *See* United States Bureau of Labor Statistics, "Union Member Summary" (January 17, 2000), *at* http://stats.bls.gov/news.release/union2.toc.htm (last visited June 1, 2003).

25. *See* Andrew Hacker, "Who's Sticking to the Union?" *New York Review of Books*, February 18, 1999.

26. The response to revitalized union activity by many Republican politicians has been to advance legislation to burden such action. For example, President Bush intends to issue an executive order requiring federal contractors "to post a notice telling workers they have a right not to pay that part of union fees used for political activities." Steven Greenhouse, "Bush Is Moving to Reduce Labor's Political Coffers," *New York Times*, February 16, 2001, at A14. A California Campaign Reform Initiative (CRI) would have barred unions from spending any portion of any member's dues on political activity without the member's written consent. There was no corresponding attempt to hold companies responsible for gaining consent from their workers or the consumers of their product (or, for that matter, their stockholders) for their uses of profits in lobbying and other

political transactions. Republican demands for placing a burden of consensus and consent are directed only to the labor union side of the ledger.

27. Stone, *supra* note 2, at 631.

28. Richard B. Freeman and Joel Rogers, "A Proposal to American Labor," *The Nation*, June 24, 2002, at 18.

29. *Id.* at 22.

30. *See* Theodore Caplow, *American Social Trends* 90 (Harcourt Brace Jovanovich, 1991).

31. *See* Daniel H. Weinberg, U.S. Department of Commerce, Pub. No. P60-191, "A Brief Look at Postwar U.S. Income Inequality," *Current Population Reports: Household and Economic Studies*, at 1 (1996).

32. *See id.*

33. A parallel examines the growth in average household income for each quintile—about 44 percent for the top quintile (from $73,754 in 1968 to $105,945 in 1994) but only 7 percent for those in the bottom quintile ($7,202 to $7,762). *See* Weinberg, *supra* note 31, at 1. The change from 1977 to 1999 for the top quintile was a positive 38.2 percent (from $74,000 to $102,300) and shockingly a *negative* 12 percent (from $10,000 to $8,800) for the bottom quintile. *See* David Cay Johnston, "Gap Between Rich and Poor Found Substantially Wider," *New York Times*, September 5, 1999, §1, at 16. *But see* W. Michael Cox and Richard Alm, "Why Decry the Wealth Gap?" *New York Times*, January 24, 2002 (citing the Treasury Department as reporting that between 1979 and 1988, 86 percent of Americans in the bottom fifth improved their status).

34. *See* Johnston, *supra* note 33, at 16.

35. *See* Peter T. Kilborn and Lynette Clemetson, "Gains of 90's Did Not Lift All, Census Shows," *New York Times*, June 5, 2002.

36. *See* Cox and Alm, *supra* note 33 (Cox goes on to dismiss these figures as being un-arbitrary and a result of progress. He further states that within a seventeen-year study, only 5 percent of the people in the economy's lowest 20 percent failed to move to a higher income group).

37. *See id.*

38. Urie Brofenbrenner et al., *The State of Americans* (The Free Press, 1996).

39. *See id.* at 56.

40. *See id.* at 58.

41. Poverty may be increasing because of the change from blue-collar

to white-collar jobs that took place between the 1970s and 1980s, a change from which workers have not completely recovered. *See* Caplow, *supra* note 30, at 63. Caplow questions whether there even is a crisis of the family: he argues that although Americans have been told the family is in crisis, they tend to see their own families as happy and successful.

42. U.S. Department of Labor, "Futurework: Trends and Challenges for Work in the 21st Century" (visited June 1, 2003), *at* www.dol.gov/asp/programs/history/herman/reports/futurework/report.htm

43. *Id.*

44. *Id.*

45. *See* Timothy M. Smeeding and Lee Rainwater, "Comparing Living Standards Across Nations, Real Incomes at the Top, the Bottom, and the Middle," *Luxembourg Income Study* (February 2002); Jeanne Brooks-Gunn and Greg J. Duncan, "The Effects of Poverty on Children," *The Future of Children: Children and Poverty,* Summer/Fall 1997, at 55.

46. *See* Center for the Future of Children, "Executive Summary," *The Future of Children: Children's Poverty,* Summer/Fall 1997, at 3.

47. *Ibid.*

48. Brooks-Gunn and Duncan, *supra* note 45, at 57. This report collects and assesses the available research in regard to each of these dimensions of the well-being of children in poverty. The authors conclude that income can substantially influence children's well-being, finding the associations between income and child outcomes are more complex and varied than suggested in simple tables. "Family income seems to be more strongly related to children's ability and achievement-related outcomes than to emotional outcomes. In addition, the effects are particularly pronounced for children who live below the poverty line for multiple years and for children who live in extreme poverty." *Id.* at 67–8.

49. *See* Louis Uchitelle, "The American Middle, Just Getting By," *New York Times,* August 1, 1999 at BU1 (citing the U.S. Census Bureau, which calculates the median family income between $46,500 and $50,000).

50. *Ibid.* at BU13 (citing the U.S. Census Bureau) (families were working 3,860 hours in 1997—up from 3,236 in 1979).

51. *Ibid.*

52. *Ibid. See also* Anne Phillips, *Which Equalities Matter?* 62–3 (Blackwell, 1999) (Phillips argues that television is a necessity in a society that derives its culture from TV programs, and that if one does not have a car, one lacks the means to access basic amenities).

53. *Id.* at 63.

54. Caplow, *supra* note 30, at 59.

55. *Id.*

56. *Id.* Even two-parent families are experiencing poverty, so revering the two-parent household as an ideal economic unit is not the answer. Indeed, two-parent families are working harder than before, when there was only one breadwinner, but they are still getting paid the same. *See* Harriet Johnson Brackey, "Survey: Workplace Is More Demanding," *Herald,* February 7, 1998, 1C.

57. *See* Schultz, *supra* note 10, at 1926 (discussing the incidence and ramifications of increasing wage inequality).

58. *Id.; see also* David Leonhardt, "Did Pay Incentive Cut Both Ways?" *New York Times,* April 7, 2002, at C1 (revealing the exorbitant income—up to $154 billion—that many chief executive officers of leading corporations enjoy, even despite company failures).

59. Isaac Shapiro and Robert Greenstein, "The Widening Income Gulf," Center on Budget and Policy Priorities (September 9, 1999), www.cbpp.org/9-4-99tax-rep.htm (June 1, 2003)

60. *See* Leonhardt, *supra* note 58, at C1; *see also* "A Prime Example of Anything-Goes Executive Pay," *New York Times,* June 4, 2002, at C1.

61. Robert H. Frank, "Higher Education: The Ultimate Winner-Take-All Market?" *at* www.ilr.cornell.edu/cheri/wp/cheri-wp02.pdf (June 1, 2003)

62. Lee Rainwater and Timothy M. Smeeding, "Doing Poorly: The Real Income of American Children in a Comparative Perspective," Maxwell School of Citizenship and Public Affairs (1995), 18.

63. See *id.* at 24–25.

64. Ehrenreich's figures are confirmed by United for a Fair Economy, "Exec-Worker Gap in Pay Gets Wider" at www.ufenet.org/press/ufenews/2001/Executive_Excess_2001_Denv.html (visited June 1, 2003).

65. Although voluntary charity and philanthropy are not the objects of the social contract configuration with which I am dealing, it is important to point out that they prove to be no substitutes for governmental mandates when it comes to business responsibility. Inventors and investors have accumulated huge fortunes, but such financial success has not make their holders socially uncomfortable. Giving is relatively miserly and much more narrowly directed than it was at the turn of the last century, which was also an era of capital consolidation and transformation. Today, phi-

lanthropy seems more industry related or self-enhancing than the generalized public institution building that occurred at the turn of the twentieth century. Andrew Carnegie may have built libraries, but Bill Gates donates to them computer equipment that will illustrate to users the wonders of Microsoft, while a scolding Ted Turner contributes funds to show the United States how to pay off its debt to the United Nations.

66. Phillips, *supra* note 52, at 12–13.

67. *See generally* Schultz, *supra* note 10, at 1922–23 (discussing how workplace restructuring trends can create worker competition and result in harassment and discrimination).

68. *See* Clark Freshman, "Re-Visioning the Dependency Crisis and the Negotiators Dilemma: Reflections on the Sexual Family and the Mother Child Dyad," 22 *Law and Social Inquiry* 97 (1997) (reviewing Fineman, *The Neutered Mother*).

69. Schultz also argues for a living wage, the right to work, empowering work conditions, and reduced hours for *all* workers. Schultz., *supra* note 10, 1942–57.

Chapter Ten: The Tenable State

1. "Contract with America" *at* www.nationalcenter.org (visited June 1, 2003).

2. In this regard, it is very interesting to examine the debates about programs to expand voter registration, such as the motor-voter proposal, or schemes to increase representation, such as supplementing more traditional census-information gathering. In both of these instances, the more exclusionary (less democratic?) policies were championed by those in legislative power—one suspects because the reforms were perceived to benefit the other party.

3. *See e.g.*, Samuel Bowles, David M. Gordon, and Thomas E. Weisskopf, in "Right-Wing Economics Backfired," *Challenge* (1991) at 4. (The three professors of economics at the University of Massachusetts at Amherst, New School for Social Research, and the University of Michigan summarize their findings as follows: "The Reagan Administration did indeed succeed in reversing many of the economic policies of the 1970s, yet the new policies now appear to have driven the U.S. economy not to new heights of achievement, but to an ignominious impasse.")

4. *See* Justin Fox, "Here We Go Again," *Fortune* (May 12, 2003), 64–71 (calling Reagan's policy of supply-side economics "dead wrong" and invoking George H. W. Bush as critic of his son's recent plans).

5. *See generally* www.libertarian.org (visited on June 1, 2003).

6. 347 U.S. 486 (1954).

7. Joel Bakan, *Just Words: Constitutional Rights and Social Wrongs* 46 (University of Toronto Press, 1997).

8. *Ibid.*, 9–10.

9. *See, e.g.,* Kathleen E. Mahoney, "The Constitutional Law of Equality in Canada," 44 *Maine Law Review* 229 (1992), at 230.

10. Bakan, *supra* note 7, 9–10. Other commentators have a more utopian vision: "[the] underlying aim [of egalitarians] is to bring about a society of equals: a classless, genderless, non-racist society in which there are, if that is possible, no social strata or at least a society where the necessary strata hierarchies are as minimal as they possibly can be and not the source of some people having power over others," Kai Nielsen, "Radical Egalitarianism Revisited: On Going Beyond the Difference Principle," 15 *Windsor Yearbook of Access to Justice*, at 125; "we will not, by the evident differences between people that obtain in many ways and in many domains be jolted from a deeply embedded and considered conviction that the life of everyone matters and matters equally, a conviction that has appropriately been called moral equality: the belief in the equal moral standing of all people." *Id.* at 126 (citing Hurka, 1992).

11. *See* Nielsen, *supra* note 10, 121.

12. This is a play on the words of President George W. Bush, who has repeatedly advertised his educational policy as designed to leave "no child behind."

13. For a brilliant analysis of how these ideas can be used by feminists in the welfare context, see Martha T. McCluskey, "Subsidized Lives and the Ideology of Efficiency," 8 *American University Journal of Gender, Social Policy and the Law* 115 (1999).

14. T. H. Marshall and Tom Bottomore, eds., *Citizenship and Social Class* (Pluto Press, 1992) at 8.

15. Martha McCluskey, "The Illusion of Efficiency in Workers' Compensation 'Reform,'" 50 *Rutgers Law Review* 657, at 683 (1998).

16. McCluskey notes that average state compliance increased from a level of 6.8 out of the nineteen "essential recommendations" in 1972 to an

average of 12.1 in 1982, when the national trend toward expansion appeared to level off substantially short of the recommended goals. During this same period, writes McCluskey, benefits and coverage in many states expanded as a result of changes in administrative and judicial interpretations of statutes. *Ibid.*, at 684. The changes in aspirations for the state that occurred during the Reagan era meant that in the 1990s, employers' cries that the expansion of benefits was a "crisis" fell on fertile ears. From 1989 to 1997, states heeded the demands of employers and insurers rather than labor groups and other representatives of injured workers, and enacted legislation that substantially limited workers' compensation. McCluskey describes the justification for this revamping as reducing costs for insurers. *Id.*, 700.

17. Sonya Michel, "A Tale of Two States: Race, Gender, and Public/Private Welfare Provision in Postwar America," 9 *Yale Journal of Law and Feminism* 127 (1997).

18. United Nations General Assembly, December 10, 1948, G.A. Res. 217A, 3GAOR, Resolutions (A/810), at 71.

19. Concluded December 16, 1966. 993 U.N.T.S. 3.

20. Adopted November 22, 1969. 1144 U.N.T.S. 123; OAS Treaty Series No. 36; Basic Documents Pertaining to Human Rights in the Inter-American System, OEA/Ser.L.V/II.71, Doc. 6 rev. 1, at 25 (1988).

21. (Banjul Charter) June 27, 1981, 21 I.L.M. 59 (1981).

22. Adopted November 4, 1950. 213 U.N.T.S. 222; *European Convention on Human Rights: Collected Texts* 3 (Kluwer Academic Publishers, 1987).

23. *See, e.g.,* International Covenant on Civil and Political Rights, concluded Dec. 19, 1966, 999 U.N.T.S. 171; American Declaration of the Rights and Duties of Man, May 2, 1948; Basic Documents Pertaining to Human Rights in the Inter-American System, OEA/Ser.L.V/II/71, Doc. 6 rev. 1, at 18 (1988) (which is unique among these documents for its overtly sexist language and lack of remedial provisions); and numerous optional protocols to the previously mentioned conventions, which provide more details as to the manner in which these rights will be guaranteed.

24. Of course, even in countries where there is favorable reception for international human rights norms, the picture is not always a cheery one. Anne Bayevsky and Joan Fitzpatrick report that while the political branches of Canada and the United Kingdom indicate a greater acceptance of international human rights standards, this ratification "does not necessarily translate into greater and more principled acceptance of inter-

national human rights norms by domestic courts." "International Human Rights Law in United States Courts: A Comparative Perspective," 14 *Michigan Journal of International Law* 1, 2 (1992). One could counter that at least they have gotten over the first hurdle—that of acceptance of universal and international opinion.

25. See 993 U.N.T.S. 3.

26. *Ibid.*

27. *See, e.g.,* Protocol to the American Convention on Human Rights, (San Salvador), November 17, 1988, OAS Treaty Series No. 69, 28 *International Legal Materials* 156 (1989), Article 17, Protection of the Elderly ("Everyone has the *right to special protection* in old age"), and Article 18, Protection of the Handicapped ("Everyone affected by a diminution of his physical or mental capacities is *entitled to receive special attention* designed to help him achieve the greatest possible development of his personality") (emphasis added).

28. *See, e.g.,* Protocol to the American Convention on Human Rights, Article 17.

29. *See, e.g.,* United Nations General Assembly, December 10, 1948. G.A. Res. 217A, 3GAOR, Resolutions (A/810), Article 25 ("Everyone has the right to a standard of living adequate for the health and well-being of himself and of his family, including . . . medical care and necessary social services, and the right to security in the event of . . . sickness [or] disability").

30. *See, e.g.,* Protocol to the American Convention on Human Rights, Article 18.

31. *Ibid.,* Article 10, Right to Health.

32. Concluded December 16, 1966. 993 U.N.T.S. 3, Article 10.

33. South Africa Constitution, Ch. II, §27.

34. *Id.,* §26.

35. *See* Ann-Marie Slaughter, "A Typology of Transjudicial Communication," 29 *University of Richmond Law Review* 99 (1994).

36. Ruth Bader Ginsburg and Deborah Jones Merritt, "Affirmative Action: An International Human Rights Dialogue," 21 *Cardozo Law Review* 253, 282 (1999).

37. 123 Supreme Court 2472 (2003) (ruling that the statute making it a crime for two persons of the same sex to engage in sexual conduct violates the due process clause of the Fourteenth Amendment).

38. *See* Professor Christopher D. Stone's discussion of income redistribution through labor market and nonworkplace measures in *Where the Law Ends: The Social Control of Corporate Behavior* (Waveland Press, 1991), chapter 12.

39. *See, e.g.,* National Child Benefit, "Canada Child Tax Benefit for July 2003," at www.nationalchildbenefit.ca/ncb/govtofcan4.shtml (visited June 1, 2003); Columbia University, "Tax Day: How Do America's Child Benefits Compare?" Clearinghouse on International Developments in Child, Youth and Family Policies, Issue Brief, Spring 2002, at www.childpolicyintl.org/issuebrief/issuebrief4.pdf (visited June 1, 2003); Health Canada Online, "Canada's Health Care System at a Glance," (November 28, 2002) at www.hc-sc.gc.ca/english/media/releases/2002/health_act/glance.html (visited June 1, 2003); "International Forum on Common Access to Health Care Services" (January 31, 2003) at http://social. regeringen.se/forum/pdf/final_statement.pdf (visited June 1, 2003); European Commission, Directorate-General XXII, Education, Training and Youth, "Press Release: Financial Support for Students in Higher Education in Europe," at www.eurydice.org/News/Communique/en/Question_ cles_EN.pdf (visited June 1, 2003); KAM International, "Canadian Education," *at* www.kaminternational.com/index.asp (visited June 1, 2003).

40. "Occupational Outlook Handbook," *National Bureau of Labor Statistics,* Childcare Workers, at www.bls.gov/oco/cocos170.htm (visited June 1, 2003).

41. Grace Chang, *Disposable Domestics: Immigrant Women Workers in the Global Economy* (South End Press, 2000), 58.

42. For a discussion of accommodation as conceived of in the Americans with Disabilities Act see Ronald D. Wenkart, J.D., "Public Employment Reasonable Accommodation and the ADA," 133 *Education Law Report* 647, 653–54.

43. *See, e.g.,* Elinor Burkett, *The Baby Boon: How Family-Friendly America Cheats the Childless* (The Free Press, 2002).

44. *See* Clark Freshman, "Re-Visioning the Dependency Crisis and the Negotiator's Dilemma: Reflections on the Sexual Family and the Mother Child Dyad," 22 *Law and Social Inquiry* 97 (1997) (reviewing Fineman, *The Neutered Mother*).

45. *See generally* Vicki Schultz, "Life's Work," *100 Columbia Law Review* 1881, 1942–57 (arguing for a living wage, the right to work, empowering work conditions, and reduced hours for all workers).

Postscript: What Place for Family Privacy?

1. For a fuller account of this theory, *see* Martha Albertson Fineman, "Cracking the Foundational Myths: Independence, Autonomy, and Self-Sufficiency," 8 *American University Journal of Gender, Social Policy and the Law* 17, note 11 (2000). Note as well that with the end of entitlement for families in need represented by welfare reform, the state might respond.

2. The common-law privacy doctrine is not an individualized concept but rather is founded on the nature of the protected relationship: it attaches to the entity of the family, not to the individuals that compose it. Historically, this has meant that in certain cases, the doctrine operates to shield the family unit from state interference, even when the request comes from one of the family members. Fineman, *supra* note 1, at 966. Fineman, "Intimacy Outside of the Family: The Limits of Privacy," 23 *Connecticut Law Review* 955, at 966. *See also State v. Black,* 60 N.C. 262 (1864) (demonstrating a court's reticence to interfere in an admittedly abusive marital relationship). From that era's perspective, "abusive" may not be the right word—the court acknowledged that there was physical violence, but stated that a husband is permitted to use "such a degree of force as is necessary to control an unruly temper and make her behave herself"—that this constitutes abuse is a concept not developed until the late 1900s. For further analysis, *see* Beirne Stedman, "Right of Husband to Chastise Wife," 3 *Virginia Regulation* 241 (1917).

3. Of course, abuses within real-life families will continue to occur. However, the issue in those cases should be how to address such abuse within the parameters of a family privacy ethic. The existence of abuse should not be sufficient to launch an attack on privacy as applied to the family. See Fineman, *The Neutered Mother,* at 187–88.

4. I do argue, however, that individual concepts of privacy are not sufficient to resist collective control in many areas of intimate and family life. This is especially relevant in the case of paternity actions, custody awards, and subsequent modification of custody orders. *See* Fineman, *supra* note 3, at 189–91.

5. *Griswold v. Connecticut,* 381 U.S. 479 (1965).

6. This limitation on the right to the marital context was clearly on the mind of a number of justices. In his concurrence, on behalf of the chief justice and Justice Brennan, Justice Goldberg asserted that our "concept of liberty protects those rights that are fundamental." *Griswold v. Connecticut,* supra note 5. In delineating which rights rise to the status of being funda-

mental, Justice Goldberg noted that judges must look at the "traditions and (collective) conscience of our people to determine whether a principle is so rooted . . . as to be deemed fundamental." *Id.*, at 493. Although marital privacy is not explicitly addressed in the Constitution, to the dismay of Justice Stewart, it was embraced as a fundamental right. *See id.* (Justice Stewart dissenting.)

7. *Id.* at 486.

8. *Id.* Justice Douglas, concerned that the use of contraceptives was what was prohibited, asked, "[W]ould we allow the police to search the sacred precincts of marital bedrooms for telltale signs of the use of contraceptives? The very idea is repulsive to the notions of privacy surrounding the marriage relationship." *Id.*

9. *Id.* at 495.

10. *Eisenstadt v. Baird*, 405 U.S. 438 (1972). Laurence Tribe has stated that the "right of access to contraceptive technology affirmed in Eisenstadt" was not limited to married couples. Indeed, in *Eisenstadt,* the court declared that just such a distinction between married and single persons was unconstitutional. Tribe further asserted that the court's decision could hardly be said to have revolved around marriage or the family. *See* Laurence H. Tribe, *American Constitutional Law* 1423 (2d ed., Foundation Press, 1988).

11. *Eisenstadt,* supra note 10, at 453.

12. The fact that the cloak, as it was spun out, had certain holes does not detract from the basic point that it was tailored for individual and not entity protection. *See Planned Parenthood of Central Missouri v. Danforth*, 428 U.S. 52 (1976). ("The obvious fact is that when the wife and the husband disagree on this decision [abortion], the view of only one of the two marriage partners can prevail. Inasmuch as it is the woman who physically bears the child and who is the more directly and immediately affected by the pregnancy, as between the two, the balance weighs in her favor.")

In cases subsequent to *Eisenstadt,* various doctrinal limitations and exceptions have been fashioned to curb the reach of this modern un–family-fettered form of privacy. While *Eisenstadt* expanded the notion of who was protected by privacy, it also seems to have contracted the possibilities of what was protected, focusing primarily on decisions concerning reproduction. Further, language about deeply rooted traditions from Goldberg's opinion in *Griswold* has proved constricting, limiting protection to the traditional. *See Bowers v. Hardwick*, 478 U.S. 1039 (1986).

13. Federal courts have relied consistently on the domestic-relations ex-

ception to decline jurisdiction in family law matters. This exception to diversity jurisdiction was established in *Barber v. Barber,* 21 How. 582, 16 L. Ed. 226 (1859). The overriding attitude of the federal bench is that state courts are, and continue to be, better equipped to handle domestic matters. *Simms v. Simms,* 175 U.S. 162 (1899); *McCarty v. McCarty* 453 U.S. 210 (1981). This general reluctance on the part of the federal judiciary may give way to increased federal activity in family law matters. Judith Resnick argues that federal intervention in family law is inevitable, however, because an "interlocking enmeshed regulatory structure covers the host of human activity." For additional discussion of federal intervention in family law matters, *see generally* Judith Resnick, " 'Naturally' Without Gender: Women, Jurisdiction and Federal Courts," 66 *New York University Law Review* 1682, 1750–7 (1991).

14. The law claims to be absent in the private sphere and has historically refused to intervene in ongoing family relations. Elizabeth M. Schneider, "The Violence of Privacy," 23 *Connecticut Law Review* 973, 976 (1991). *See also* Nadine Taub and Elizabeth M. Schneider, "Perspectives on Women's Subordination and the Role of Family Law" in *The Politics of Law: A Progressive Critique* 121 (D. Kairys, ed., Pantheon Books, 1982).

15. *McGuire v. McGuire,* 157 Neb. 226 (1953).

16. *Id.* at 238. There are many other contemporary cases embodying this principle of family privacy. Tort law has traditionally been held inapplicable to injuries inflicted by one family member on another. Under doctrines of interspousal and parent-child immunity, courts have consistently refused to allow recoveries for injuries that would be compensatable but for the fact that they occurred in the private realm. In the same way, criminal law has failed to punish intentional injuries to family members. This principle can also be seen in common-law and statutory definitions of rape that continue to carve out a special exception for a husband's forced intercourse with his wife. Furthermore, wife beating was initially omitted from the definition of criminal assault on the ground that a husband had the right to chastise his wife. *See* Schneider, *supra* note 14, at 976.

17. I William Blackstone, *Commentaries,* 447.

18. This line of family privacy was given constitutional protection fairly early by the Supreme Court, in cases such as *Meyer v. Nebraska,* 262 U.S. 390, 399 (1923) (holding that substantive due process guarantees the right "to marry, establish a home, and bring up children"). The right to marry is a family formation issue. The rights to use contraception (*Griswold*) and bring up children are family conduct or function issues. *See also Wisconsin v.*

Yoder, 406 U.S. 205 (1972); *Prince v. Massachusetts*, 321 U.S. 158(1944); *Pierce v. Society of Sisters*, 268 U.S. 510 (1925).

19. It is this sense of privacy that I define as an ethic or ideology. It transcends law as such and informs the way that laws are interpreted and understood. Law can be utilized in the ideological project, but it cannot be a substitute for it. *See generally* Fineman, *supra* note 3, at 14–24.

20. The far-reaching potential of the individual, constitutional version of privacy to protect a wide range of intimate decisions has been limited in subsequent cases. Privacy has been limited to conventional, heterosexual expressions of sexuality (*see Bowers v. Hardwick*, 478 U.S. 1039 [1986]); eroded from its initial, expansive application in the abortion context (*see Planned Parenthood v. Casey*, 510 U.S. 1309 [1994]); and generally not applied to much beyond a narrow category of intimate decision making, notably family (*see Meyer v. Nebraska*, 262 U.S. 390 [1923]), marriage (*see Griswold v. Connecticut*, 381 U.S. 479 [1965]), and procreation (*see Roe v. Wade*, 410 U.S. 959 [1973]; *Skinner v. Oklahoma*, 400 U.S. 995 [1971]).

21. The feminist critique of our common-law family privacy doctrine concludes that it is unavailable to protect women and children because as individuals they are then subjected to potential dominance and oppression. *See generally* Taub and Schneider, *supra* note 14. *See also* Fineman, *supra* note 2, at 968. Elizabeth Schneider asserts that in the private sphere of domestic and family life, which is purportedly immune from law, there is a selective application of the law. That by invoking privacy, Schneider argues this selective application of the law serves as a rationale for immunity in order to protect male domination. *See* Schneider, *supra* note 14, at 977.

22. Privacy appears to rest on a division between public and private realms that has been oppressive to women and has supported male dominance in the family. The notion of marital privacy has been a source of oppression to battered women and has helped to maintain women's subordination within the family. *See generally* Schneider, *supra* note 14.

23. The contrived ties are those the law constructs between biological strangers through such devices as marriage (which creates husband and wife) or adoption (which creates parent[s] and child). Ties of a "natural" nature are those of consanguinity, although only some of these family ties are reinforced by law in modern societies. Interestingly, while parents have a legal obligation to their minor children, adult children are not generally responsible for their parents.

24. The Supreme Court recognized this conception of family in *May-*

nard v. Hill, 125 U.S. 190 (1888). Marriage "is an institution in the mainte-nance of which in its purity the public is deeply interested, for it is the foundation of the family and of society, without which there would be nei-ther civilization nor progress." *Id.* at 211.

25. I am not asserting that this is how families actually operate; rather, this image is aspirational or idealized. Law certainly reflects a bias for the reproductive unit as the appropriate family form, as evidenced by the fact that the basic family relationships in our jurisprudence are those of hus-band and wife and parent and child. Those outside of these specified rela-tionships will often analogize their intimate relationships to one of these paradigmatic ones in order to argue for benefits conferred upon the tradi-tional family.

26. For a historical account of parental rights, *see generally* Barbara Ben-nett Woodhouse, "Who Owns the Child? Meyer and Pierce and the Child as Property," 33 *William and Mary Law Review* 995 (1992). For a discussion of the modern trend in parental rights, *see* Woodhouse, "A Public Role in the Private Family: The Parental Rights and Responsibilities Act and the Pol-itics of Child Protection and Education," 57 *Ohio State Law Journal* 393 (1996).

27. In "Hatching the Egg: A Child Centered Perspective on Parents Rights," 14 *Cardozo Law Review* 1747 (1993), Barbara B. Woodhouse first ad-vocated this new approach to the parent-child relationship, terming it the "generist perspective." It is based on the view that the nurturing of the next generation is the touchstone of the family. An adult's relationship with children is one of trusteeship rather than ownership. Adults' "rights" of control and custody yield to the less-adversarial notions of obligation to provide nurturing, authority to act on the child's behalf, and standing to participate in the collaborative planning to meet the child's needs. For more on the generist perspective, *see* Woodhouse, " 'Out of Children's Needs, Children's Rights': The Child's Voice in Defining the Family," 8 *Brigham Young University Journal of Public Law* 321 (1994).

28. Woodhouse, "Out of Children's Needs, Children's Rights," supra note 27, at 394.

29. *Id.*

30. The claim is that caretaking is society-preserving work and entitled to subsidy for that reason. See Fineman, *Neutered Mother,* at 394.

31. I have done this in regard to the dichotomies of independency-dependency and self-sufficiency–subsidy in another context, taking the

stigmatized component of the comparison and arguing that it is both inevitable and universal. *See* Fineman, supra note 1. This phase of the project involves considering the concept of autonomy. I think this is what we should be arguing for—the freedom to self-govern, which is not the same as perceiving ourselves as independent and self-sufficient.

32. This is the position of the nuclear family today. It is afforded privacy, and for the state to intervene, it must provide sufficient justification. For more on this, see Fineman, *supra* note 2, at 968.

33. Here, privacy and subsidy are conceived of as intertwined rights that support an entity against the state. As such, they would actually facilitate a move away from form to function. Autonomy carries with it the ability to define the unit.

34. For example, marital rape and domestic violence would be treated under the same set of rules that would apply to legal strangers (which is what they become without or outside the family label).

35. Perhaps this is why so many scholars neglect the family. This is also an illustration of the way in which we are fixated on gender relations, the way that ordering (symbolically or otherwise) the relationship of sexual affiliates dominates our attention and distorts analyses in regard to other relationships.

36. I recognize that this will happen in some cases, but this realization should not provide the operative assumption for parent-child relationships. If it becomes the operative assumption, it creates a culture for state intervention and control.

37. I find that sort of belief underlying statements such as Woodhouse's "children are people in their own right." Woodhouse, *supra* note 26, "A Public Role in the Private Family," at 394.

38. *See* Fineman, "Cracking the Foundational Myths," *supra* note 1.

39. A clear concept of entity-focused privacy could make a difference in a number of areas. For example, in custody determinations, the initial decision would be made under a primary caretaker standard because it is this standard that respects the autonomy and decision making of the prior unit and respects decisions that were made within the marital family by validating them at divorce. In addition, entity privacy would require that once a determination was made, it would be final. Modification, absent abuse or neglect findings that apply to all entities, would not occur simply because there were changed circumstances, as is now the rule in most jurisdictions. Entity privacy would require the same respect for postdivorce

caretaking units as is shown to two-parent units. There would also be implications for the welfare context, because single motherhood would not be stigmatized. Certainly the current official coercive conduct and investigation of sexual activities associated with paternity proceedings would be affected.

40. A functional approach to the family is a process. Each generation must struggle with the question of what public expectations and aspirations are to be placed on the family. Further, we must explicitly not only consider the roles or functions we want our families to play, but also ask what resources they will need to perform those functions. The question of what sources can be tapped to supply necessary family resources must also be addressed. This process places the family in the context of other societal institutions. Finally, the question of family privacy must be addressed. Society must resolve how porous the family will be, and how much autonomy is to be ceded.

Index